FROM SIN
TO INSANITY

FROM SIN
TO INSANITY

*Suicide in Early
Modern Europe*

EDITED BY JEFFREY R. WATT

First published 2004 by Cornell University Press

Printed in the United States of America

Design by Scott Levine

Library of Congress Cataloging-in-Publication Data

From sin to insanity : suicide in early modern Europe / edited by
   Jeffrey R. Watt.
      p. cm.
   Includes bibliographical references and index.
   ISBN 0-8014-4278-8 (cloth)
      1. Suicide—Europe—History.   2. Suicidal behavior—Europe—
   History.   3. Social history.   I. Watts, Jeffrey R. (Jeffrey Rodgers),
   1958–
   HV6548.E9F76 2004
   362.28'094'0903–dc22

                                          2004010277

Cornell University Press strives to use environmentally responsible suppliers and materials to the fullest extent possible in the publishing of its books. Such materials include vegetable-based, low-VOC inks and acid-free papers that are recycled, totally chlorine-free, or partly composed of nonwood fibers. For further information, visit our website at www.cornellpress.cornell.edu.

Cloth printing   10 9 8 7 6 5 4 3 2 1

FROM SIN
TO INSANITY

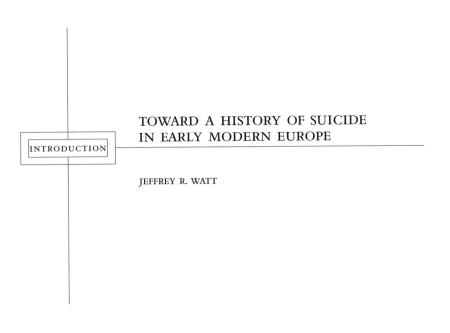

TOWARD A HISTORY OF SUICIDE
IN EARLY MODERN EUROPE

JEFFREY R. WATT

In October 1555, Jean Jourdain, twenty-six, a bachelor farmer living near Geneva, was distraught because he had contracted venereal disease and had been summoned to appear before the Consistory, a type of morals court, on account of his sin of fornication. One Sunday morning Jourdain went into the woods where he stabbed himself, but immediately felt remorse when he heard the ringing of a church bell. Asking God for forgiveness, the wounded Jourdain staggered to a nearby village where he languished eight days before expiring. Before he died, authorities asked the wounded Jourdain if he had given himself to the devil. The dying man admitted that he had called out in the woods, entreating Satan to come kill him. He heard no voice, however, and no demon put Jourdain out of his misery. In the mind of this humble young man, "self-murder" was so closely associated with the devil that he invoked diabolical intervention to put an end to his days. Genevan authorities expressed their utter repugnance toward this act by ordering that Jourdain's body be dragged on a hurdle and then impaled and left exposed outside the city.[1]

The suicide of Claude Dalloz, occurring more than two centuries after Jourdain's death, could not have been more different. A French aide-de-camp who shot himself in Geneva in October 1793, Dalloz, thirty-five, had been a revolutionary but became most disillusioned with the Jacobin Dictatorship and the Reign of Terror. In a suicide note, Dalloz wrote of his desire to emulate Cato, the Roman Republican leader who stabbed himself rather than surrender to the forces of Julius Caesar. Dalloz proclaimed, "I have seen the disgrace of France being tyrannized by the most vile scoundrels. . . . I die calm and content that I have not knowingly offended anyone. . . . I have never hated anyone except the brigands who are tearing France apart."[2] Dalloz chose to end his life only because he could not tolerate the "destruction" of France by Robespierre and other Jacobins. In Dalloz's mind, the devil and sin played no part in this deed, a view shared by Genevan magistrates, who imposed no restrictions on either his burial or the distribution of his modest estate.

These two radically different scenarios bear witness to the fact that the early modern period was a watershed in the history of suicide, a topic now recognized as an important subfield of historical research. The ten essays of this volume show that dramatic changes took place in the attitudes toward and experiences surrounding voluntary death in the centuries stretching from the Renaissance to Napoleon. European archives have abundant sources that can tell us much about the men and women who took their lives during the early modern era. By studying self-inflicted deaths, one can learn much not only about suicide itself but also, as the two Genevan cases suggest, about prevailing mores and mindsets.

Indeed, suicide and attitudes toward self-inflicted death offer an invaluable window to the collective mentality of a given society. Contrasting attitudes toward suicide in the ancient Greco-Roman world, on the one hand, and medieval Christian Europe, on the other, reflected the fundamental differences in the dominant mores of these two epochs. In ancient Greece and Rome, suicide caught the attention of the great philosophers, playwrights, and statesmen, who pondered whether it was legitimate to end one's life voluntarily. Many in the ancient world admired certain individuals, such as Socrates and Cato, who took their own lives.[3] This at least partial principled toleration of suicide among ancient pagans gave way to inflexible opposition to self-inflicted deaths among Christians. Augustine was the thinker most responsible for the strong traditional abhorrence of suicide that held sway in Europe for over a thousand years. Condemning self-inflicted death in all circumstances, Augustine equated suicide with refusing to submit to God's will: having given life, God alone had the power to determine when people were to leave this world.[4] Well into the early modern era, many Christian thinkers also associated suicide with diabolical possession and temptation, a belief clearly seen in the case of the farmer Jourdain discussed previously.[5]

While ancient and medieval writers were most concerned with the ethics of taking one's life, modern scholarship on suicide has concentrated on the causes of suicide. The work on suicide that has garnered the most attention in the past two centuries has largely been the scholarship of two sorts of researchers: psychiatrists and psychologists, on the one hand; sociologists, on the other. Some pioneers in psychiatry argued in the nineteenth century that all suicides are caused by mental illness, and psychiatrists have paid special attention to the physiological causes of suicide, often associating it with manic depression.[6] For Sigmund

Freud (1856–1939) and other psychoanalysts, suicide results not from physiology but from intrapsychic conflicts. According to one hypothesis based on Freudian thought, suicide can result when people concentrate their libido entirely on one object. If, for example, a man invests all his romantic and sexual interests in one woman and that relationship fails—be it through unrequited love or the departure or death of the woman—life for him may no longer seem worth living, and suicide may follow.[7] Whether they stress biological imbalances or psychic conflicts, both psychological and psychiatric approaches to suicide emphasize the inner causes that push a person to take his or her life.[8]

Sociologists, by comparison, have argued that societal forces or external impetuses, are the most fundamental causes behind suicide. Many have insisted that suicide has been endemic ever since modernization or industrialization. In 1879 Enrico Morselli, for example, argued that the rural societies of premodern Europe provided an unquestioned culture based on seemingly timeless traditions. Changes brought about by urbanization and modernization resulted in cultural confusion, allegedly leading to growing despair and increasing numbers of suicides.[9] The figure who still towers above the rest in sociological research on suicide is Emile Durkheim (1858–1917), who studied official statistics and concluded that variations in suicide rates reflect differences in social organization. For Durkheim, suicide rates vary inversely to the degree of religious, domestic, and political integration of a particular society: the stronger the support one receives from one's religion, family, and state, the less likely a person will commit suicide.[10]

In spite of their differences, sociologists, psychologists, and psychiatrists all certainly treat suicide in an entirely secular manner, viewing social or mental ills, not sin or diabolical possession, as decisive factors behind self-inflicted deaths. Their various approaches all point to the secularization and, to a considerable degree, the medicalization of suicide, reflecting a monumental shift away from the medieval period in the collective attitudes in Western societies. In tracing the changes over time in suicidal actions and attitudes toward voluntary death, historians make a vitally important contribution to our overall knowledge of suicide. While authors writing from the ethical/religious, medical/psychological, or sociological perspectives all contribute to our understanding of suicide, historians play an essential role by showing that suicide must be considered, at least in part, a constructed phenomenon that can be experienced and understood in radically different ways in different cultures.

Historians have demonstrated that much can be known about suicide in past centuries. They first turned their attention to the intellectual history of suicide, examining the attitudes toward voluntary death of philosophers, jurists, theologians, and creative writers from various epochs.[11] While historians continue to evaluate the actions and writings of "great" men and women of the past, the past few decades have witnessed a revolution in the study of history, as scholars pursued social history, endeavoring to learn as much as possible about common folk and private life. Inspired by sociology, some specialists in modern European history have written fine quantitative studies based on official statistics in an effort to establish suicide rates for a given society.[12] In archives throughout Europe, social historians have looked at a wide range of sources, such as death records, police reports, and judicial proceedings that can provide valuable information about suicide in the past. Consequently, the history of suicide can be looked at both from above—from the perspective of moralists and intellectual leaders—and below—from the way self-inflicted death was experienced by common folk.

The ten essays of this volume make a vitally important contribution to our knowledge of suicide in early modern Europe, approaching the subject from various perspectives and contexts. They treat suicidal activities from the fifteenth to the early nineteenth centuries in geographical settings as diverse as Scandinavia, Hungary, Paris, northern Germany, England, Switzerland, Spain, and Amsterdam. Although these studies make numerous references to the views on suicide of philosophers, theologians, and essayists, intellectual history is not the primary focus of any of them. Previous research has already shown that virtually all intellectual leaders of sixteenth- and early seventeenth-century Europe viewed suicide as utterly abominable. By contrast, many of their counterparts of the eighteenth century, the era commonly known as the Enlightenment, took issue with the traditional abhorrence of suicide. The so-called philosophes, the intellectual leaders of the Enlightenment, celebrated reason and rejected as superstitions many Christian traditions, often embracing deism or even atheism. Earlier studies have shown that many of these thinkers—including Montesquieu, Voltaire, and most emphatically David Hume—defended voluntary death under certain circumstances. This volume, however, places greater emphasis on the social, legal, and cultural history of suicide.

Several of the book's chapters examine the legal dimension of suicide. Whereas suicide was itself not a crime in pagan Rome, in medieval Europe various legal penalties were often imposed against the bodies and estates of those who took their lives. Essays in this volume show that during the course of the early modern period, European magistrates became more reluctant to pass such sentences against suicides, a trend evident in the divergent reactions of Genevan magistrates in the instances of Jean Jourdain in 1555 and of Claude Dalloz in 1793. In the sixteenth century, European judicial authorities regularly denied funerary rites for suicides, often casting further dishonor on them by ordering the desecration of their corpses and the confiscation of their goods. In his essay, Machiel Bosman traces changing sentences against suicide in Amsterdam. Extant records indicate that judicial authorities ceased imposing penalties against the bodies and estates of suicides in Amsterdam in the later seventeenth century. Although this put the

Dutch in the vanguard in the de facto decriminalization of suicide, Amsterdam's judges nonetheless ordered the desecration of the corpse of a criminal who took his life as late as 1792, long after such desecrations had fallen into disuse in most European states. The reason for this apparent paradox stemmed from the growing importance of Roman law in Dutch legal practices. Dutch jurists increasingly embraced the notion, derived from the Roman Empire of the first century, that those guilty of serious crimes should not be able to escape punishment by taking their lives. The postmortem penalties were accordingly intended to punish the previously committed crime rather than suicide itself.

In his contribution, Paul Seaver finds that the diocese of London granted a substantial number of licenses to permit Christian burials of suicides in the years 1610–1641, a rather surprising discovery given the fact that the British clergy aggressively denounced suicide well into the eighteenth century. In making their requests, survivors were apt to stress the pious lives the deceased had led while attributing the suicide to grief, melancholy, or some other form of mental illness. Significantly, from the late sixteenth century, Londoners could also see suicide depicted in drama and literature as legitimate or at least pardonable in some circumstances. This evidence suggests that Londoners showed a certain leniency toward voluntary death that anticipated by generations the changing opinions on suicide that would eventually spread throughout England.

The decline in penalties cannot be attributed to the influence of Voltaire, Montesquieu, and other Enlightenment writers who criticized these judicial practices. Sentences that went beyond the denial of burial rites were becoming less common already in the mid-seventeenth century, well before these critics raised their voices. For example, these judicial changes predated by a century Cesare Beccaria's famous condemnation of penalties against suicide in his *On Crimes and Punishments* (1764). Consequently, the views on penal reform of Beccaria and other Enlightenment thinkers were more an expression of changing mentalities already under way than the agents of change themselves. Rather than a response to learned criticisms of these practices, the de facto decriminalization of suicide stemmed from the growing sentiment that sentences against the bodies and estates of suicides harmed only innocent survivors.

Suicide could also play an important role in shaping the political culture of various regions of Europe. Craig Koslofsky's essay examines the disposal of the bodies of suicides, which caused a major jurisdictional conflict between church and city officials in Electoral Saxony in the early eighteenth century. Leipzig city officials found support for their position in the thought of Christian Thomasius, the preeminent German political philosopher of the early Enlightenment, who called for the complete subordination of the church to the state. Thomasius promoted the secularization of the body of the suicide by calling for secular control over all burials and criticizing the denial of Christian funerary rites to those who took their lives. Such an attitude, however, conflicted with popular fears concerning the bodies of suicides and with the ambitions of church authorities, who ultimately were successful in reacquiring jurisdiction over these and other burials. This Saxon dispute ably demonstrates the role that suicide could play in questions concerning the secularization (or desecularization) of jurisdiction.

Several chapters in this volume shed light on how suicide was experienced at the popular level, demonstrating that attitudes toward suicide were changing among broad segments of the population. By examining the testimony of people who survived suicide attempts and the secondhand accounts of close associates of completed suicides, Vera Lind studies the feelings of people as they approached voluntary death. Throughout the early modern era, rural residents of these northern German regions viewed suicide as wholly repugnant. In the seventeenth century, those who survived their suicide attempts often described themselves as being overcome by diabolical powers. As suicide became increasingly medicalized in the eighteenth century, survivors of suicide attempts more often blamed their acts on melancholy or other mental and physical maladies over which they reputedly had no control. Although popular understanding of suicide was thus changing in important ways, northern Germans continued to adhere to a cultural taboo that precluded openly expressing the wish to die.

In his work on Stockholm, Arne Jansson studies an unusual form of violent death in the late seventeenth and early eighteenth century: suicidal murder, killing another person with the sole intent of then being sentenced to death and executed. Found also in Lind's work, these actions involved people who wanted to die but not by their own hands—they feared that damnation necessarily awaited suicides because they had no opportunity to repent of their sins. By killing an innocent person, they expected to be sentenced to death and to have plenty of time to ask forgiveness of God for this and other sins. Growing suicidal tendencies apparently stemmed from increased social isolationism associated with economic change and Stockholm's substantial population growth, the result of steady immigration into the city. Sweden remained a thoroughly Lutheran state at this time, and Stockholm's congregations became much larger, resulting in fewer contacts with pastors and the weakening of religious communal ties. It was the unique combination of these loosening communal bonds, the strong fear of damnation, and judicial authorities' consistency in imposing the death penalty for murder that was responsible for Stockholm's remarkable number of suicidal murders.

Myths about self-inflicted deaths could also be quite prominent in certain communities or nations. Suicide could be a two-edged cultural sword, as seen in the chapter on early modern Spain by Elizabeth Dickenson and James Boyden. On the one hand, Spaniards celebrated national pride in their literature and theater by lauding the inhabitants of the ancient Spanish town of Numantia, who committed suicide rather than surrender to the Romans. On the other hand, the Spanish Inquisition could be extremely harsh in dealing with alleged heretics or apostates who took their lives while imprisoned. When a suspected Judaizer—a person who had formally converted to Christianity but secretly maintained Jewish practices—committed suicide in prison in 1513, inquisitors ordered her body burned and her property confiscated. More important, they declared that all her heirs were barred in perpetuity from holding ecclesiastical or public office, from exercising certain professions, from carrying arms or riding horses, and even from owning precious metals, gems, or rich fabrics. These eternal penalties imposed on the heirs of suicides—punishments unique to early modern Spain—were tied to the Iberian concept of honor and reflected anti-Semitic hatred.

In his essay, David Lederer examines the emphasis on patriotic self-sacrifice in early modern Hungary. Having been invaded and occupied by Germans, Turks, and others, Hungarians long extolled in their literature the virtues of heroes who actively sought martyrdom on behalf of their people. As nationalistic fervor grew strong in the mid-nineteenth century, Hungarian artists and writers romanticized the patriotic self-sacrifices of late medieval and early modern martyrs in poems and paintings. This same era witnessed a dramatic increase in the number of recorded suicides. Lederer proposes that the legends of self-sacrifice that thoroughly imbued Hungarian popular culture might reduce inhibitions toward self-inflicted deaths. And the stress on the preservation of the group through the sacrifice of the individual could demean self-worth, making Hungarians, who have had the world's highest official suicide rate for the past century, more prone to suicidal proclivities.

The growing numbers of suicides, a key social development, is even more central to Jeffrey Watt's essay. He finds that in the late 1700s, the small city-state of Geneva witnessed an explosion of suicides and the first appearance of a suicide gender gap: in virtually all modern societies, males comprise the large majority of those who take their lives. While earlier generations had stoically borne financial woes, the loss of loved ones, and the mental and physical infirmities that might push people to take their lives, late-eighteenth-century Genevans were more likely to succumb to such travails primarily because of changes in their religious culture, most notably the emphasis on the love of rather than the fear of God and the de-emphasis on hell and diabolical power. With the removal of religious deterrents, men were more susceptible to suicide because, while enjoying higher expectations for economic and political success, males were also much more likely to fall short of their goals.

Jeffrey Merrick looks at suicide in Paris in the year 1775, another setting that purportedly witnessed an increase in self-inflicted deaths. Police investigations reveal that witnesses most often blamed these voluntary deaths on personal reversals or especially on physical and mental illnesses. No testimony suggested that

Parisians viewed suicide as a sin or even a crime in itself. Nonetheless one can also find expressions of disapproval of those who impetuously put an end to their days without sufficient reason. An intendant or royal administrator, was criticized as showing weakness of character, for example, when he impulsively slit his throat because he felt his honor was impugned by reports of mismanagement of funds. In most respects, Parisians appeared quite modern in their attitudes toward voluntary death. Ultimately, like most people today, Parisians of the late eighteenth century embraced the very important "meaning" of suicide, based on common sense, that "something is fundamentally wrong with the situation" of those who take their lives, that suicide is "directly dependent upon the situation in which the individual existed at the time of the action."[13]

Donna Andrew examines the public reactions in the early nineteenth century to the suicide of Sir Samuel Romilly, a prominent British politician. The very broad press coverage of this death reveals both the widespread outpouring of grief in England over the loss of Romilly, and the simultaneous anger at any attempt to exculpate his act. While some of the growing number of popular dailies and monthlies provided accounts that tended to explain his death sympathetically—he was said to have been a victim of overwork and of his overwhelming grief at the death of his wife—others said he lacked fortitude to go on living, and that his act showed a disregard of God's providence. Had he died a century earlier, public reactions almost certainly would have been overwhelmingly negative, condemning this self-inflicted death as a grievous sin and a cowardly act. In the early 1800s, both the popular press and learned opinion were torn between seeing suicide as a product of sickness or of sin, as acts of mental anguish or opprobrious vice. These findings show that even by the nineteenth century, one of Europe's most "modern" societies was still quite ambivalent about voluntary self-destruction, an attitude that persisted long after the death of Romilly. Indeed, the English Parliament did not officially decriminalize suicide until 1961.[14]

Together, these essays indicate that the period stretching from the Renaissance to the Romantic era witnessed dramatic changes in the judicial treatment of, popular attitudes toward, and frequency of suicide. It is no exaggeration to say that the modern suicide was a product of early modern Europe. Suicide as we know it—decriminalized, secularized, and medicalized—had taken hold among Europeans by the late 1700s.

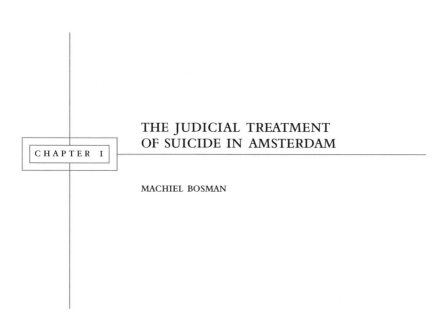

THE JUDICIAL TREATMENT
OF SUICIDE IN AMSTERDAM

CHAPTER I

MACHIEL BOSMAN

In 1792 Hendrik Roseboom, a twenty-nine-year-old man from Varel, was arrested in Amsterdam. He was thought to have perpetrated "tremendous thievery." Roseboom, who was obviously aware of his guilt and of the fate at hand for him, decided not to await his verdict and hanged himself in jail. Death, however, did not shield Roseboom from all legal consequences. The sheriffs, Amsterdam's judges, ruled that his corpse must be dragged on a hurdle to the harbor and then shipped to the other side of the IJ River. There the body was to be hanged by the legs in the gallows field, "to be consumed by the air and the birds."[1]

This was the last judicial sentence against a suicide in Amsterdam, the largest and most influential city of the Dutch Republic. In many other European cities, the postmortem punishment of suicides had fallen into disuse decades earlier. Be that as it may, Amsterdam was actually in the vanguard in the decriminalization of suicide. This apparent paradox can be explained by the fact that authorities in early modern Amsterdam made a strict distinction between criminals who killed themselves and suicides without a criminal record. In fact, Amsterdam's last known conviction of a suicide with no criminal past was in 1668.

How did this sharp distinction come to be made? To answer this, I have studied selected judicial proceedings of early modern Amsterdam from 1532, the date of the first extant case of suicide. In addition, I have examined the legal opinions of early modern Dutch scholars along with the traditions of Roman law, which had a profound impact on the legal treatment of suicides in Amsterdam.[2]

Legal Opinions on Suicide in the Dutch Republic

Roman law was originally very lenient on the subject of suicide. Among the Romans, the possessions of those condemned to death or to lifelong banishment were confiscated. Roman law, however, also applied the principle that death precluded trying or punishing a person for any crimes that he or she may have committed (*crimen extinguitur mortalitate*). As a result, suspects had the opportunity of safeguarding their estates by committing suicide before being convicted. This practice was abandoned in the first century AD, when the emperor Tiberius ordained that confiscation should also be imposed on suicides who had been brought to this act by a moral awareness of having perpetrated a crime (*ob conscientiam criminis*).[3] Thereafter, criminals who took their lives were in serious danger of having their estates confiscated by Roman authorities. Three conditions had to be met before such a confiscation could be effected. First, this penalty had to be justified by the severity of the crime committed. Second, the suspect had to have been either caught in the act or charged with the crime before taking his life. And finally, there must be no other plausible motives for suicide, such as weariness of life (*taedium vitae*), unendurable suffering, or mental illness. Only suicides meeting this profile were considered to have been committed *ob conscientiam criminis*. Even then, it was still possible for surviving relatives to contest confiscation, but they bore the burden of proving the deceased's innocence.[4] Most important, Roman law prescribed no penalties against noncriminals who took their lives.

The fall of the Western Empire put an end to the more lenient treatment of suicide in the West. Although the Bible mentions a half dozen suicides and contains no explicit condemnation of voluntary death, various church fathers took an aggressive stand against taking one's own life. Augustine, the fifth-century church father, was the thinker most responsible for the development of Christianity's long abhorrence of suicide. In *The City of God (De Civitate Dei)*, he stated that he who kills himself is a murderer, interpreting the sixth commandment as forbidding both suicide and murder.[5]

The early medieval church followed Augustine's lead, classifying suicide as a mortal sin, regardless of motive. As suicides lost their lives in the very act of committing this sin, they were deemed beyond redemption. Augustine's views on suicide were confirmed by the Council of Orléans in 533, and thirty years later the Council of Braga denied funerary rights to suicides: "for those who voluntarily kill themselves either by a blade, poison, throwing themselves off precipices, hanging themselves, or violently by any other method, let there be no commemorative prayer for them at Mass and let not their bodies be brought to burial with Psalms: for out of ignorance, many are wrongfully performing these ceremonies."[6]

In the second half of the Middle Ages secular courts came to prominence in the administration of justice on suicide. Regional customary law, which in this period was the most pervasive form of law, shared this abhorrence of suicide but went beyond the canonical denial of funerary rights. Various European regions developed different ways of defiling a suicide's body and memory. In Zurich the penalty reflected the manner in which suicide had been committed. Those who had jumped to their deaths found their resting places at the foot of a mountain; those who had drowned themselves were buried in sand. In Metz and in Strasbourg a suicide's body would be committed to the river after packing it into a barrel, while in England it would be buried at a crossroads.[7]

In most of the Low Countries a suicide's body would be hanged "to feed the ravens."[8] The corpse would be put on a hurdle and dragged through the mire on its way to the gallows field, where it was put on display on a gallows formed by a two-pronged stick. The same penalty was applied in parts of Germany and France. The Flemish lawyer Filips Wielant (ca. 1441–1520) gave the following explanation of these rituals: "And the reason is the enormity of the crime. For if someone kills another person, he kills only the body, but if he kills himself, he kills both body and soul."[9] A suicide's estate as well as his body could suffer legal consequences. From the thirteenth century on, sources in various European regions record confiscation of a suicide's belongings.[10]

The earliest softening of legal opinions on suicide in medieval Europe was found in Bologna. Significantly, Bologna in the twelfth century became the most important center for the study of both canon and Roman law, giving stimulus to the creation of the world's first university. There, some scholars revived the notion, found in Roman law, that suicide out of madness was pardonable. After some time this attitude penetrated secular justice in the Low Countries: in the fifteenth century it was decreed that a suicide was punishable only if committed "intentionally" or "knowingly."[11]

The late Middle Ages also witnessed the beginning of a process of centralization of power in the Low Countries. The machinery of more centralized governments was established, including tribunals overseeing different jurisdictions. These courts were increasingly staffed with educated lawyers who tried to apply the traditions of Roman law they had studied. As a result, while the judgments in courts of first instance were based on local unwritten customary laws, appellate courts, increasingly staffed by university educated jurists, were likely also to apply provisions from Justinian's code.[12]

The year 1510 marked the first time that the prevailing customary law was written down for any of the provinces of the Netherlands. In that year, the Fleming Wielant published his *Pracktyke Criminele (Criminal Practice)*, providing a description of the law then current in Brabant and Flanders, two of the southern provinces. In 1555 Wielant's compatriot Joost de Damhouder (1507–1581) published a document under the same title, which in part plagiarized the work of Wielant. De Damhouder, who discussed suicide more extensively than had Wielant, noted the discrepancy between written law and customary law:

> According to written law, whoever takes his own life out of desperation and despair or out of fear of losing his life, his honor or his estate, or from similar causes and evil intentions, will be dragged on a hurdle and hanged on a gibbet. . . . But if he has done so out of illness, having been speedily and suddenly overpowered by some frenzy, profound melancholy, or the loss of the senses, he will receive a Christian burial and not be hanged on a gibbet, and such according to written law. . . . According to customary law, whoever takes his own life (for whatever cause or reason) will be hanged on a gibbet as his own murderer, and his goods will be forfeited.[13]

If under customary law suicide was punished without fail, under written law suicide out of madness was pardonable.

The sixteenth and seventeenth centuries were of monumental importance for the history of the Netherlands. In the later 1500s, a number of provinces of the Netherlands, motivated in part by their Protestant convictions, revolted against the very Catholic Philip II, King of Spain and sovereign of the Low Countries. After some time, the Netherlands were partitioned, with the southern provinces remaining loyal to Philip while their northern counterparts pursued permanent independence under the leadership of Holland. Thus was born the predominantly Protestant Dutch Republic, which signed a twelve-year truce with Spain in 1609, though the King of Spain did not renounce his claims to the Netherlands until 1648.

During the truce with Spain, strong internal dissensions brought the young Republic to the brink of civil war. One of their victims was Hugo Grotius (1583–1645), the great pioneer in the study of natural law. From 1619 to 1621 he was imprisoned in a castle, from which he eventually escaped by hiding in a book chest which was then removed from the castle. While in confinement, Grotius passed his time by writing a description of the law that currently prevailed in the province of Holland. The result of this project, *Inleidinge in de Hollandsche regtsgeleertheit (Introduction to the Law of Holland)* is now praised as "the most fundamental document on law in the Republic"[14] and was considered "the basis of our national law" in the eighteenth-century Republic.[15] On the criminal consequences of suicide, Grotius wrote, "But no one has an unlimited right over his life. Therefore in Holland persons who deliberately do away with themselves have always been subject to punishment, even though not accused of crime: for their bodies were dragged on a hurdle and hanged on a gibbet, and their goods forfeited. And this went on so far that some privileges which permitted forfeited

DESPERATIO.

Effudit vitam desperans Iscariotes.,
Sublimi ligno triste pependit onus.

Die Verzweiflung.
Iudas Verräther nicht bedenckt,
waß er gethan, und sich erhenckt.

Eichler del.

Hertel excud:

Figure 1. Cesare Ripa, *Desperatio,* engraving, early seventeenth century, reprinted in
Baroque and Rococo Pictorial Imagery: The 1758–1760 Hertel Edition of Ripa's "Iconologia",
ed. Edward A. Maser (New York: Dover, 1971), 59.

goods to be redeemed for a small sum made an exception in the case of such a desperate deed, along with other great offences."[16] During his confinement, Grotius lacked the means of supporting his statements with sources and texts of law. But it appears that his view on the penalization of suicide was based, among other things, on the aforementioned decrees of the fifteenth century. As noted previously, these decrees also mandated penalties only if suicide was committed knowingly and deliberately.

It is questionable, however, whether these decrees adequately reflected legal practice in seventeenth-century Holland. Simon van Groenewegen (1613–1652), a lawyer who in 1644 published an annotated edition of Grotius's *Inleidinge,* thought that other rules applied to suicide. He provided the following comment on Grotius's discussion of self-inflected death:

> But according to De Damhouder and Zypaeus [1580–1650], the afore-
> mentioned practice and punishment is not imposed upon those who have
> done away with themselves out of madness or otherwise, if they are not
> guilty of any crime. . . . According to Roman Law, even those who do
> away with themselves out of dejection and despair are not liable to pun-
> ishment, if they have not been accused of any prior crime. . . . This inter-
> pretation of the law is also found in two sentences of the Court of Holland
> given on the 30th of September 1616 in the case of the guardians of the
> children of Pieter Iansz.[17]

This might well be the first time that a description of a law current in a European region has been so explicitly derived from a correct understanding of Roman law. Like De Damhouder before him, Van Groenewegen distinguished three motives for suicide. If not committed out of madness or from fear of punishment, it must have been committed out of despair; there were no other options. In judicial terms, suicide out of desperation was deemed no more than killing oneself "without any cause," as a Dutch bailiff phrased it in court in 1610.[18] Van Groenewegen, taking his line from Roman law, could see no reason for punishing the suicide without cause.

Van Groenewegen's lead was widely followed and all subsequent Dutch lawyers subscribed to his views.[19] In 1659 Simon van Leeuwen (ca. 1625–1682) simplified the suicide case by recognizing two categories of motive only. In his words there were "those who, convinced of having committed serious crimes, do away with themselves in order to escape punishment and . . . are dragged through the streets on a hurdle and hanged on a gibbet"; and there were "those who wrong themselves merely from despair or dejection, and . . . are not liable to corporal or financial punishment."[20] Since suicide out of despair was not punishable, it went without saying that suicide motivated by madness was also not subject to punishment.

By the eighteenth century, the penalization of suicide was no longer even an issue among Dutch lawyers. On the one hand, few if any calls were made for the decriminalization of suicide committed in order to escape punishment; on the other hand, the impunity of suicide without cause was rarely if ever contested. In 1777 the Genootschap van Rechtsgeleerden (Society of Legal Scholars) even felt called on to prove that the punishing of suicide out of despair had been "in use with us in ancient times." As for the standards of its own days, the Genootschap stated, "Finally we note that the punishment of those who have done away with themselves while not accused of crimes, went out of use . . . years ago . . . and nowadays is not administered anymore."[21] In 1809 the introduction of the *Crimineel Wetboek voor het koninkrijk Holland* (Penal Code for the Kingdom of Holland) rendered the old Dutch criminal law inoperative. The Code contained no provisions on suicide, marking the last step in the process of the decriminalization of suicide in the Netherlands.

Sixteenth-Century Suicides

Of all violent crimes suicide is probably the most poorly documented in the judicial records of early modern Europe. It is different from other offences in that both the perpetrator and the victim die, leaving neither to be interrogated. Amsterdam's legal archives contain two collections of sentences from the sixteenth century: the Book of Justice (1524–1709) and the Book of Confessions (1534–1811).[22] The latter contains records of the sheriffs' interrogations of suspects. This collection generally sheds little light on suicide since those who took their lives obviously could not be questioned. The Book of Justice was drawn up by the bailiff, whose responsibilities comprised those of today's commissioner of police, examining magistrate, and public prosecutor. In the Book of Justice, the bailiff made notes on those offences that were publicly punished on conviction. This is a very useful source of information on sixteenth-century suicide because it contains autopsy reports. Whenever an unnatural death occurred, the bailiff and two sheriffs held a postmortem examination of the body. Witnesses were also interrogated to establish the facts surrounding the untimely death.

The historian Jean Jungen examined the earliest Book of Justice, covering the years 1524–1565, and the succeeding Book of Justice for the years 1570, 1580, and 1590. This research revealed twenty-two suicides: eleven by stabbing, seven by hanging, three by drowning, and one whose method is undocumented.[23] In only eight of these cases is it known what happened to the corpses, a reflection of the fact that discharge or acquittal generally went unrecorded in the Amsterdam Book of Justice.

The earliest suicide known in Amsterdam was that of Ael Heinricxdochter in 1532. The Book of Justice recorded, "Today the bailiff and the sheriffs of the court . . . held a postmortem on the body of Ael Heinricxdochter, married to a Jan Brouwer, who, it was said, stabbed herself under the left breast in the heart with a small bread knife while lying on her bed in her vest, and died instantaneously."[24] Although the Book of Justice says nothing more about this death, another source is more revealing. Heinricxdochter's estate was contested before the Court of Holland, and its verdict yields more information on a suicide in sixteenth-century Amsterdam than any other known source.[25] At the inquest into Heinricx-dochter's suicide, the bailiff "could conclude only that the event in question had occurred out of desperation."[26] The bailiff then entered into negotiations with Heinricxdochter's widower, Jan Brouwer, who ultimately paid a sum of three hundred pounds to prevent the public display of his wife's corpse. The body, rather than left exposed, was buried in unconsecrated ground, possibly in the *Ellendigenkerkhof* (Churchyard of the Wretched) where "the only burials are those of convicted criminals and those who are deemed unworthy of consecrated ground."[27]

A criminal case was usually considered settled after such a buy-off, but it was not so in this case. The steward, an official responsible for fiscal matters in the county of Holland, demanded the "separation" of Ael Heinricxdochter's possessions, meaning confiscation of half of her estate. Refusing to give up, Brouwer appealed to the Court of Holland in 1537. During the trial Brouwer argued that confiscation contravened written law, while the prosecutor referred to unwritten customary law, which did provide for confiscation. The Court chose an intermediate position, allowing confiscation but not in excess of one hundred pounds. In doing so, the Court based its decision on a privilege granted to Amsterdam in 1404, according to which no subject of this city could forfeit more than his life and one hundred pounds of his estate.[28]

Jan Brouwer did not take this lying down but appealed to the Great Council of Mechlin, the highest court in the Low Countries. This court ruled entirely in his favor in 1538.[29] All the same, the Court of Holland's earlier verdict shows that a sentence of confiscation was not out of the question at this time. This is noteworthy since in Amsterdam confiscation was hardly ever imposed except as an additional punishment in the event of a death sentence. But a buy-off, such as that presented by Jan Brouwer, ordinarily amounted to settling a case without a sentence. Why then did authorities try to confiscate part of Heinricxdochter's belongings anyway? The answer to this requires a short digression. When someone died under suspicious circumstances, the bailiff and the sheriffs held a postmortem investigation to establish the cause of death. If a crime had been committed, they normally tried to identify the culprit through investigation, prosecution, and a trial which might ultimately result in a death sentence. But in an undisputed case of suicide, the offence and the offender were discovered simultaneously, and death had already occurred. In such cases the Amsterdam authorities considered prosecution and a trial unnecessary: the suicide had sentenced himself by his very deed, and the sheriffs could order the confiscation without a trial and conviction.[30]

Although Ael Heinricxdochter was apparently the only Amsterdam suicide whose case reached the Court of Holland, the Book of Justice provided varying degrees of information about other suicides. In five cases, this source contains only an autopsy report similar to that for Heinricxdochter, making no mention of any possible sanctions pertaining to the burial of the corpse or the estate of the deceased.[31] The autopsy reports for eight other suicides note mitigating circumstances. Some of these were described as insane, while others found windows of opportunity to confess their sins between their deeds and their deaths.[32] The very fact that such circumstances were recorded so often suggests that they influenced the way a suicide was judged. This was definitely the case in the handling of Jan Pouwelsz's suicide. In 1551 he stabbed himself in the abdomen six times, dying from his wounds some two or three hours later. Since he showed "great contrition" after inflicting the wounds, Pouwelsz was permitted to be buried in consecrated ground.[33]

By contrast, seven suicides from the sixteenth century are known to have been subjected to postmortem punishment. In most cases, these sentences were imposed on people who had committed a serious crime before taking their lives. For example, Andries Jacobsz, whose body was convicted to the gallows, had murdered his wife prior to taking his own life.[34] Three others who were hanged postmortem had committed suicide while on remand or on the run from justice. Although it is not clear in all cases what crimes they were suspected of, a crime preceding the suicide was obviously viewed as an aggravating circumstance.[35]

However, apart from those with criminal records, suicides generally were not subject to postmortem penalties. Among those whose bodies were left exposed, only Symon Aertsz in 1548 and Cornelis Wesseltsz in 1553 were not specifically said to be guilty or suspected of felonies prior to their suicides.[36] One other suicide, who probably had not committed a crime before taking his life, was buried in the gallows field.[37] That sentence possibly stemmed from the fact that he was the only one to hang himself in a public area. The Amsterdam authorities were inclined to be more severe with crimes committed in public.

All told, judicial records show that already in the sixteenth century, Amsterdam authorities were most aggressive in passing sentence against the suicides of criminals and that insanity could exculpate, to a degree, voluntary death.

Seventeenth-Century Suicides

The 1600s, Amsterdam's golden century, yield little information on the subject of suicide. Diligent research has turned up only four decisions concerning suicide. To a degree, this lack of data stems from the fact that the administration of criminal justice in seventeenth-century Amsterdam has thus far been poorly researched.[38] Another problem is that the richest source for the previous years, the autopsy reports, ran dry in the 1600s. This was because the autopsies were no longer performed by the bailiff and the sheriffs but by the *gezworen chirurgijns van den gerechte* (sworn surgeons of the court). The surgeons usually gave a medical opinion only, with no legal conclusion attached. To make things worse, their reports are missing for the years up to 1666. In reports from a later date, a number of deaths were attributed to "strangulation." Although some of those who died in this manner were probably suicides, searching for them in the books of sentences bears little fruit.[39] In his research on the Book of Justice for the years 1650 to 1708, Pieter Spierenburg found only one suicide, occurring in 1658.[40] The Book of Confessions mentions no cases at all in the second half of the seventeenth century.[41]

Significantly, Spierenburg did not come across verdicts of criminals who killed themselves either. This is remarkable since suicides *ob conscientiam criminis* were punished in both the sixteenth and eighteenth centuries; it is implausible that they were treated differently in the 1600s. Also, Hans Bontemantel (1613 – 1688), a sheriff of Amsterdam, mentions a convicted suicide in 1668 that is not found in the sentence books.[42] This seems to imply that in the second half of the seventeenth century, verdicts for suicide were not regularly recorded in the books of sentences. It is not known where they were recorded.[43]

In spite of the challenges endemic in this archival research, some important insight to the judicial treatment of suicide in seventeenth-century Amsterdam can be gathered. There is specific reference to two cases in the notes of Bontemantel and two in the judicial archives.[44] Serving six times on Amsterdam's board of sheriffs between 1654 and 1672, Bontemantel left a very rich collection of notes on the administration of criminal justice in his day. He referred to suicide on a number of occasions, providing, among other things, the following description of the treatment of suicides with no criminal records:

> The custom in Amsterdam is for someone who has hanged himself to be examined or inspected by the bailiff in the presence of two sheriffs, who will draw up a report on this inquest. The sheriffs will then order the corpse to be buried at night by police officers, even though the bailiff will demand that the corpse be pulled underneath the door, dragged on a hurdle

through the streets with its face down, and buried beneath the gallows. . . . [The corpse] will sometimes be interred in the evening by friends, provided that the sheriffs consent.[45]

Bontemantel's account clearly indicates that in contrast to the previous century, suicides were tried by sheriffs in the 1600s. This stemmed in part from the increasing acceptance of Roman law which contributed to the standardization of the administration of justice. In addition, the bailiff and the sheriffs were no longer responsible for collecting all the evidence, as physicians performed the autopsies. This meant that it was for the court to determine the weight of the evidence gathered from all sources.

More important, Bontemantel revealed that the sheriffs could be relatively lenient in handling suicides, as they were usually buried in silence. Quiet burials—interments that took place, often at night, without prayers or ceremonies—were commonly prescribed for the corpses of suicides in early modern Europe. This denial of funerary rites might be accompanied by further dishonor concerning the site of the burial—the bodies could be consigned to the gallows field or to a separate part of the churchyard. Amsterdam was also familiar with this practice, as a verdict from 1647 shows. Plaus (?) Michielsen, who had hanged himself in an inn on the Zeedijk, was "laid on a sledge pulled by a horse and brought to the Churchyard of the Wretched in order to be buried there."[46]

According to Bontemantel the bailiff's demand for burial in the gallows field was little more than a formality that he did not really expect to be imposed. Nonetheless, this demand was met occasionally. In 1658 Michiel Straatsburg, a seventy-two-year-old sailor, committed suicide by hanging. The sheriffs took a firm stand: not only was his body sentenced to be buried in the gallows field in "a pit without a coffin," but his goods were confiscated as well.[47] This second part of the punishment is particularly interesting as Bontemantel made no mention of seizure at all in his description of the treatment of suicides with no criminal record.

In considering the case of a German who committed suicide in 1669, Bontemantel addressed the issue of confiscation head on. The German was granted a silent burial in light of his melancholy nature, but the sheriffs disagreed as to whether his estate should be confiscated. Bontemantel was resolutely opposed to confiscation because "those who wrong themselves merely from despair or dejection . . . are not subject to corporal or financial punishment."[48] This argument prevailed, and the German's estate remained intact. Nevertheless this case implied that the confiscation of goods could occur even when permission for a silent burial had been granted.

For Bontemantel, a quiet burial alone was the appropriate sentence for most suicides, but not all his judicial colleagues concurred. In his notes, Bontemantel referred to a suicide in 1668 who, though not suspected of any criminal activities, was nonetheless publicly displayed on the gallows anyway. It is a sad story:

> A man, . . . who was in the habit of asking his wife for money to buy brandy, would on her refusal say that he would go hang himself. When on 23 June 1668 he again asked for two pennies to buy brandy, his wife said she had no money, whereupon he replied, "I will hang myself or may the devil take me." His wife replied, "Do whatever you like, you always say that," and went back to her cleaning. Shortly thereafter, she found that her husband had hanged himself in their home. She then called for the neighbors, who have all made declarations and given evidence. On a charge by the bailiff, his corpse has been taken to the Volewijk [Amsterdam's gallows field] on 26 June 1668 and hanged on a gibbet.[49]

Bontemantel, who often showed more clemency than his fellow sheriffs, did not attend the trial and reacted with indignation to the sentence; in the margin next to his summary of this case, he wrote, "I am not responsible for this [sentence] and it is against the law."[50]

These irate comments are quite revealing. Although the extant sources are patchy, Bontemantel was correct in suggesting that this "punishment" of suicide was against customary law; beyond mandating quiet burials, penalties against suicide were in fact falling into disuse by this time. Excluding suicides with criminal records, we have no record of any penalty imposed after 1668 on the bodies—other than night burials—or estates of those who took their lives. The evidence suggests that by the later seventeenth century, suicide per se was becoming decriminalized. This does not mean that in the eighteenth century suicide was no longer a matter for the law. Autopsies were still undertaken, and witnesses were still interrogated, but these inquests were intended above all to ensure that the deceased was not the victim of foul play. Once the sheriffs concluded the death was self-inflicted, suicides who had committed no other crime were to be buried, either with traditional honors or in silence.[51]

The denial of funerary rites to suicides also begs the question as to whether the Protestant Reformation had any impact on the administration of justice in cases of suicide in the Netherlands. The conversion to Protestantism in theory eliminated the distinction between consecrated and unconsecrated burial ground. More broadly, Reformed Protestant leaders, such as Calvin, hoped to demystify burials entirely, which they considered heavily laden with pagan superstitions. But although Calvin would have liked to do away with burial rituals altogether, nowhere did rank-and-file Protestants ever fully embrace this aspect of Calvinist morality. Throughout early modern Europe, Reformed Protestants conducted funerary processions to cemeteries, where mourners offered prayers and sang Psalms. Although Protestants of course believed that funerary ceremonies had no impact on one's eternal fate, burials that occurred quietly in the evening without ceremony were nonetheless intended to impugn the honor of the deceased.[52] As Amsterdam's legal practices governing suicide had parallels in Catholic regions, the conversion to Protestantism apparently had little impact on decisions concerning the bodies and estates of those who took their lives.

Eighteenth-Century Suicides *"Ob Conscientiam Criminis"*

Judicial records for eighteenth-century Amsterdam show unequivocally that, among suicides, only criminals had anything to fear from the law.[53] Although no evidence exists of any action against the bodies and estates of other suicides, criminals who took their lives continued to be punished through the late 1700s. Suicides committed in prison in Amsterdam can easily be identified from 1732, the date from which are extant the bills of wardens of De Boeijen, an Amsterdam remand center. Wardens kept detailed records of detainees, in part because prisoners were supposed to pay for their jail accommodations themselves. As most of them could not afford these charges, wardens could make claims to the bailiff for prisoners' unpaid fees. Their bills contain concise information about the offenders, the length of their stays in De Boeijen, the nature of their offences, and the sheriffs' verdicts.

De Boeijen not only housed prisoners but also served as a storage place of corpses that were to be punished. Consequently, the bills of wardens shed light not only on those in custody who took their lives but also on miscreants who committed suicide before being arrested. Authorities were aware of the penchant of prisoners, especially those who might face capital punishment, to do away with themselves and took measures to prevent such voluntary deaths. If prison and judicial officials feared that certain prisoners might make an attempt on their lives, guards were posted to watch over them. A failed suicide attempt resulted in tightened security, as was evident in the case of J. F. Humbert Droz, who eventually died on the scaffold. While awaiting execution in 1766, Droz attempted to take his life by slitting a vein in his arm with a piece of glass. Guards immediately intervened, preventing him from completing the suicide. The sheriff further reported, "After he had been bandaged by the doctor and the surgeon, it was reported that [Droz] was out of danger but should be kept quiet and well guarded lest he do himself further harm. Thereafter, the Board [of sheriffs] decided to strap his hands to his body in such a way that he could not join them and to assign to him six guards instead of two, all six of whom were strongly advised to make sure that he not harm himself any further and that they would be held accountable if he did."[54] In spite of such measures, several eighteenth-century criminals did manage to cheat the hangman. Between 1732 and 1795 Amsterdam officials took action against fourteen suicides who had criminal records.[55] Three of these committed suicide before being arrested, all of whom were accused of murder. The other eleven took their lives while in custody, either in De Boeijen or in guardhouses where people who were arrested at night were kept until the following morning. Most of these suspected criminals hanged themselves, though one stabbed himself.

Of the fourteen suicides with criminal backgrounds, nine were sentenced to postmortem punishment. The form that these sentences took was apparently related to the preceding crime. For example, the body of Arnoldus Wensing, who had been arrested for sodomy, was thrown into the IJ River; sodomites who had been executed met the same postmortem fate. The bodies of the other eight suicides were taken to the Volewijk. Two of these, both swindlers, were buried under the gallows, while the remaining murderers and thieves were "hanged . . . by the legs on the gibbet, until they will have been consumed by the air and its fowl."[56] Being hanged by the legs had a symbolic meaning, indicating that this criminal had evaded the normal judicial process through his or her death.[57]

All nine of these were convicted of suicide "committed, as it were, *ex conscientia sceleris* [out of a moral awareness of the crime] and to escape well-deserved punishment."[58] By taking their lives, the suicides had shirked the judicial process for their previous misdeeds. In most cases the self-inflicted death was the sole offence listed in the indictment. Only one suicide confessed his earlier crime before taking his life, while three murderers committed suicide while on the run. Under either of these circumstances, the sheriffs considered the earlier offence proven, and the sentence then spoke of "two utterly abominable crimes."[59] It should be noted that none of the sentences mentions the confiscation of goods. In fact in Holland in 1732, authorities had forbidden the seizure of all a person's belongings, regardless of the crime that he or she may have committed.

No sentences can be found for the five other people who committed suicide while in jail. The bodies of these were transferred from De Boeijen to the hospital. From there they were buried it seems—undoubtedly in silence and without ceremony. In these cases, judicial authorities apparently deemed that the deceased's crimes were not severe enough to merit postmortem punishment. Three of them were accused of theft; as the sources do not reveal what was stolen, they might well have been petty thieves. Another prisoner had merely been "impudent," while the crime of the remaining suicide is not known. Had they been guilty of crimes considered more serious, their bodies probably would have been subject to hanging or burial in the Volewijk. In short, the judicial treatment of criminal suicides in eighteenth-century Amsterdam aimed at punishing not the self-inflicted death per se but the crimes committed prior to the suicide.

When dealing with those who had committed serious crimes, however, Amsterdam officials did not mitigate the treatment of the bodies of suicides *ob conscientiam criminis* until the very end of the eighteenth century. The last time a suicide's corpse was publicly displayed in the Amsterdam gallows field was as late as 1792. It took a Revolution to get suicide *ob conscientiam criminis* decriminalized. In 1795 the French Revolution spread to the Dutch Republic, resulting in the overthrow of the Stadtholder and the establishment of a parliament. On 6 March 1795 the Provisional Representatives of the People of Holland consigned the gallows fields to the dustbins of Dutch history, issuing the following decree:

> As the experience of many years has shown that the gallows, racks, and whipping posts put up in many places along the public roads serve merely to present a sorry spectacle of past barbarism . . . , so have we now decided to decree that everywhere in this Province all traces of this ancient barbarism shall be removed as soon as possible and at the latest within six weeks after this promulgation. . . . Whereas we also decree that henceforth the dead bodies of all those that may be subjected to capital punishment within the Province of Holland shall be removed immediately after execution and be decently buried.[60]

Though not issued for this specific purpose, this decree effectively did away with postmortem punishment of suicide in Amsterdam.

Conclusion

In 1721 Montesquieu published his famous *Persian Letters.* Its leading character, Usbek, a Persian traveling through Europe, described European mores concerning suicide: "In Europe the law treats suicides with the utmost ferocity. They are put to death for a second time, so to speak; their bodies are dragged in disgrace through the streets and branded, to denote infamy, and their goods are confiscated."[61] In some parts of Europe the law was every bit as severe as Montesquieu suggested. But in Amsterdam, and possibly in the Republic as a whole, the Dutch were clearly in the vanguard in the decriminalization of suicide.[62] At the time that Montesquieu wrote these words, only the suicides of criminals received sentences that went beyond prescribing quiet burials.

The roots of this pattern can be traced to earlier centuries. In the sixteenth century, the first extant records reveal that authorities were considerably more severe in handling the suicides of criminals than those of noncriminals. The seventeenth century marked important legal changes in the province of Holland. Hugo Grotius, the preeminent early modern Dutch jurist, was the first to write down the province's law code, heretofore unwritten customary law. The writing down of customary law nurtured the further standardization of the administration of justice. In 1644 the jurist Simon van Groenewegen asserted that according to both Roman law and the jurisprudence of the Court of Holland, only those suicides committed *ob conscientiam criminis* were to be penalized, further emphasizing the distinction made by Amsterdam officials in the previous century. As noted previously, the city witnessed the last known conviction of a suicide without a criminal past in 1668.

Of interest, although Amsterdam was in the forefront in the decriminalization of suicide, its authorities continued to punish criminals who took their lives through the late eighteenth century, well after such practices had been abandoned in many other areas of Europe. As in Roman law, criminals who killed themselves were subjected only to those penalties that could still be carried out. From the time of Tiberius, this involved the confiscation of the estate among the Romans; in Amsterdam, where confiscations were abolished in 1732, this involved the display of the corpse. Clearly, the adoption of Roman law was a major influence on the legal approaches to suicide in early modern Amsterdam.

In spite of the attacks of Cesare Beccaria and a host of philosophes on the penalties against suicide, the Enlightenment did not play a significant role in the decriminalization of suicide in Amsterdam. If we leave aside criminals who took their lives, suicide in Amsterdam was effectively decriminalized a century before the publication of Beccaria's *Crimes and Punishments* (1764). Moreover, the "enlightened" debate on suicide paid scant attention to the punishment of criminal suicides, who continued to be punished in Amsterdam more than a century after penalties had fallen into disuse for those who killed themselves out of madness, melancholy, despair, or reasons unknown.

When the French Revolution reached Holland and a new republic was created in 1795, the legal treatment of suicide had in effect gone full circle. With the abolition of the gallows field and the de facto decriminalization of all suicides, the Dutch had, wittingly or unwittingly, returned to the judicial traditions of the Roman Republic—death precluded punishment, and suicide itself was not a crime.

CHAPTER 2

SUICIDE AND THE VICAR GENERAL IN LONDON

A Mystery Solved?

PAUL S. SEAVER

On 10 September 1601, Richard Hill, a parishioner of St. Sepulchres in the city of London, appeared before Dr. Edward Stanhope, the chancellor and vicar general of the diocese of London and alleged that Richard Allen of the parish of St. Mary Magdalen in Milk Street, "being lately sick and in his sickness so perplexed as that he did by instigation of the devil . . . attempt to have cut his own throat and did partly effect the same;" although dying, he was able to summon the parson to whom "he made a great confession of his hearty sorrow and repentance . . . , and with acknowledgment of his fault and desire of pardon at God's hand made a very good and christian-like confession of his faith and so ended his life the same day." Despite the testimony of the surgeons in attendance that Allen's wound would not have proved deadly had he not been so debilitated by his long sickness, the coroner returned a verdict of *felo de se,* thus denying the suicide the possibility of a Christian burial under ordinary circumstances. Nevertheless, it was precisely the wish to secure a Christian burial that had brought the suicide's friend before the vicar general, and the latter, having heard testimony backed by the parson that Richard Allen had indeed expressed his "hearty repentance," granted a license in the name of the bishop for a burial to take place in the parish church of St. Mary Magdalen, so long as the parson consented and the interment "be done without any great pomp or show."[1]

The right to give Richard Allen a Christian burial was of course precisely the reason for his friend and his parson to appeal to the vicar general. A bishop's chancellor and vicar general was the chief judicial officer of a diocese, in this period a layman with training in civil law who both presided over the bishop's courts and over an office that granted licenses to marry, to practice midwifery and surgery, to probate wills and bequests, to elect parish clerks and alter the furnishing or structure of parish churches, to enter into a benefice and to preach, and a variety of other acts requiring episcopal approval. Burial in consecrated ground was, as is well known, a right (and a rite) that was normally denied to a suicide, to a person convicted by a coroner's jury of self-murder, of *felo de se*. Thus, the parish clerk of St. Botolph's Aldgate noted in his register on 28 November 1595 that a coroner's jury had met "to inquire out how Elizabeth Wickham, a widow, being an incontinent person did come to her death, who had hanged herself upon a garden pale by her apron strings." Once it was determined that she had previously attempted to take her life, the jury came to the conclusion, perhaps foregone, that she had murdered herself, and returned a verdict of *felo de se,* in consequence of which she was buried "in the alley where she hanged herself, according to her deserts, having a stake driven through her in remembrance of her wicked [act?]; she was about some thirty-six years old."[2]

What follows is not a study of suicide as such, but rather of the reactions to it and explanations offered for it in extenuation of what both church and state regarded as a crime against God, nature, and the Commonwealth. It is not an attempt to revise what is known about suicide in early modern England, but rather to suggest that the treatment of suicide in early seventeenth-century London in particular points to the new and powerful role the metropolis was coming to play in English society and culture. The city's dominant role as a media center both in the production of books and of manuscript newsletters and, as the century wore on, as a center of polite opinion and manners, was to make it not only the leader in new kinds of fashion, entertainment, and consumption, but perhaps more importantly in new attitudes and cultural change.[3]

The early Tudor state had strengthened the machinery of detection and increased the probability that possible deaths by misadventure would nevertheless be identified as self-murder. By statutes of 1487 and 1510 coroners were required to report all suspicious, unexplained, or "unnatural" deaths twice yearly to King's Bench. Jurors were given only four possible verdicts—misadventure, homicide, suicide, or "an act of God"—and coroners were given the not inconsiderable incentive of one mark (13s.4d.) for each homicide discovered and reported, including *felo de se*. The king's almoner or his deputies had the right to the goods and chattels of suicides, and from the late 1530s this right was strengthened by the almoner's capacity to sue in Star Chamber. However, a jury could obviate the sanctions imposed on homicides, including suicides, if the jury judged the perpetrator to have been mad at the time of the act, in which case a verdict of *non compos mentis* (not sound of mind) could be returned. Michael MacDonald has shown in his pioneering study how the growth of such *non compos mentis* verdicts from the 1680s to the 1760s can be used as an index of an important change in cultural attitudes toward suicide. Nevertheless, it was not until 1823 that a parliamentary statute abrogated the penalty of bodily desecration and permitted suicides to be buried in the churchyard or other burial ground of the parish, and not until 1870 that the government finally ceased to demand the forfeiture of a suicide's chattels.[4] The point obviously of such a bizarre and ancient custom of interment, as that visited on Elizabeth Wickham of Aldgate, was not so much to punish the suicide—she was in any case beyond the reach of the authorities— as it was to dramatize the horror of the act of self-destruction and to deter similar acts by jeopardizing the survival of a suicide's family. As a contemporary wrote, it was customary "to bury such as lay violent hands upon themselves, in or near to the highways, with a stake thrust through their bodies, to terrify all passengers, by that so infamous and reproachful a burial, not to make their final passage out of this present world. The fear of not having burial, or having an ignominious and dishonorable burial, hath ever affrighted the bravest spirits in the world."[5] The deterrent effect, if any, as with most sanctions against criminalized acts, is hard to measure.

The episcopal licensing of burial of a suicide was not totally unprecedented. A manuscript license, apparently granted by Bishop John Aylmer, exists from Elizabeth's reign, which is in form remarkably similar to that recorded in 1601 in the vicar general's book:

> John by permission of God, Bishop of London, to all Christian people to whom these presents shall come, greeting. Whereas Thomas Leech, Gent. late (while he lived) of the parish of St. Mildred in the Poultry, London, of our diocese and jurisdiction of London, did before his death lay violent hands on himself and cut his own throat with a knife, whereby he had and received such a mortal wound, that he died of that hurt: by reason whereof it might be doubted, whether he had such an interest in Christian burial, as other persons of this realm have.

As was true in the Allen case in 1601, the episcopal license then went on to cite mitigating circumstances:

> Yet notwithstanding, forasmuch as it hath been testified before Sir Henry Martin, Knight, our Chancellor, that the said Thomas Leach falling into deep melancholy passions, whereof he languished six or seven months, was thereby many times distracted of his wits, and had no reason in those distractions to govern himself; and that after the wound he had received, he lived some little time, and when he could not speak, was found groaning and lifting up his hands, whereby it appeared, that he had an apprehension

of, or was penitent for, the sin he had committed in laying violent hands on himself, and died a good Christian. And thereupon petition has been made to us, that leave and license may be granted to bury the body of Thomas Leach, and our said chancellor hath decreed the same to be granted. We, therefore, the Bishop aforesaid, for the reasons set down, so far as in us is, and by law we can or may, have and do give and grant license and leave, &c.[6]

The formulaic nature of Bishop Aylmer's license and that of Bishop Richard Bancroft's vicar general, recorded in 1601, suggest that earlier licenses of a similar nature might have been granted, but, if so, these remain unknown. However, although Aylmer's episcopal license closely resembles those recorded in the vicar general's book in 1601, it was not itself recorded in any of the vicar general's books for the years of Aylmer's London episcopate (1577–1594), nor does such a license appear in the vicar general books at any time prior to 1601.[7] In the course of the next four decades a series of vicar generals in the name of the bishops of London granted thirty-one licenses for the Christian burial of suicide, but these petitions never challenged or extenuated either the fact of self-murder or the moral opprobrium attached to the act.[8]

The Christian case against suicide was by the seventeenth century very ancient. In his *The Theatre of Gods Judgments,* Thomas Beard, the well-known Calvinist preacher and schoolmaster of Huntingdon, began his chapter, "Of such as have murdered themselves," by noting that

Saint Augustine in his first book *De Civitate Dei* doth most strongly evince and prove, that for no cause voluntary death is to be undertaken: neither to avoid temporal troubles, least we fall into eternal; nor for fear to be polluted with the sins of others, least by avoiding other men's sins, we increase our own; nor yet for our own sins that are past, for which we have more need of life that we might repent of them; nor lastly, for the hope of a better life, because they which are guilty of their own death, a better life is not prepared for them.[9]

By the sixth century church councils in Western Europe followed Augustine and ruled first against funeral rites and masses for those who killed themselves after being accused of a crime, and then extended this prohibition to any whose death was self-inflicted.[10] The Reformation brought no change in this respect, and Protestant clergy in England continued to cite Augustine and to condemn suicide. In 1594 John King, the future bishop of London, preached in a sermon on Jonah that the sixth commandment condemned suicide and that Augustine and Aquinas both ruled against it. A few years later George Abbot, the future arch-

bishop, preaching on Jonah as well, also cited the sixth commandment and excused Jonah's challenge to God by casting himself into the sea on the grounds
that Jonah had a prophetic knowledge of God's intention and therefore was an
example that "may not be followed by us." Puritan divines in no way differed in
their condemnation of self-murder, Thomas Cartwright seeing it, as did others,
as forbidden by the sixth commandment.[11]

When the Puritan John Sym devoted a lengthy treatise to the subject in the
1630s, he was, then, treading a familiar trail. Self-murder was unlawful, he wrote,
"because it is unlawful by religion, most harmful in effect, and contrary to reason." He then went on to invoke the sixth commandment and Augustine's statement that, "he that kills himself, kills no other thing in so doing but a man."
Self-murder, Sym went on, was contrary to the general meaning of the law,
"which is love and justice," for we are enjoined to love ourselves and our neighbors like ourselves. Self-murder destroyed the image of God, which we all bear;
it is against God's sovereignty, for God gives us life as a gift, which we cannot reject or destroy without committing an act of gross disobedience; finally self-murder is against the providence of God, for God determines "after what fashion we
should die, or live." Self-murder was not only an offence against God, but contrary to Nature, for it was against that "natural affection and propenseness whereby it endeavors to preserve and cherish itself," for "religion and nature's laws are
not repugnant but differ in extent and degrees of perfection." It was almost as an
afterthought that Sym noted that suicide hurt both Church and Commonwealth
"by bereaving the same unjustly of their members," and added that the state quite
justly seized the good of suicides "for recompense to the Commonwealth for de-
priving the same of a member."[12] As Sym remarked in his Epistle Dedicatory to
Robert, Earl of Warwick, his patron, "the theme of self-killing is the subject both
of divinity and of humanity, of religion and of law."[13] Sym provided a lengthy
catalogue of all the calamities of fortune, the discontents and "troubles of mind"
that lead to self-murder, but fundamentally he was convinced that the causes of
such a heinous sin and crime was one's own will, "far more prone to evil than to
good," and to the suggestions of the devil, ever ready to exploit human weakness.[14] For all its length, Sym's treatise said nothing that had not been said by orthodox clergy before him and, allowing for a change in rhetoric, for a century
after.

Where these divines joined hands was in their conviction that suicide had become a national disease, requiring all the efforts that could be mustered by physicians of the soul to prevent its spreading.[15] In an epistle to the reader, which
prefaced Sym's *Lifes Preservative against self-Killing,* William Gouge, the Puritan
preacher at Blackfriars, echoed Sym's claim, justifying "an entire tractate" on suicide, "seeing how requisite and needful it is . . . in these days," for Gouge was
convinced that "scarce an age since the beginning of the world hath afforded

more examples of this desperate inhumanity, than this our present age."[16] The seven suicides recorded in the Bills of Mortality for 1636 were only .055 percent of the 12,650 deaths recorded in the London Bills for that year.[17] However, given the well-known limits of suicide statistics at any time, and the particular problems facing those who compiled the Bills in early seventeenth-century London, where suicide by drowning was so easy to disguise as, or mistake for, misadventure, statistical evidence is dubious at best.[18] In any event no evidence exists that Dr. Edward Stanhope, the vicar general of the diocese of London in 1601, was responding to the writings of moralizing divines or to the statistics of the Bills of Mortality. Rather he and his successors were responding in the first instance to individuals and small groups of the friends and kinfolk of suicides petitioning for a license to give the suicide a Christian burial in consecrated ground.

There is another possibility. At the beginning of act 5, scene 1 in *Hamlet,* the two grave diggers discuss Ophelia's burial:

> First Clown: Is she to be buried in Christian burial that willfully seeks her own salvation?
> Second Clown: I tell thee she is, and therefore make her grave straight. The coroner hath sat on her, and finds it Christian burial.
> First Clown: How can that be unless she drowned herself in her own defence?
> Second Clown. Why, 'tis found so.

After the two consider the problem further, the Second Clown cynically asks: "Will you ha' the truth on't? If this had not been a gentlewoman, she should have been buried out o' Christian burial." Status always counted for something in early modern England, usually for a great deal. Michael MacDonald notes that "with the exception of [the Earl of] Essex, none of the noblemen who is known to

TABLE 2.1.
Mortality in London, 1629–1636

Year	Total mortality	Drowned	Murdered	Suicides	Licensed to bury
1629	8,771	43	0	8	1
1630	9,237	33	0	8	1
1631	8,288	29	3	6	1
1632	9,527	34	7	15	2
1633	8,392	37	0	0	3
1634	10,899	32	6	3	2
1635	16,501	32	5	8	1
1636	12,650	45	8	7	0

Sources: Graunt, *Natural and Political Observations,* Table of Casualties, found between pages 74 and 75; LMA, Vicar General Book, 1629–1636.

have killed himself after 1680 was judged a self-murderer. Gentleman's suicides were routinely classified as *non compos mentis* or as deaths by natural causes."[19] Of course if this were routinely the case before 1680, if coroners' juries regularly returned verdicts of misadventure or *non compos mentis* in cases involving members of the gentry and nobility, as the grave-diggers in *Hamlet* supposed, there would have been no need for the vicar general to issue a license, since only those convicted of the felony of self-murder were denied Christian burial. Nevertheless, the possibility of social bias is always worth considering. Of the thirty-one suicides licensed by the bishop of London to be buried in a churchyard between 1601 and 1641 one knight, four gentlemen, and one gentlewoman were so licensed, 19 percent of the total number. Evidently London coroners' juries had no hesitation about rendering verdicts of *felo de se* against the social elite in their midst. The one knight, Sir George Southcote, had been a resident of Kensington, an aristocratic parish not part of the city but well to the west of it, where one might expect that more consideration would be given to a family of such social standing. He had, however, done away with himself by hanging, apparently an act so unambiguous as to leave the jury little choice. The story, testified to by Sir George's father, also a knight, and two other parishioners, that Sir George had fallen into a "deep melancholy" for "divers years" and as a consequence was "distracted of his wits" and "had not reason to govern himself," evidently was seen as both plausible and sufficient, and license was granted for his "Christian burial in some outward place of the churchyard of Kensington, so that the same be done privately in the night without solemnity, prayers, or ringing of bells."[20] The entry for Dorothy Gale, widow and gentlewoman of St. Stephen Coleman Street, differs in no respect from other entries of city suicides. She had "occasioned her own untimely death by falling out of a garret window." Testimony to the effect that she was "well disposed and not only conformable to the orders of the Church of England but also very religiously and piously given," was provided on oath by "many persons of good rank and quality." Her suicide was explained and excused by the fact that "for divers years before her death [she was] much troubled with a megrim [migraine] in her head," during which she was "even quite deprived both of her sight and understanding." It was due to "that kind of agony or distraction and not out of any distrust either of God's mercy or any discontent through worldly affairs" that "looking out of her garret window, very dangerous by reason both of the height and wideness thereof, did fall forth . . . into a court or yard under the same. And by the fall broke her neck and died." The coroner's jury (and this is the only entry that mentions one) "for want of evidence cannot yet give their verdict," in consequence of which her body could not be buried without license, which was then granted on 23 December 1628.[21]

Other than the knight and the five identified as gentry, the London suicides on the whole were not recorded in the vicar general's records with either titles or other social markers of status. Perhaps the clearest evidence of a lack of social bias in the issuing of these special licenses is the fact that four of the thirty-one licenses were granted for the burying of servants who had committed suicide, three women and one man. All told, thirteen of the thirty-one were women, a sex ratio of men to women of 1.3:1. MacDonald and Murphy give the sex ratio for selected groups of suicides from 1485 to 1714 as 5.2:1.[22] Clearly a larger proportion of London suicides who appear in the vicar general's records were women than was true of a national sample over a much longer period, but the London numbers are so small that there is uncertainty that they are representative even of London suicides. Michael Zell's study of Kentish suicides in the second half of the sixteenth century shows that 37 percent were victims of drowning.[23] Of the thirty-one recorded in the London vicar generals' books, thirteen hanged themselves, nine cut their throats, five took poison, two jumped to their deaths, and two stabbed or cut themselves mortally. None were recorded as having drowned, and yet the Bills of Mortality show large numbers of Londoners perishing in this way, and Forbes noted that eight of the thirty-five London coroners' verdicts he found for 1590 were the result of investigations of drownings.[24] If some of the London males who were alleged to have entered the Thames to bathe or swim and subsequently drowned had actually entered the river with the intention of doing away with themselves, the ratio of male to female suicides might have looked more like those found elsewhere. The high percentage of victims of poisoning among the vicar generals' suicides (16.6 percent compared to the 2 percent Zell found among his Kentish suicides), if representative of the total population of London suicides, may have been occasioned by the ready access to apothecary shops in the city.

Whatever the means employed, the petitioners usually had no difficulty in finding an apparent cause for the act of self-destruction. Although Anne Thatcher, an ancient widow of seventy "or thereabouts," was reputedly "of good life and conversation," she had hanged herself "by reason of some bad debtors who deceived her of her money." Her unhappiness about these bad debts had led to "some discontents and in these discontents that she hung and strangled herself and thereof died." Despite that act, the three parishioners of St. Andrew Undershaft who appeared on her behalf, testified to their belief that she still retained a clear conscience, and a license was granted on 22 January 1617/18.[25] In the case of Anne Grinder, the wife of an upholsterer of St. Mildred in the Poultry who had hanged herself, John Sherston of Lincoln's Inn, gent., testified that Anne had suffered "extreme pain and grief . . . in childbed," losing her "only child and daughter" before she had well "recovered her senses;" it was, Sherston alleged, the combination of prolonged illness and grief that led to "a distraction and frenzy" and thence to the taking of her life. Her burial in her parish churchyard was licensed in July 1626.[26] The two women petitioning on behalf of Susan

Smallman of St. Margaret Lothbury explained that she had lost one of her eyes four or five years before, and that "being in extremity of pain in the [other] eye, sent for mercury water and drank the same as a medicine for her eye (not being sensible, as it is presumed) that she should thereby receive her death." Although the parenthetical remark suggests skepticism about her ignorance, the petitioners went on to note that on learning that she had poisoned herself, she denied that she would have taken the mercury water had she known its lethal effects, and the parson having been summoned, she confessed her sorrow for the offence "and prayed pardon of Almighty God." The vicar general (by this time Dr. Arthur Duck) then issued a license dated 8 February 1630/31.[27]

The petitioners had offered a real motive—extremity of pain—in making a case for Susan Smallman. In that of Benjamin Standish of St. Martin Ludgate the petitioners only specified that he had been "much afflicted with sundry crosses and hindrances, and was much decayed in his estate;" the fear of falling "into further poverty" apparently also led to the suicide of Anne Page of St. Martin in the Fields. For others illness or simply old age, rather than grief or anxiety, led to lunacy and the mad act of self-destruction: Anne Reynolds of St. Martin's Ludgate was apparently driven mad with the pain caused by the cutting and lancing of a fistula "growing upon her," whereas in the case of Margaret Porter of St. Swithin's the petitioners only alleged her age as causing "fits of distraction and lunacy." Motivation was not invariably seen as important to the petitioners, and in most instances the petitioners' stories omitted either personal motivation or physical cause, such as sickness, pain, or old age.[28]

Nevertheless, the petitions always offered grounds that might explain or excuse the act, mitigating circumstances that might justify making an exception to the treatment ordinarily meted out to those who took their own lives. First of all, where it was possible to make the claim, the petitioners invariably noted evidence of penitence prior to the suicide's death. Henry Thorneton of Fulham had cut his own throat,

> yet did not so presently die, but that God gave him some respite of time to call to him for mercy, and at that time . . . Henry Thorneton signified that he was heartily sorry that he had committed that offence and presently seemed exceedingly penitent and sorrowful for that all other his transgressions, and conceived good hope of his atonement to God and salvation in and by the death and merits of Christ Jesus whom only he acknowledged to be his redeemer and savior, earnestly praying that He would speak peace unto his conscience and in full confidence and assurance thereof earnestly desired to receive the sacrament of the Lord's supper, and so did with good comfort to all outward appearance receive the same.[29]

Few petitions presented such elaborate circumstances pointing to repentance followed by tokens of grace granted and salvation gained, but, where plausible, claims of penitence were presented. Thus when Anne Gibson of St. Nicholas Olave in Bread Street followed Thorneton's example and cut her throat, she also reportedly "did not presently die, but that God gave her some respite of time to call to him for mercy, in which time . . . the said Anne Gibson shewed herself very penitent and sorrowful for that fact, and humbly desired God for Christ his son's sake to forgive her this and all other her offenses and did much joy in the prayers of others that prayed with her."[30] Humphrey Maddock of St. James Clerkenwell, another who "cut his own throat," nevertheless managed to live

> more than a night and a day after the hurt received in which time he, the said Humphrey Maddock shewed himself very penitent and sorrowful for [what] he had done, protesting that if it were to do again, he would not do it for all the world, and acknowledged that this sin was grievous and required great repentance (which if God lent him life, he would impose upon himself during life) and acknowledged the infinite merits and mercies of Christ, desiring, hoping and trusting that Christ would save him and intercede for pardon for him.

Needless to say, after such an affecting story, license was granted to bury him.[31]

Sometimes when penitence was not directly claimed by the petitioners, it was nevertheless strongly implied. Marie Playe, a servant living in St. Botolph's Aldgate, who was alleged to have been frantic with grief for the past three months or more, then drank a "potion of strong and deadly poison," but lived for three hours after taking the draught, during which "she did confess and acknowledge what she had done and was sorry for it and desired to have salad oil and other things which she took and drank in great quantity to expel the said poison and prayed heartily to God to forgive her this great offence and all her sins." The fact that she drank salad oil in a vain attempt to stop the poison from working was evidently seen as evidence that her expressions of regret were genuine, and the bishop's license to bury her in the Christian fashion, though privately "without solemnity," was subsequently granted.[32]

Sometimes penitence was taken to have been implied by the gestures of the dying suicide; sometimes it was simply presumed. As previously mentioned, after Thomas Leach, gent., of St. Mildred in the Poultry, cut his throat, he survived "some little time." Unable to speak, the dying Leach was "found groaning and lifting up his hands," gestures which, it was suggested, could be interpreted as a sign of contrition for his sin of self-murder. It was an affecting claim, as well as a compelling one, and license was duly granted.[33] In the case of Gresham Hogan, gent., who had leaped to his death from "a high turret . . . of his dwelling house in Hackney," it was argued that "after his fall God gave him life by the space of two hours during which time he had the faithful and devout prayers of many good friends, and it may charitably be presumed that God dealt mercifully with his soul." It was perhaps a case of penitence by proxy, and if it was only a charitable thought that God dealt mercifully with his soul, certainly the vicar general was prepared to deal mercifully with his body, for a license to bury his remains was granted on 18 August 1617.[34]

Actual or implied penance was important, not to say crucial, at least in theory. As William Ames wrote in his influential *Conscience with the Power and Cases Thereof,*

> If God of his great mercy add a change of mind, with an appealing by faith to the judgment seat of God's mercy in Christ, then is that true (which some use to say) that the judgment of repentance maketh void the judgment of punishment, that the accusation, witnessing, and condemnation to wrath to come are prevented by these actions which supply their rooms; yea, that God himself in Christ shall be an advocate, a witness, and judge, for those that have pleaded against themselves in the court of conscience by repentance.[35]

On being asked in the 1580s whether a suicide might be saved, the Reverend Richard Greenham replied that "the jailer in the Acts [of the] Apostles would have hurt himself, but converting and repenting his thought and purpose did not hinder him of his salvation."[36]

Testimony to the sincere penitence of a suicide obviously provided the vicar general and bishop with grounds for granting a license for the Christian burial of the suicide, but such testimony was necessarily limited to those who lived at least for hours, if not days, beyond the act that led to their death. Those who cut their throat or took poison seemed in most cases to have lived long enough to express regret for the act and to pray for forgiveness, and one can imagine the vicar general wishing to put the best construction on such evidence of contrition and penitence. However, petitioners only offered testimony concerning the penitence of thirteen of the thirty-one granted licenses; others, in particular the twelve who hanged themselves and the two who jumped to their deaths, had no opportunity to repent, nor did petitioners in their behalf offer such unbelievable testimony.[37]

The first four petitions for license to bury suicides implied or actually presented testimonial evidence of repentance. The fifth, that of Anthony Gurling of St. John Zachary presented a unique case. While admitting that Gurling had indeed caused his death by laying "violent hands" on himself by "strangling himself in a bridle," the petitioners, including the parson, Henry Hamond, and one of the churchwardens, argued that Gurling "at the time his death [was] a youth but of fifteen years or thereabout, so as he had not sufficient discretion for the ordering the course of his life, nor was so capable of good or evil as persons ripe and full [of] years."[38] Other petitions scattered across the years explicitly claimed that the self-murderer was in fact mad, the implication being that the coroner's jury should have returned a verdict of *non compos mentis*. While in "the hospital of Bethlehem in the parish of St. Botolph without Bishopsgate," William Ellys had hanged himself. Why the evidence of his incarceration in Bedlam was not alone sufficient to obtain a verdict of *non compos mentis* is not explained, but the petitioners did testify that Ellys "was distracted of his wits for the space of five months last past before his death."[39] Much the same was claimed about Richard Gilles or Gyles of St. Olave Hart Street who hanged himself.

> [I]t hath been testified . . . that he, the said Richard Gilles, for the space of six weeks or two months next before his death was much grieved and dis-contented and possessed with melancholic and was much troubled with fits of distraction or lunacy, and that within the time aforesaid he being at the house of the said Robert Kirkham in Thames Street in the parish of St. Dunstan in the East, London, fell into a violent fit of distraction or lunacy, and then and there pulled and teared himself and raged and stamped and showed sundry other such like signs of a distracted man, sometimes by whistling, sometimes by running to and fro, and that he then and there pulled himself by the throat in such a violent manner as it is conceived he would have done mischief or hurt to himself in case he had not been pre-vented by them.

The petitioners also noted as other signs of his distraction his "idle and senseless talking," and his "knocking of his head against the wall."[40] In effect, these peti-tioners seem to have been requesting the bishop to remedy an injustice done by the coroner, for in each case they presented the kind of evidence that should have led to a *non compos mentis* verdict.

It was a case, dating from October 1616, that was to prove paradigmatic for many of the remaining petitions that led to the granting of licenses. Marie Playe, a servant to a merchant family living in St. Botolph Aldgate, had occasioned her own death by "drinking some potion of strong and deadly poison." Although she lived long enough to pray for the forgiveness of her sins, the petitioners' central case seemed to rest on different grounds. Before committing this act, the peti-tioners claimed, she was "in the course of her life honest, sober and of good con-versation, and one that was diligent in resorting to church and hearing God's word preached and hath good friends and was religiously brought up." Despite this exemplary life—and this appears to have been the crucial argument—during "the space of this three months past and more, upon some instant occasion [she became] much grieved and grew so perplexed in that her grief that she seemed many times distracted of her senses and frantic and committed that great offence in the time of this her great distemperature and distraction." What seems to have been important to the petitioners was this sudden change in a woman, formerly sober and pious, who suffered some secret sorrow or grief that led to a distraction of her senses and to the frantic act of self-murder. In short, it was a recent but unexplained psychological state that led to aberrant behavior.[41]

Similar examples abound. Thomas Leach, gentleman, of St. Mildred in the Poultry, had killed himself by cutting his throat. Before that act he had fallen "into deep melancholy passions whereof he languished six or seven months, was therein many times distracted of his wits, and had no reason in those distractions to govern himself."[42] Edmund Needham, of Gray's Inn, who hanged himself in November 1623, had been "much distracted with a deep melancholy wherewith he was possessed, and in the time of those distractions was not able or fit to govern himself."[43]

All but one of the petitions after 1630 used the language of distraction and melancholia. Susan Smallman "was much troubled in her mind and affections, as it were, distracted, through the extremity of pain in her eyes;" Benjamin Standish "was greatly possessed with deep melancholic, insomuch as he was many times distracted, and that he oftentimes used signs of distraction and lunacy by raging and stamping with his feet," so that "at such times he seemed as a senseless man, not knowing what he did."[44] The only exception during this period to the rhetoric of melancholia, discontentment, and distraction of mind, which was repeatedly offered by petitioners to the vicar general as an adequate explanation for acts of self-destruction, occurred in May 1635 when the master of Anne Page, and the curate of her parish of St. Martin in the Fields, both testified that Anne, "fearing to fall into further poverty did upon the temptation of the devil (as she herself confessed upon her death bed) give herself the said wound in her throat" from which she died.[45] This was the only other case (besides Richard Allen in 1601) among the thirty-one with any mention that the act of self-murder was done at the instigation of the devil, although the ministerial treatises on suicide invariably invoked the great Tempter. As Thomas Beard observed, although it was clearly not intended as a comforting thought, the "many which seem to make away with themselves, are murdered and made away by the Devil, and not by themselves;" John Sym argued that one of the general motives that led people to murder themselves was "the strong impulse, powerful motions, and command of the Devil, who is himself a murderer, and also moves man to practice it."[46] And yet even in this exceptional instance, in which the power of the devil as tempter is invoked in a license granting permission for a Christian burial, the very next sentence noted that, "the reason why she laid violent hands upon herself was the fear of want, having no friends."[47] Granted that spiritual causes are not incompatible with mundane motivations, it nevertheless seems as though the devil is mentioned almost as an afterthought.

Certainly the conviction that the devil really existed, that the devil could take on a physical shape perceptible to people and was capable of causing real harm, was not simply a metaphor or analogy for wicked temptations, continued through the seventeenth century.[48] What is surprising about the thirty-one petitions to the vicar general was the omission with the two exceptions mentioned of what was, after all, a standard trope in such circumstances: that self-murder had been committed by the temptation or at the instigation of the devil. The petitioners were after all addressing an officer of an ecclesiastical court; they did not describe self-murder as merely a crime, rather than a sin, against God. The penitence described in so many petitions of those who had killed themselves but lived long enough to express contrition only made sense in a theological setting in which penitence for sins of omission and commission was a prerequisite for an appeal to God for mercy and forgiveness. Nevertheless, the extenuating circumstances offered were mundane causes and human motivations, fears and griefs that led to confused thoughts and irrational actions, and these the vicar general in the name of the bishop accepted and rehearsed in writing in the licenses granted and recorded in the vicar general's book.

Although the language of states of mind, of physical pain, and mental anguish, used to explain and excuse suicide became a dominant refrain in the licenses granted in the 1630s, it was present much earlier. Marie Playe's suicide in 1616 was explained as a consequence of being "much grieved and . . . so perplexed in that her grief that she seemed many times distracted of her senses and frantic." In 1618 William Ellys hanged himself, having been "distracted of his wits for the space of five months last past," and in 1620 Thomas Leach cut his throat after "falling into deep melancholy passions."[49]

In the absence of any statement of policy by either the vicars general or the bishops of London it is impossible to do more than speculate about what led to the granting of such licenses.[50] There is no way of knowing either why the friends of some suicides petitioned for their Christian burials and not others, nor how such friends learned that it was possible to petition for such a license. The numbers in any one year were tiny in the rapidly expanding metropolis, where death occurred with mind-numbing frequency. It is, of course, impossible to know how many actual suicides took place, but what matters are those believed to have taken place and which therefore became subject to coroners' investigations. In this latter respect John Graunt's figures abstracted from the surviving Bills of Mortality are suggestive. In the absence of the reports of London coroners to King's Bench there is no way of knowing how the figures in the Bills correspond to those in which coroners' juries returned a verdict of *felo de se* and by so doing prevented the suicide from being buried in consecrated ground. Nevertheless, the fact that in 1633 the Bill of Mortality showed no suicides in a year in which the friends of three suicides petitioned and were licensed to give them a Christian burial raises questions about the possible correspondence, if any, of the Bills' figures for those who "hanged and made away with themselves" and the number of coroners' verdicts of suicide.[51] Bureaucratic precedent may explain why licenses were granted by the vicar general following the spate of licenses issued in 1615, but how the friends of suicides learned about the possibility of obtaining licenses remains a mystery, though it does suggest that despite the explosive growth of the metropolis in these decades, gossip kept Londoners aware of such possibilities, that it was in some sense common knowledge.[52]

What is evident in these years, despite the apparent unanimity of clerical opinion that self-murder was a sin against God, nature, and the state, is that the legitimacy of suicide was in fact discussed and even debated both in treatises and on the stage. Sir Thomas More had famously raised the issue as early as 1516 in the *Utopia,* where Hythloday describes "voluntary death" as justified and permissible, if only under limited and circumscribed circumstances.[53] In 1578 while still a student at Cambridge, John Harington wrote a dialogue in which Samuel, Saul, and Solomon debated "Whether it be damnation for a man to kill himself." Samuel spoke for the orthodox in condemning "he that killeth himself" under any circumstances. Saul replied that on the contrary he himself is the example to follow:

> Was it not better for me to kill myself, seeing that I see death present before mine eyes, than suffer mine enemies to abuse me ignominiously, to triumph over me despitefully, and to revile me contumeliously? If a man be condemned to die, is it any matter whether he or the hangman shall tie the halter about his neck and cast him off the ladder? Did not the martyrs of Queen Mary's days willingly offer themselves to the flames? Were they therefore reproved? If I had come to the hands of the Philistines alive, they would have labored and forced me, if God had not been with me, either to have forsaken Jehovah, and to have worshiped their idols, or with exquisite torments to have blasphemed God, dishonored Jehovah, and offended the spirit of God. . . . He that will save his soul in the next life, he must lose his life in this.

Ignoring anachronism, Saul then goes on to cite with approval not only the example of Samson, "whom Jehovah blessed and fortified him with strength" to kill himself by pulling down the temple on his own head, but also Cato, who "killed himself, knowing that Caesar had conquered Pompey," as well as Socrates and Themistocles in a catalogue that ended with Sir James Hales, whom Harington pictured as a latter day Samson, committing suicide rather than abjuring the true faith in Catholic Queen Mary's time. Solomon weighs in at the very end to announce enigmatically that he would "leave all to the secret judgment of God, . . . referring all rather to his mercy."[54]

If Harington's slight piece can be passed off as a bit of undergraduate daring, the same cannot be said of John Donne's much more extensive manuscript, *Biathanatos*, written in 1608 when he was well into his thirties, some years before he took orders. Admittedly Donne did not publish the tract during his lifetime, but his son, in committing it to the press some years later confessed that his father in bequeathing the manuscript "forbid both the press and the fire." In his preface Donne admitted that he often contemplated suicide, but that his conscience had assured him "that no rebellious grudging at God's gifts nor other sinful concurrence accompanies these thoughts," but only the conviction that "I have the keys of my prison in my own hand, and no remedy presents itself so soon to my heart as mine own sword."[55] Some of his arguments sound remarkably like those offered by the petitioners to the vicar general. For example, while admitting the necessity of repentance, he nevertheless denied that the act of self-homicide, as he called it, necessarily precluded it, for "to presume impenitence, because you were not by, and hear it, is an usurpation." Further, he noted that "of one who died before he had repented, good Paulinus would charitably interpret his haste," which again sounds remarkably like one of the extenuating arguments offered in the petitions.[56]

Donne's strategy was not to deny that the law of nature, of reason, and of God seem to rule against the legitimacy of suicide, but rather to suggest that none of the three do so in all circumstances. Thus, while admitting that the law of nature seems to forbid self-homicide because "self-preservation is of Natural Law," nevertheless, "though this be ill for conservation of our species in general, yet it may be very fit for some particular men." Quoting Aquinas, he noted that "the lower you go towards particulars, the more you depart from the necessity of being bound by it," and the prime example of this principle is martyrdom, for "though the body perish," the principle of self-preservation is not denied, for "thereby, out of our election, our best part is advanced." That self-homicide is against natural law under all circumstances is contradicted by the laws and customs of Athens and Rome and in his imaginary state by Sir Thomas More, "a man of the most tender and delicate conscience."[57] Civil law "hath pronounced nothing against this self-homicide, which we have now in disputation," with the exception of the case in which a criminal to escape conviction, kills himself before judgment, in which case his goods are forfeit. But the very existence of the exception suggests other circumstances in which suicide is legitimate. Again while admitting that the canon law forbids a Christian burial to a suicide, it also does so in the case of those under an interdict, and yet that fact means even "the holiest man which dies in that place cannot be buried." Hence, Donne argued, "one may be subject to that punishment, (if it be any in the law) and yet not guilty of such a crime as this is reputed to be."[58] Donne admitted that suicide is punishable as murder in England, but suggested that, "since therefore, to my understanding, it hath no foundation in Natural nor Imperial Law, nor receives much strength from those reasons, but having by custom only put on the nature of law, as most of our law hath, I believe it was first induced amongst us, because we exceeded in that natural desire of dying so."[59]

St. Augustine's strictures were not so easy to dismiss, and Donne agreed that "neither to avoid temporal trouble, nor to punish our own past sins, nor to prevent future, nor in a desire of the next life, (where these considerations are only, or principally) it can be lawful for any man to kill himself," but then having conceded so much, Donne adds that "neither St. Augustine nor we deny, but that if there be cases, wherein the party is disinterested, and only primarily the glory of God is respected and advanced, it may be lawful."[60] In fact *Biathanatos* suggests that Donne not only knew biblical and classical examples, and the opinions of Church fathers and schoolmen, but also of the debate that set in with the advent of humanist learning in Northern Europe.

When Donne wrote *Biathanatos* in the early seventeenth century, Stoic and Epicurean arguments, as well as those that privileged aristocratic honor and the older courtly love tradition, had long been familiar to European intellectuals. Donne may have been bolder in confronting the contradictions inherent in espousing these arguments in a Christian world and in seeking exceptions even in the Christian tradition itself, but awareness of the contradictions and the debate itself was scarcely novel. Michel de Montaigne's *Essays* and Sir Philip Sidney's *Arcadia* had anticipated Donne, and if Sidney's Pyrocles does not in the end kill himself, Sir Walter Raleigh did make the attempt, while incarcerated in the Tower in 1603, justifying his action in a last letter to his wife on the grounds that "I know it is forbidden to destroy ourselves, but I trust it is forbidden in this sort, that we destroy not ourselves despairing of God's mercy."[61]

However, familiarity with these arguments was not the sole province of intellectuals; they would have been known to any Londoner with the price of admission to the theater. Marlowe's Faustus had declaimed

> My heart is harden'd, I cannot repent:
> Scarce can I name salvation, faith, or heaven,
> But fearful echoes thunders in mine ears,
> 'Faustus, thou art damn'd!' Then swords and knives,
> Poison, guns, halters, and envenom'd steel

> Are laid before me to dispatch myself;
> And long ere this I should have done the deed,
> Had not sweet pleasure conquer'd deep despair.[62]

Faustus, of course, does not kill himself, and briefly comforts himself with the thought that "Christ did call the thief upon the Cross; / Then rest thee, Faustus," before being escorted off the stage and out of life by Mephistopheles in the final scene.[63] However, if Marlowe's Faustus contemplates suicide within a Christian framework, Shakespeare's Hamlet a few years later famously debated the issue entirely in secular terms, for Hamlet's debate is not between Christian hope and despair, but simply fear of the unknown: but for "the dread of something after death," "who would bear the whips and scorns of time."[64] If Hamlet debated the issue but failed to act, Brutus in *Julius Caesar,* defeated by Octavius, runs upon his sword: "Caesar, now be still. / I killed not thee with half so good a will," and rather than condemning the act, Antony praises Brutus, pronouncing him "the noblest Roman of them all."[65]

The point is not that the popular theater became an arena in which Londoners witnessed the Christian condemnation of suicide giving way to Stoic approval. What a playgoer would have witnessed was a variety of dramatic responses, of ways of experiencing and understanding an act that remained officially condemned. Alongside those plays in which suicide was the final sinful response to despair were those tragedies of courtly love in which suicide was presented as the appropriate response to the death of a lover, as in *Othello* and *Romeo and Juliet*. In Robert Wilmot's *Tancred and Gismund,* suicide is seen not simply as the tragically inevitable response to a lover's death but as the necessary step on the journey to join the dead lover. So Gismund on learning that her father has murdered her lover, takes poison: "Now pass I to the pleasant land of love, / Where heavenly love immortal flourisheth."[66] The classical story of the virtuous Lucretia, raped by Sextus Tarquinius, provided another type of suicide, justified because done to protect her husband's honor, a story on which changes were rung from Chaucer on through the Renaissance.[67]

In addition to these tales of the dilemmas of virtuous love for which the only solution was suicide, the history of republican Rome provided tragedies in which the hero's death represented a blow against tyranny and a refusal to surrender republican virtue. So in Ben Jonson's *Sejanus,* Arruntius mourns the lack of such heroes in the decadent Rome of Tiberius:

> Where is now the soul
> Of god-like Cato? he, that durst be good,
> When Caesar durst be evil; and had power,
> As not to live his slave, to die his master.[68]

Figure 2. Peter Simon, *The Suicides of Romeo and Juliet,* engraving, 1874, after a painting by James Northcote in 1792.

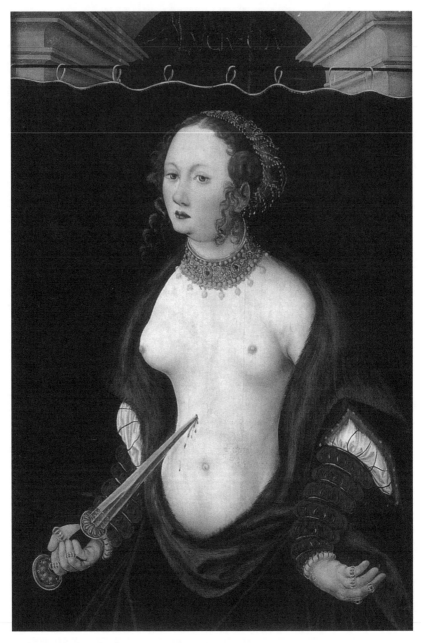

Figure 3. Unknown Dutch painter, *Lucretia,* first half of sixteenth century. Reproduced with the permission of the National Museum, Cracow..

As Rowland Wymer has argued, "the confident manner in which playwrights built scenes, or even whole plays, round these different connotations presupposes an audience capable of responding positively as well as negatively to a suicide in the theater."[69] It also presupposes a society in which conflicting social values were not so much resolved as played out in all their contradictions. Like the duel, suicide could under certain circumstances be viewed as an honorable act, however contrary to Christian values, and however much condemned by Church and monarch alike.

It was precisely in the middle of this Elizabethan and Jacobean debate carried on in pamphlets and dramatized in plays that the vicar general of the diocese of London began to entertain petitions requesting licenses to give suicides a Christian burial. Is it not conceivable that the debate in the popular theater, as well as among intellectuals, created a climate of opinion in which it became plausible for petitioners to request, and a series of vicars general to grant, such petitions in the four decades between 1601 and the closing of the church courts in the early 1640s? Such licenses imply a public opinion sufficiently ambivalent about suicide to permit these vicars general, who were, it must be remembered, civil lawyers, not churchmen, to take a permissive stance toward the issue of Christian burial, and to encourage the laity to seek such Christian rites for their friends who had murdered themselves in some publicly obvious fashion.[70] The licenses, after all, never condoned the act and never suggested that to kill oneself was virtuous.

A license did offer a parish priest official sanction for an exceptional act, but no evidence suggests that the burial of suicides in London provoked much comment. Certainly the parish registers recording such acts give no evidence of parochial protest or outrage. In the burial register for St. Botolph Bishopsgate, the parish clerk with typical brevity recorded the interment of "William Ellis [who] hanged himself per license 26 May [1618] [age] 26;" two years earlier the register noted that "William Hutton gent buried the 2 of November [1616]" but makes no mention of the fact that Hutton had committed suicide. Even when the act is mentioned, as at St. Swithin, the register merely records the event without comment: "Margery, wife of Roger Porter, was buried the 10th of May 1633 in the churchyard, who strangled herself."[71]

Deaths by suicide were noteworthy, and without question Londoners noted them. Nehemiah Wallington wrote "A Memorial of those that laid violent hands on themselves," beginning in 1632, and noted eleven suicides in the city in 1634 and 1635 alone, one, a neighbor's maid who "did hang herself there by the bedside with a garter, I did see myself." Having penned their cases, he went on to note what "uses" should be made of such lamentable incidents. First, such events "should make us watch ourselves and to be warned by them, as the Apostle saith. 1 Cor. X.ii." Further, one should avoid "melancholy and solitariness, for Satan works much upon such;" but above all "take heed of judging, as the Apostle Paul saith." It is that last comment which is of particular interest, for Wallington, a Puritan artisan, neither went to the theater nor read such learned works as Robert Burton's *Anatomy of Melancholy.* The neostoicism of the intellectuals was foreign to his mental world, which was formed by the sermons he heard and the Puritan tracts he read. Having experienced suicidal tendencies himself, he knew the dangers of such temptations; having recorded the suicides of several godly laymen and ministers, he knew that conscientious introspection was dangerous even for those he assumed were better armored against such dangers than himself. Yet his response was not to condemn those who gave way to the promptings of Satan and to their own melancholia, but rather "in God alone I put my trust: his wonders will I tell."[72] He never mentions the burial of a suicide, but it is hard to imagine that he would have opposed interment in a parish churchyard, for who but God could judge such an act? And if even a conscientious Puritan, ideologically far closer to Beard and Sym than to the Donne who wrote *Biathanatos,* refused to pass judgment on suicides, it is perhaps not surprising that no evidence suggests that other Londoners objected to the licenses granted for a Christian burial by the diocesan vicar general.

Perhaps less mystery arises about how Londoners scattered across the metropolis from suburban Fulham and Kensington in the west to Hackney in the east came to the knowledge that it was possible to petition for a licensed burial. If face-to-face communities were normally limited to a handful of contiguous city parishes, livery companies drew members from across the urban wards and beyond.[73] The diocesan courts were in St. Paul's, itself a well-known center of gossip and news. London was the center of a vast communication network of word, manuscript, and print, an expanding network symbolized by the printed pamphlet and the scribal newsletter, but by no means limited to the written word.[74] London's insatiable demand for the latest court gossip and European news was satirized by Ben Jonson, who had no sympathy for it, in his late and not very successful play, *The Staple of News,* "wherein the age may see her own folly," and where information is perceived as a commodity to be traded and "vented forth."[75] In such a packed and alert urban community it is difficult to imagine that the exceptional granting of a license to bury a suicide could have remained unremarked, even had the vicars general sought to keep it secret, and there is no evidence that any did so. Licenses specified that burial should be late at night at the edge of the churchyard and without due pomp and solemnity, but by such measures the vicar general (and bishop, if he was ever actually involved) clearly wished to obviate the offending of conservative opinion, not the keeping of such burials secret.

Finally, it is significant that the petitions offered as their primary justification the allegation that the suicide had acted in a fit of distraction, acute melancholia, or lunacy. Obviously, if such had been self-evident, the coroner's jury should have returned a verdict of *non compos mentis,* in which case no felony would have been involved and the issue of a Christian burial would not have arisen. However, as Michael MacDonald has shown, coroners' juries did not begin to reach (or were not permitted by the coroner to reach) such verdicts with any regularity until the last decades of the seventeenth century and in fact such verdicts did not reach 30 percent of the cases reported to King's Bench until 1695.[76] Yet evidently the language of psychological distress was well known in early Stuart London, and even the godly Nehemiah Wallington interpreted his own suicidal tendencies as arising from the fact that he was "troubled in my mind and melancholy."[77] As in so many other ways, it appears that in this, too, London led the country both in opinion and in practice, anticipating later changes perhaps by as much as two or three generations.

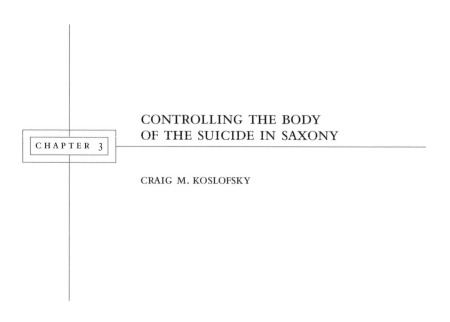

CHAPTER 3

CONTROLLING THE BODY
OF THE SUICIDE IN SAXONY

CRAIG M. KOSLOFSKY

In March 1702 a suicide in the town of Taucha, outside Leipzig, set off a four-year administrative dispute between the Leipzig city council and Saxon church authorities over the burial of suicides.[1] The city council sought to maintain its de facto control over the bodies of suicides against the claims of the Lutheran state church in the Electorate of Saxony. Ultimately, with the support of the Saxon Privy Council in Dresden the church officials won out: all secular administration of the burial of suicides was transferred to the church authorities.

The Leipzig dispute over the burial of suicides surfaced during a period of extraordinary political tension and intellectual ferment in Saxony. The absolutist ambitions of King-Elector Frederick Augustus I (1694–1733; as Augustus II, King of Poland, 1697–1733) threatened the authority of the Lutheran state church and the privileges of the Saxon nobility. The burial dispute centered on the practical, local implications of territorialism, a new theory of church subordination to state authority articulated in the 1690s by the Saxon jurist Christian Thomasius (1655–1728). The most influential German political philosopher of the early Enlightenment, Thomasius adapted the political theory of Thomas Hobbes and Samuel Pufendorf to the principalities of the Holy Roman Empire. In Thomasius's view, the political pretensions of the clergy were antithetical to the moral and political functions of the state, and he argued energetically for territorialism as the solution to this problem. In the Leipzig dispute Thomasius recognized an important struggle over the local application of the territorial principle. His bitter intellectual adversaries, the leaders of the Lutheran state church in Saxony, also felt that the burial dispute raised crucial issues of church and state authority. The conflict concerning who had jurisdiction over the burial of suicides was informed by prevailing administrative practice, changing views of suicide, and the legal theory of the early Enlightenment in a distinctive Saxon political context.

Research on suicide in early modern Europe has focused on changing popular views of self-destruction and on learned debates over the causes of suicide and the fate of the soul of the suicide. This research has identified a clear secularization of attitudes toward the act in the course of the seventeenth and eighteenth centuries. In England by the mid-eighteenth century "the causes of suicide," to quote from Michael MacDonald and Terence R. Murphy's landmark study, "were located more in the quality of a person's social relationships and his success or failure in the market economy, and less insistently in his relationship with the spiritual forces of God and the devil."[2] The recent study of the detailed discussion of suicide in the autobiography of the Leipzig author Adam Bernd (1676–1748) also reveals an almost entirely secular understanding of suicide and its origins in "melancholy."[3] In his study of melancholy and suicide in early modern Zurich, Markus Schär also identifies "the devaluation of supernatural forces" as the dominant trend in attitudes toward suicide over the seventeenth and eighteenth centuries.[4]

Secularization is a fundamental aspect of the history of suicide in the early modern era. However, the interest of modern scholars in changing attitudes toward self-destruction can obscure one of the most salient aspects of suicide for early modern men and women: the body of the suicide.[5] The historian's focus on the mind in the study of suicide collides with the intense concerns of early modern people with the body. The suicide's body was thickly overlaid with folk beliefs; its disposal was fraught with conflict, often reflecting after death the tensions which provoked the suicide itself. Whatever theologians, physicians, or philosophes might argue about the mind or the soul of the suicide, self-destruction left behind a material body—a silent yet awful challenge to some of the most basic assumptions that held the community of the living together. Secular and ecclesiastical authorities had to determine the legal status of this body and see to its disposal. The body of the suicide, intensely significant in popular belief, Christian theology, and local politics, lay at the threshold of any practical early modern concern with self-destruction.

By all accounts popular concerns about the body of the suicide were widespread, and disputes over the Christian burial of these outsiders were a common consequence of self-destruction across early modern Germany. As the work of David Lederer on Bavaria and Michael Frank on Lippe has shown, conflicts over the burial of individual suicides can give valuable insight into the exercise of power within village communities and between local authorities and territorial administrators.[6] In each case an array of factors came to bear, from estate and privilege to ongoing local conflicts. These factors played themselves out within the general framework of authority over the burial of suicides, but this question of administration has received little attention. We know that learned attitudes toward suicide were changing, but who would apply the new attitudes in specific cases? Like no other crime, self-murder transgressed against both secular and ecclesiastical authority, in an age when the only honorable disposal of a corpse was through local Christian burial. Thus a central question emerged: was the body of the suicide under secular or ecclesiastical jurisdiction?

This question was the basis of the Leipzig dispute (1702–1706), an administrative conflict between civil and church authorities that has not been explored in any of the recent research on the burial of suicides. Several detailed studies have examined the law and administration of burial in Nuremberg, Würzburg, Zurich, and Geneva; in each of these territories little or no separation occurred between secular and ecclesiastical authority, and thus little opportunity for conflict at an institutional level over the burial of suicides.[7] In the Catholic Electorate of Bavaria and in the Lutheran Duchies of Schleswig and Holstein, secular administrators emphasized the secular crime of suicide and thus claimed the authority over the disposal of the body.[8] In most cases the Catholic clergy in Bavaria cooperated with the Bavarian Court Council when the burial of suicide was at issue, leaving the final decision to the Court Council.[9] In Schleswig and Holstein, individual pastors often petitioned the duke to allow for a less dishonorable form of burial, but the clergy never challenged secular authority over the burial of suicides.[10]

In Electoral Saxony, however, the political ambitions of Frederick Augustus I antagonized all the Saxon estates and fostered the church-state conflict over the burial of suicides. The Lutheran state church, governed by its Upper Consistory in Dresden, was a powerful institution which could claim to be the truest heir of the Reformation of Martin Luther and Philipp Melanchthon. By the late seventeenth century the Upper Consistory generally numbered about eight members including the court preacher (*Oberhofprediger*), all of whom were theologians.[11] It was supported by two regional consistories in Leipzig and Wittenberg; the local superintendents who oversaw the pastorate answered to these regional consistories. The entire state church was subject to the Elector of Saxony in his role as *summus episcopus*—literally, "highest bishop," reflecting his role as the supreme head of the church—but Lutheran theologians argued that the consistories exercised the *ius in sacra*—jurisdiction over things internal to religion—while the territorial ruler maintained only the *ius circa sacra*—jurisdiction over things related but tangential to religion. The Saxon church was in many ways an organ of the state, but the Saxon Elector was also a member of the church, subject to its moral and doctrinal authority. This relationship between prince and church, usually termed episcopalism, had developed during the Reformation and was fully articulated by the early seventeenth century.[12]

The political and confessional basis of Saxon episcopalism was destroyed by Frederick Augustus I. His political ambitions (based on his election to the Polish throne in 1697) and his cultural preeminence (centered on the spectacular court at Dresden) made him the very image of a Baroque absolute monarch. But the image was far from reality. The Saxon nobility still met regularly in a parliament (the *Landtag*) and had considerable power and authority. Unlike their counterparts in Brandenburg-Prussia, the Saxon nobles increased their political role after the Thirty Years' War, maintaining control over taxation, their right to assemble, and the Saxon Privy Council.[13]

The Lutheran state church of the Electorate was also an obstacle to Augustus' ambitions of absolutism. In 1697 Augustus, ruler of the heartland of the Lutheran Reformation, secretly converted to Catholicism to make himself eligible for election to the Polish throne. After making public his conversion, he assured his Lutheran subjects that their religion would be untouched, but the Lutheran clergy nonetheless were forced to abandon their episcopal view of church-state relations.[14] After the conversion of Augustus to Catholicism, the Saxon Privy Council replaced the Elector as the *summus episcopus* of the Lutheran church in Saxony and as speaker for the Lutheran estates (*Reichsstände*) in the Imperial Diet. The Privy Council was closely tied to the Lutheran nobility of the principality: during the long periods when the King-Elector was in Poland it ruled without consulting him on most matters, including the Leipzig suicide dispute.[15] Augustus was not especially interested in day-to-day administration; his political ambitions moved on much higher levels.

Through his conversion, election to the Polish throne, and attempts at absolute rule, Augustus created a set of new conflicts and alliances in the Saxon Electorate. Foreign (that is, non-Saxon) noble courtiers and administrators (some Catholic!) struggled with the local nobility over taxation, official corruption, and estate privileges. The state church resisted the religious pluralism inherent in the new situation and attempted to ally with the Saxon nobles.[16] At the same time, Augustus demanded more revenue from Leipzig and other Saxon cities, thus alienating another estate that might have supported his political agenda.

During the Leipzig dispute over the burial of suicides, new ideas about ritual, the body, and the relationship between church and state flowed into the turbulent political waters of Electoral Saxony in the early eighteenth century. In this chapter, I first examine the body of the suicide in popular belief and in Saxon church law, then discuss ritual and the body in the political theory of Christian Thomasius and in the practice of the Leipzig city council. The Leipzig dispute ultimately resulted in an administrative "desecularization" of suicide: Thomasius's arguments in favor of secular control and the de facto administration of the city authorities were offset by the cooperation of the Saxon Privy Council with the Lutheran clergy. The outcome of this dispute shows that the secularization of ideas about suicide led only indirectly to a secularization of authority over the body of the suicide.

The Body of the Suicide

In early modern German popular belief, pastoral theology, and law, the body of the suicide could be both a source of power as well as a compelling sign of transgression. Folklorists tell us that pieces of a suicide's clothing might have been used to strengthen livestock. The hand of a suicide was sometimes believed useful both in healing and in magical theft, and the skull was considered to have healing powers. Soil from the grave of a suicide was also believed by some to have magical powers. As recorded in the voluminous *Dictionary of German Superstition* (*Handwörterbuch des deutschen Aberglaubens*), these beliefs lack the necessary regional and chronological specificity to be applied directly to this Saxon case, but they certainly illustrate a broad range of belief in the power of the body of the suicide.[17]

The suicide's body was no less important to churchmen and jurists, who were concerned with its burial. From the first centuries of the Christian tradition, burial location was a powerful and evocative symbol of inclusion or exclusion. Although Lutherans rejected the concept of "consecrated ground," the place of Christian burial still signified inclusion or exclusion, marking the communal status of the deceased.[18] This status was dangerously ambiguous in cases of self-murder: in an instant, suicide could transform an honorable member of the community into an outsider, leaving a dishonored body whose proper place of burial was uncertain.

In early modern Germany Christian burial was typically, though not always, denied to the "dishonorable," including suicides, criminals, and those who practiced dishonorable professions such as prostitutes and executioners.[19] Suicides might be buried with somewhat more respect.[20] In a 1635 case the Saxon Upper Consistory allowed a suicide to be buried "in the churchyard in a separate place, in the evening or early morning without tolling, singing, or any such ceremonies, and without any long delay."[21] In 1690 a Brunswick man who had led an otherwise pious and upright life hung himself because of "*Melancholie.*" He was buried in the children's cemetery, in a separate area near the wall. The burial took place in the evening in silence ("*in aller Stille*").[22] The continua of space (burial with the other adults, among the children, near the wall, or outside the cemetery completely) and ritual (burial in silence, with or without the pastor, at night, or in the evening) could give an almost quantitative sign of the dishonor accorded to the deceased by the religious and secular authorities of the community.

The traditions of dishonorable burial were never applied indiscriminately. In early modern Saxony the burial of suicides ranged from the *sepultura asina* (literally, "donkey burial," amounting to burial under the gallows) to burial outside the communal cemetery or just inside the cemetery wall (certainly the most common form of interment for suicides).[23] Given the range of possible rites, from the utter denial of Christian burial to an honorable funeral that might include a sermon, the body of each suicide raised potentially divisive questions of ritual form and administrative authority. Conflicts erupted because the body of the suicide remained a powerful but ambiguous sign for common folk and learned officials alike.

How did officials determine the "appropriate" form of burial for a suicide? From the mid-seventeenth century on, Lutheran administrators confronted with the body of a suicide would turn to the work of the Leipzig jurist Benedict Carpzov (1595–1666) for guidance. The church law of Lutheran Saxony was first treated systematically in Carpzov's *Jurisprudentia ecclesiastica seu consistorialis* of 1649, a landmark work of Protestant church law. Carpzov based the *Jurisprudentia ecclesiastica* on the actual decisions and rulings of the Saxon consistories; while denouncing the canon law of the Roman church, he maintained many of its principles, including the terms of the canonical distinction between honorable and ignominious burial.[24] Carpzov's authority, based on his pioneering and systematic works in criminal, civil, and church law, was extensive: his works were published and cited throughout central and northern Germany and Scandinavia for over a century. The subsequent discussions of the law of burial by the Leipzig city council and by Christian Thomasius in 1702–1705 began with Carpzov's treatment of the law of burial.

Carpzov dealt with questions of burial in title 24, definitions 373 through 395 of the *Jurisprudentia ecclesiastica*. The burial of suicides takes a prominent place in Carpzov's discussion, due not to the frequency of suicide but rather to the central questions of ritual and authority it raised within the framework of the Lutheran funeral. Was the disposal of the body of the suicide a secular or an ecclesiastical matter? Willful suicide could be punished by the rites of dishonorable burial and desecration, but those self-murderers judged mentally incompetent might be given an honorable burial, in some cases with a funeral sermon.[25] By focusing on the intent of the suicide, Carpzov raised two interlocking questions. First, what was the mental state of the deceased? Second, who held the authority to assess this mental state and so determine the appropriate form of burial?

Carpzov stated that the assessment of the mental state of the suicide and the decision to deny or permit Christian burial, as well as the degree of honor shown by the funeral, were in the hands of church authorities alone.[26] For Electoral

Saxony and most other Lutheran territories the Consistory, the highest body of the state church, was to make such decisions. According to Carpzov, church law placed the burial of suicides solely under ecclesiastical authority, delegated in some cases from the Consistory to a local church official. Carpzov's understanding of church law was reinforced by an Electoral Saxon decree (*Reskript*) of 1664 which explicitly gave the church authority over the burial of suicides, in particular when melancholy was judged to be the cause.[27]

Early in his explication of the law of burial, Carpzov considered the burial of suicides ("autochirios") in general, and presents four cases concerning their burial. In two cases burial in the churchyard was permitted, though "in a separate place" at night or early in the morning. In two further cases burial was designated outside the churchyard or cemetery. In each case the decision was made by the Upper Consistory in Dresden.[28]

Carpzov then discussed those who took their own lives when prompted by melancholy, rage, or other mental weaknesses.[29] He cited three cases in which the suicide was given a Christian burial, though in a separate area of the churchyard or cemetery. These decisions were made either by the Saxon elector (acting, in legal terms, as *summus episcopus*) or by the Dresden Upper Consistory. In summary Carpzov quotes a ruling of the Saxon Upper Consistory: "The Electoral Saxon Church Ordinance makes clear that . . . matters regarding the dead and their burial should be brought before the Consistory and handled there."[30] This authoritative affirmation of ecclesiastical control over funerals in general and over the burial of suicides in particular was challenged at the end of the seventeenth century: both the practice of the Leipzig city council and the political theory of Christian Thomasius sought to secularize the burial of suicides.

The Leipzig-born jurist and philosopher Christian Thomasius was forced from his position at the University of Leipzig in 1690 when his criticism of the traditional faculties of the university provoked the hostility of the Lutheran orthodoxy dominant there. He fled to Berlin, then served as one of the founders of the Brandenburg-Prussian university in Halle, where he continued to develop his legal philosophy, which systematically distinguished law, decorum, and morality and subordinated the church to civil authority.[31] Deeply troubled by his expulsion from Leipzig, Thomasius saw the reform of "clerical tyranny" as his special intellectual calling. His importance as a founder of the German Enlightenment rests on his relentless and thorough destruction of the confessional basis of the early modern state and his support for religious toleration.[32]

Directly influenced by Hobbes and Pufendorf, Thomasius argued for a "territorial" understanding of church-state relations, which placed the secular ruler over all the religious communities of his dominion as a supraconfessional authority.[33] Thomasius presented his work on church law as a defense of the rights of territorial rulers against the attempts of "papistical clerics" to aggrandize to themselves aspects of civil authority. He saw his views on church-state relations as truly Protestant, continuing the struggle against clerical tyranny begun by Luther.[34] The counterpoint to Thomasius's territorialism was the episcopal system of traditional Lutheran political theory.

Thomasius articulated the principle of princely authority over the church and its ritual in the 1695 dissertation of his student Enno Rudolf Brenneysen, *On the Law of the Prince Concerning Adiaphora* (*De jure principis circa adiaphora*), also published in German translation for a broader audience in 1705.[35] The 1695 treatise enraged Lutheran theologians in Saxony, who attempted to ban it and published a series of countertreatises to which Thomasius and Brenneysen responded over the next five years.[36]

For Thomasius, the authority of Protestant princes over church ritual was one aspect of a larger struggle to anchor state authority completely outside the traditional legitimization of the church. To do this, Thomasius was willing to stretch the traditional Lutheran concept of "adiaphora" to its widest possible extent. Thomasius held everything except the fundamental doctrine of the church as indifferent or morally neutral, and all these adiaphora could be legitimately regulated by secular authority.[37] Following Hobbes, he argued that the conscience was free from secular authority, but that the body and the rites and ceremonies of the church(es) within a state were subject to the secular ruler, who has authority "over the actions of his subjects, in secular as in spiritual affairs."[38]

In 1702 Thomasius focused this argument on funeral ceremonies, discussing a range of issues related to burial that served as further examples of the attempts of the "papifying" clergy to seize the rights of Protestant princes. Thomasius's treatise on the law of burial (*Solennia Sepulturae*), was prepared as a dissertation in Halle and published on 8 April 1702. In this work, also published in the German collection of 1705, Thomasius applied the territorial principle, based on his understanding of ritual as adiaphora, to the Protestant law of burial.[39] He saw controversies over the law of burial as one example of the struggle against clerical pretensions: "I have recently learned that persons in a certain place are struggling with all their might . . . to deny to the princes and secular authorities the right to change or eliminate funeral ceremonies."[40] In Thomasius's words, this Lutheran clerical attack on secular authority over funerals "stinks of the Papacy" and was the work of "the secretly papist clergy disguised as Lutheran theologians."[41] He argued forcefully that "the administration of funeral ceremonies belongs not to the law of internal things [the *jus in sacra*], but to the law of external things [*jus circa sacra*]."[42] In his treatise on the law of burial, Thomasius dealt with the punishment of suicides, burial in churches, the simplification of funerals, the rise of nocturnal burial, and the role of the funeral sermon. Burial ritual became an important "test case" in the application of the territorial principle.

The *Solennia Sepulturae* examined the contemporary trend to simplify and reduce the clergy's role in the traditional Lutheran funeral. Thomasius endorsed this development, begun around 1670 by courtiers and urban elites, in terms of the right of the Protestant ruler to alter the order of burial "with good cause."[43] Thomasius's interest in extending secular authority over funerals was especially clear when he argued against his main legal authority, Benedict Carpzov.

Accordingly, the burial of suicides was prominent first in Carpzov's discussion of the Lutheran funeral and then in Thomasius's treatise. He reinterpreted Carpzov's commentary in order to argue that the Consistory had only a delegated authority over the burial of "those who in a rage or in melancholy murdered themselves."[44] This authority over the body of the suicide was exercised in the name of the territorial ruler and revocable at any time: "when the jurists say that the authority over funerals belongs to the consistory . . . , they speak only about what normally happens on the direction or instigation of the prince, as when the consistory or ministry does something on express or implicit command of the prince."[45] Beyond this, Thomasius suggested that even lesser organs of secular government, such as city councils, might overrule a church consistory on such matters.[46] In the administration of burial, Carpzov had placed consistorial authority above the secular authorities. Thomasius reversed this position by arguing that Carpzov's detailed presentation of clerical authority referred only to authority delegated by the secular ruler case-by-case.

The arguments Thomasius presented on burial law tended to secularize the body of the suicide in two ways. First, Thomasius argued for secular authority over all funerals; the clergy would merely provide the appropriate form of burial. He also criticized the denial of Christian burial to suicides, arguing that punishing the body did not punish the suicide or deter others from the crime, but that it allowed "papists or papistical pastors" to treat "the most pious and innocent people as if they were godless and despisers of the Word of God."[47] Ignoring the intense significance of the body and its final resting place in Lutheran church law and in popular belief, Thomasius sought to lessen the importance of the body, which he viewed as merely mundane and neither sacred nor powerful.[48] Like all worldly things, it belonged under secular authority.

Funeral rituals, including the burial of suicides, provided an excellent opportunity to make these two arguments because the rituals were embedded in daily life. As Thomasius noted in his own remarks at the conclusion of the *Solennia Sepulturae,* "such a topic . . . is of daily use."[49] In fact, as Thomasius's arguments supporting secular authority over burial were discussed and published in Halle in 1702, the same issue arose in Leipzig.

The Leipzig Dispute over the Burial of Suicides, 1702–1706

It was no coincidence that Thomasius presided over a dissertation on the law of burial in April 1702. In nearby Leipzig, where Thomasius still had many connections, the city council was embroiled in a struggle with the regional Consistory regarding the council's jurisdiction over the burial of suicides. Like Thomasius, the council argued that the administration of burial, and in particular the burial of suicides, properly belonged under secular authority.

The archival record of the dispute begins with the suicide of Anna Altner of Taucha, who hanged herself a few days after Laetare Sunday (March 26) 1702. The city council of Leipzig was the manorial lord (*Gerichtsherr*) of Taucha, and the suicide was reported to the administrators of the city's rural holdings (the *Landstube*).[50] These territorial administrators in turn reported the case to the Leipzig city council, who ordered an investigation into the life and character of the deceased.[51]

To determine "the probable causes of the suicide," the territorial administrators questioned Altner's pastor and confessor, Johann Gottlieb Hoffmann, as well as her neighbors and those with whom she had lived. The investigation by the Leipzig officials showed that Anna Altner had lived a "Christian and peaceful" life, and that she attended church regularly and received communion often (for the last time on the fourth Sunday in Lent, a few days before she took her life). The city officials concluded that her suicide resulted not from "evil despair" ("*boshafften Verzweiffelung*"), but rather from an "emotion of melancholy" ("*affectu melancholio*"). This was a crucial distinction in seventeenth-century discussions of suicide. Despair was a grave sin, understood as an utter loss of faith in the promise of salvation; melancholy, on the other hand, described a disturbed state of mind generally considered exculpatory.[52] After deciding that the woman was not guilty of any crime, the Leipzig administrators ordered the body to be cut down and placed in a coffin obtained by the deceased's daughter.[53] Because Altner was not morally responsible for the crime of self-murder, the secular administrators decided she could be buried quietly in a corner of the communal cemetery.[54]

Nearly two months later, on May 26, the Leipzig Consistory informed the Leipzig council's rural administration (the *Landstube*) that the Taucha pastor Johann Gottlieb Hoffmann had reported Altner's suicide to the Consistory immediately and requested instructions "on how the burial of the body should be held." The Consistory members then learned that the Leipzig council administrators had allowed the burial of the body in the Taucha cemetery without consulting them. The Consistory asked the *Landstube* in curt tones "on whose order that had occurred" and why the suicide had not been reported to them first, requesting a reply within eight days.[55]

The reply of the Leipzig territorial administration to the Consistory, dated June 17, reflected the city authorities' sense of the proper administration of the burial of suicides. They argued to the Consistory that they were authorized to rule on the burial by the manorial lord of Taucha, that is, the Leipzig city council. They further pointed out that no "prohibitive law" limited the council's authority. Finally, they argued that the established practice was to consult the Consistory only when there was doubt over the proper form of burial; as Altner's family had not requested any funeral ceremonies involving the clergy, there was no need to report the suicide to the Consistory.[56] The argument presented here by the territorial administrators of the Leipzig council places the burial of suicides entirely under secular administration. Only when doubt arose over the degree of honor shown by the funeral of the suicide would the Consistory be consulted—and the secular authorities alone decided if the case was doubtful. This argument presented a subtle functionalization of the church: after secular officials had decided on the fate of the body of the suicide, the church as a subordinate institution would then bury it accordingly.

The Consistory's prompt reply to the rural administration insisted that the burial of suicides was entirely subject to the "ecclesiastical jurisdiction": every instance must be reported to the Consistory. The secular authorities were to report on the circumstances of the suicide and the reputation of the deceased, then wait for the "resolution" of the Consistory, which would determine "if the body should be buried in the cemetery or in another place; further, what sort of ceremonies should be used."[57] The Consistory did not dispute the propriety of Anna Altner's burial itself; the administration of the burial of suicides in general was the issue.

By July 13 the conflict had escalated: the Leipzig city council itself defended its jurisdiction over the burial of suicides in a lengthy letter to the Leipzig Consistory. This was a tense time for the Leipzig council itself: in 1702 it was led by Franz Conrad Romanus (1671–1746), an Electoral administrator whom Augustus forced the council to accept as mayor in 1701. Feared and hated by the other councilmen, Romanus was a courtier-mayor who had studied law with Thomasius in Leipzig and was certainly no friend of the leaders of the Saxon church.[58] The council began by restating the arguments that the rural administrators had made: only when the form of burial was uncertain would the Consistory be informed and the judgment of the "ecclesiastical authority" be required. Otherwise, all burials of suicides were subject to the "secular magistrates."[59]

The report emphasized that the council had no obligation to inform the church authorities before the burial of a suicide, citing the *Jurisprudentia ecclesiastica* of Benedict Carpzov. In fact, the cases cited by the council (title 24, definitions 376–378) all *support* the authority of the Dresden Upper Consistory over the burial of suicides. The general authority of the consistories over the burial of suicides, which Carpzov's commentary affirmed, was presented by the council as a series of special cases in which the form of burial was uncertain, implying that the council held authority over all "straightforward" or unambiguous cases.[60] This echoes Thomasius's general subordination of church authority, and his specific point that burial is ultimately a secular matter.

The council reinforced its position by referring the practical issue of suicides in remote areas of the Electorate, then citing established practice ("older and recent cases") to show that suicides had often been buried without consulting church authorities, a claim upon which they would later elaborate. Furthermore, the council argued, neither the Consistory nor anyone else had ever before protested this practice.[61] The council's argument from precedent was plausible, considering the slow initial response of the Leipzig Consistory to the "unauthorized" burial of Anna Altner.

The Leipzig Consistory then brought its complaint to the Privy Council (*Geheimer Rat*) of King-Elector Frederick Augustus. In a ruling of November 13, 1702 the Privy Council affirmed the position of the Consistory: henceforth every case of suicide required the secular authorities to investigate the life and death of the victim, provide the appropriate consistory with this information, then await the consistory's decision on the disposal of the body. The ruling of the Privy Council removed the issue from the secular authority: "the deliberation regarding the burial of those who have committed suicide does not proceed from the high courts; instead, it comes solely, alone, and without exception before the ecclesiastical authority, and belongs before our Consistory."[62] Referring to the established practice cited by Leipzig city council, the ruling stated that the secular authority had no jurisdiction over the burial of suicides and could not acquire it through any "clandestine act."[63]

About a month later Leipzig city council defended its position in a detailed response to the ruling of the Privy Council. Again the council argued that the "disposition" over the burial of suicides belongs to the secular authorities unless there were doubts about the "ceremonies of the funeral." The council argued that no law removed the burial of suicides from their jurisdiction, and that their public administration of the burial of suicides had never been challenged by the Consistory or any other institution. The church law elaborated by Carpzov, they argued, gave the consistories jurisdiction only when "a question regarding the form of the ceremony arises."[64] Carpzov also stated, according to the council, that the secular authorities were explicitly charged to settle disputes over funerals.[65] The reply was sent to the Privy Council on December 21, and a copy was sent to the Upper Consistory in Dresden on February 25, 1703.

No record of any response from Dresden to the Leipzig council's letter exists, but the dispute continued: in June 1703 a potter's apprentice hanged himself in a suburb of the city outside the Grimma gate.[66] The relatives of the deceased requested from the council permission for an honorable burial, but in this case the Leipzig council noted that "doubts had arisen over the form and ceremonies of the funeral," and decided to request advice from the Consistory. The council noted explicitly that this report to the Consistory would in no way limit their authority over the burial.[67]

The council's report on the suicide of the apprentice, dated June 15, was never sent to the Consistory. The relatives of the deceased withdrew their request for an honorable funeral, and the body of the suicide was carried away at night "on a litter" and buried in the city's main cemetery at St. John's (the *Johannisfriedhof*), "but in a separate place off to the side."[68]

Again the council had disposed of the body of a suicide without consulting the Leipzig Consistory. On June 15 the Consistory requested a report on the life of the young man, only to learn that the council had already gone ahead with the burial. Consistory members immediately appealed to the Privy Council in Dresden, reporting that the council had failed to await their decision on the burial of the suicide. They noted that the burial had taken place "in such wild haste" that it was necessary to exhume the body shortly afterward to check for signs of violence and confirm that the death was a suicide.[69]

In response to the Consistory's report of June 1703, the Privy Council informed the Leipzig city council that the city council's distinction between "undisputed" burials (for which no consistorial permission was necessary) and cases in which the form of burial was uncertain (in which case the Consistory should be consulted) was groundless. The Privy Council affirmed the terms of its decision of November 1702: all authority over the burial of suicides lay in ecclesiastical hands.[70] In its defense the Leipzig city council challenged the accuracy of the Leipzig Consistory's report in a letter to the Upper Consistory in Dresden (June 28, 1703), then drafted a lengthy report to the King-Elector and the Privy Council which was prepared by August 27 but withheld until the fall trade fair, when the King-Elector was expected to visit Leipzig personally. The city council may have hoped to appeal to Augustus directly and circumvent the Privy Council.[71]

In this report the council repeated (sometimes verbatim) the arguments it had made in its letter of July 13, 1702. To support its argument from precedent, the council described six recent cases of suicide in the city and its suburbs over which it had adjudicated, "each time freely and publicly, without inquiry from the Consistory or the superintendents, without any . . . controversy, and also without presenting a report or receiving instructions."[72] If the council's argument is accepted, then these cases document the council's *de facto* authority over the burial of suicides back to at least 1690.[73]

Of the six suicides listed, the first three took place in the city prison where a Jew, a shepherd, and a corporal all took their lives while jailed for theft. A contemporary chronicle, the *Leipzigisches Geschicht-Buch* records the suicide of the shepherd in 1693: "On July 7, . . . a shepherd imprisoned for theft hanged himself . . . in the city hall jail."[74] The form of burial he received marked him as an utter outsider: "The executioner cut down [the body], wrapped it in a black linen cloth and had his servants carry it down, drag it out, and inter it under the gallows."[75] Vogel records the suicide of the Jew in 1687 but makes no mention of the corporal's suicide; as with the shepherd, both of these suicides were probably buried beneath the gallows.

Of the other three suicides listed by the council (a soap-maker, a turner's wife, and a rope-maker's apprentice), Vogel reports only the death and burial of the turner's wife: "On July 26 [1690] in the evening around 10 o'clock, the wife of a turner hanged herself in her bedchamber." The chronicle emphasizes her Christian burial: "after numerous persons had given testimony that she often suffered from melancholy, [the body] was taken by the gravedigger on the following evening and buried in the cemetery."[76] The council may have allowed Christian burial to the other two suicides in this group as well. These examples were meant to document both the council's long-standing uncontested authority over the body of the suicide and its careful use of this authority, which distinguished between the honest poor and dangerous criminals.[77]

This final appeal to the King-Elector displays the council's fundamentally secular interpretation of suicide: when it was clear that the suicide was committed "out of weakness" ("*aus Schwechheit,*" denoting mental incapacity rather than moral weakness), then the form of burial would be determined by secular authority. Only in "atrocious, scandalous, and wicked" (and by implication rare) cases would ecclesiastical authorities deal with suicide as a moral issue.[78] The Leipzig city council put into practice the new view of ritual and the church developed by Hobbes, Pufendorf, and Thomasius by subtly reducing the Lutheran state church to a mere provider of burial, subordinated to the decisions of the secular authority. The council's defense of its authority over the burial of suicides echoes the arguments of Christian Thomasius for secular authority over funerals in general. Indeed, its practice preceded Thomasius's arguments.

No record exists of any response from the King-Elector or the Privy Council to the Leipzig council's lengthiest appeal. The question of jurisdiction was settled: despite the precedent of secular authority over the burial of suicides (which no one disputed), the rulings of the Privy Council placed all decisions regarding the burial of suicides firmly in the hands of church authorities. The Leipzig council continued to protest the ruling through 1706, but to no avail.[79] Despite (or perhaps due to) the arguments of Thomasius, their *de facto* control was not made legitimate. A 1719 Saxon ordinance confirmed the 1702 ruling that "the secular authorities shall refer the burial of suicides . . . from melancholy . . . to the consistories" but did allow secular jurisdiction over the bodies of those who killed themselves while in jail.[80]

In the burial dispute, the Leipzig city council was unable to ally with any of the other political forces in the principality.[81] The Saxon nobles on the Privy Council supported the Lutheran clergy, and the "foreign" (that is, non-Saxon) nobles of the court, the leading advisors of the King-Elector, had no interest in the issue.[82] Augustus himself was willing to intervene directly in Leipzig affairs, but only when he stood to benefit financially. In return for generous financial donations, Augustus allowed Reformed Protestants to worship in private homes and awarded the court Jew Isaac Behrend numerous special privileges at the Leipzig trade fairs. For Augustus, financial concerns simply overrode confessional politics.[83] The Leipzig city council could rely on the support of its prince only, it seemed, when the council had enough money to offer. No financial incentive was involved in the burial controversy.

Secularization and the Body of the Suicide

The *de facto* administrative secularization of the burial of suicides established in Leipzig at the end of the seventeenth century was reversed by the regional consistory, which successfully asserted its authority over all burials of suicides, even when nothing more than the humblest interment was desired. In 1702 neither the Leipzig Consistory, the Upper Consistory in Dresden, nor the King-Elector's Privy Council denied that for some years the Leipzig city council had exercised general authority over the burial of suicides. Why did the Leipzig Consistory first contest the city council's practice in 1702–1703?

The publication in nearby Halle of Thomasius's *Solennia Sepulturae* must have intensified the conflict; in fact, it may have provoked it. In this treatise Thomasius made the law of burial a prime example of the daily application of the territorial principle of church authority. His ringing proclamation of secular authority over the burial of suicides (and of funerals in general) alerted Lutheran church leaders in Saxony to implications of the Leipzig council's burial of suicides. In the mundane issue of burial location, the secularizing practices of the city council preceded the theory of territorialism that justified it. We know that Thomasius's opponents, such as Valentin Ernst Löscher in Dresden and Johann Benedict Carpzov II (nephew of the renowned jurist) in Leipzig, followed his publications closely.[84] They may have seen the *Solennia Sepulturae* as a continuation of the bitter debate sparked by Thomasius's 1695 treatise on *adiaphora*. For Thomasius, the body was *adiaphora*, literally "a thing indifferent," devoid of the meaning it carried in popular belief and in Lutheran theology. By arguing that funeral ceremonies were *adiaphora* and as such entirely subject to secular authority, Thomasius placed the long-standing practice of the Leipzig city council in a new and threatening light: suddenly, the authority to define the community and its outsiders was at stake.

The body of the suicide thus emerged as a conspicuous and contested issue in the early Enlightenment reformulation of the relationship between the church and civil authority.[85] This secular body, subject to civil authority in life and in death, was anathema to the church authorities of Electoral Saxony.

For reasons specific to Electoral Saxony, the intellectual and administrative attempts to secularize the burial of suicides failed. The would-be absolute monarch Augustus, the political actor with the most to gain from the establishment of territorialism, never addressed the issue. With no financial incentive, he was unwilling to intervene on behalf of the Leipzig city council; his Privy Council, closely tied to Saxon Lutheranism, decided the dispute in favor of the traditional clergy. The body of the suicide remained under the jurisdiction of church officials.

Considered in its intellectual and institutional contexts, the Leipzig dispute illustrates the importance of the body and ritual to our understanding suicide in the early Enlightenment. Despite the arguments of Thomasius and the Leipzig city council in favor of secular authority over the burial of suicides, the connection between a secular understanding of the state, ritual, and the body, on the one hand, and the secular administration of the body of the suicide, on the other, appears both complex and indirect. In this Saxon case the rising tide of secularization produced powerful countercurrents which moved in an entirely different direction.

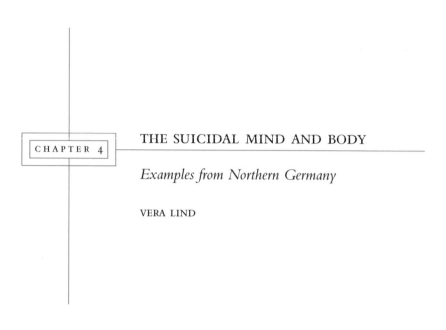

CHAPTER 4

THE SUICIDAL MIND AND BODY

Examples from Northern Germany

VERA LIND

Confrontations with self-inflicted death have touched the basic questions of human existence and provoked criticism in every age. Today most Western societies understand suicide as a medical and psychological problem that is treatable with medication and therapy. Until the eighteenth century, however, suicide was perceived and sanctioned as the sinful and criminal act of an individual. It might be an unscrupulous, conscious act, or it might result from an inner struggle, melancholy, and temptation by the devil. These beliefs were based on the medieval Christian theological definition of suicide as a deadly sin and the equivalent of committing a murder. The impulsive and violent separation of body and soul by one's own hand was seen as a breach of duty to God and society. Also, contemporaries who believed in the human instinct of self-preservation could not accept that someone could voluntarily resist this instinct.[1] The Reformation did not change these perceptions, and in local criminal statutes of northern Germany one can even see a hardening of attitudes in the sixteenth and seventeenth centuries. Counter to the Caroline Imperial law which explicitly stated that suicide could not be punished, these new statutes declared suicide a crime, punishable by the refusal of an honorable Christian burial. In addition, relatives could be denied their inheritance rights in suicide cases, and authorities punished survivors of suicide attempts with prison sentences.[2]

During the course of the eighteenth century, however, the perception of suicide changed fundamentally. Theologians, philosophers, and jurists, as well as common folk ultimately reinterpreted suicide as the sign of a physical and/or psychological illness, the basis of the modern understanding. Many came to believe that the new criminal laws concerning suicide were ill conceived and should no longer be enforced. A different view of self-destructive behavior influenced by medical opinion gained acceptance, and the criminal legal perspective became less relevant. All of this was connected to a growing trend to recognize human beings as individuals and to reject the traditional worldview and morality that had called for strict standards of punishment. This led to a more flexible view by authorities, which began to judge individual actions on a case-by-case basis. By the nineteenth century, the change became visible in legal texts too, as suicide disappeared from the penal codes as a criminal offense.[3]

A number of studies have informed us on the philosophical, theological, criminal, and legal history of suicide in Germany.[4] New research in cultural history and in the social sciences has enlightened us on the collective experience of suicide in early modern societies, the interaction between religion and secular authorities, and the relationship of these issues to the development of modernity.[5] Yet, few historians of suicide have explored the experience of the individual who is affected by suicidal thoughts and feelings. Our knowledge of how people facing self-destructive wishes in the early modern period perceived and interpreted their psychological and physical condition is extremely limited. This question could easily be dismissed as unanswerable due to the lack of adequate sources. Other than the accounts of people who survived their suicide attempts and the occasional goodbye letter or diary entry, there is little, it seems, that could provide insight into the individual experience of suicidal thoughts and feelings.

The problem of finding adequate sources to study suicide is not limited to the early modern period: it applies to all eras and is of prime interest to students of suicidology. Most twentieth- and twenty-first-century explanatory models and theories focus on the individual, namely on the innerpsychological or innerphysiological realm of suicide. Thanks to recent developments in suicide prevention, the medical and psychological evaluation of the people affected has attained the highest priority, and our understanding of the central biochemical and physiological processes in the body and mind of a (potential) suicide has increased to the extent that medication is available for treatment. In addition to questioning suicidal individuals and survivors of suicide attempts, today's suicidologists typically decipher the psychological profile of a suicide *after* death has occurred. As difficult as this process may be, they do have information available and opportunities to employ methodologies that are theoretically available to historians who face the same problem when analyzing suicides that occurred several hundred years ago.[6]

But although modern medical doctors and psychologists have investigated the emotions and sensual perceptions of suicides for decades, this is a relatively new field in historical research.[7] Some historians employ the "psychohistory" approach, in which they use psychoanalytical techniques in order to explain human emotions, behavior, and experiences. This approach is based on an analytical framework largely developed in the late nineteenth and early twentieth centuries, in which it was assumed that the essential human experience is largely biologically determined and unaffected by social and cultural change.[8] Others, such as those who work in cultural history and are interested in the history of the body and the emotions, take a different approach. They are less concerned with the explanation of specific emotions and behavior and instead consider the human experience as something largely conditioned by culture, which means that the emotional makeup of individuals and groups changes according to time and place. Anthropologists and cultural historians, for example, have demonstrated that pain, which on the surface seems to be a constant and clearly defined human sensation, is actually culturally conditioned.[9] They view the body on the whole as a socially and culturally constructed phenomenon, wherein certain signs of physical perception receive meaning to the person affected only through a cultural code.[10] This kind of research focuses on how physical and psychological perceptions and experiences were expressed over the centuries and how they changed.

In the following essay, I employ cultural-anthropological methodology and search for cultural codes that shaped the internal experiences and perceptions of early modern suicides. This can help us answer a number of questions, such as how suicides experienced the body and the mind. Did they articulate their feelings? Were their experiences guided by contemporary stereotypes of melancholy? Did they have a certain perception of suicidal and self-destructive tendencies and their possible consequences or of how society would react to their behavior? How did they connect a specific physical-psychological sensation with the desire to end their lives? Did these perceptions shift as new conceptualizations of suicide as an illness developed during the eighteenth century?

Determining the cause of death by dissecting the body seems a plausible and largely successful procedure today, as it was in the early modern period, but how can we gain insight into the mind and feelings of a suicidal person after his or her death? In the majority of early modern suicide cases in rural northern Germany, no suicide notes or diaries were left behind by people who took their lives.[11] But since suicide and attempted suicide were criminal offenses well into the nineteenth century, criminal court records of these cases can provide important clues. I have investigated the records of three hundred suicidal acts of men and women in Lutheran northern Germany between 1650 and 1820 to try to answer these questions. If the persons in question survived, then the court records include their own testimony. If not, the records consist of the testimony of relatives, neighbors, doctors, and pastors. These second-hand views are often the only clues of how a potential suicide might have felt before the act, and when critically and carefully interpreted can function as a mouthpiece for those who could no longer speak and left no written statement about their acts.[12]

My argument is that in spite of decriminalization in theory and practice in the early modern period, suicide remained an unthinkable, unspeakable taboo that led men and women who attempted it to develop innovative measures to justify the act to themselves and to protect themselves and their families from its consequences. By the end of the eighteenth century people in northern Germany still considered suicide to be a terrible religious offense and a threat to society because it acknowledged individual agency and interference with something given by God: human life. For a rural society still largely shaped by religious beliefs, taking one's life was difficult to view as something other than an ungodly act, regardless of the individual circumstances. Thus a suicide remained alienated from the rest of society. Individual suicides handled the problem of the taboo in a number of ways. Essentially they consciously and subconsciously worked within cultural codes—some of which were gender specific—that were acceptable and used them to explain their behavior to themselves and to others. For example, some experienced their bodily signs and feelings within the culturally constructed stereotype of melancholy—including religious melancholy which involved no taboo—which was not directly connected to a wish to die. Many who survived their suicide attempts later described themselves as passively enduring some external force that overcame them, thus allowing them to escape responsibility for what then happened. The way they identified those external forces changed during the eighteenth century, reflecting intellectual currents of the era. Whereas diabolical temptation seemed to explain individual suicidal feelings in the seventeenth and early eighteenth centuries, illness and personal problems caused by others increasingly became the causes from the early to mid-eighteenth century. Another way of dealing with the enduring cultural taboo was the phenomenon of suicidal murder, in which individuals who wished to end their lives committed a capital offense in order to let the unknowing authorities carry out the deed for them by passing a death sentence. The suicidal murder was one of a number of ways in which men and women creatively and strategically planned their own deaths in order to minimize the consequences for themselves or their families for having violated the taboo against self-inflicted death.[13]

From Diabolical Powers to Medical Explanations

The experience of passive suffering is a phenomenon found among suicidal men and women throughout the seventeenth and early eighteenth centuries. These people experienced physical and psychological troubles as sensual impressions that an external force imposed on them and directed within them, as something that could not have originated within their own bodies. This experience functioned as an explanation for thinking about the taboo of suicide without having to ascribe it to the self.

The external force could take various forms, including the power of the devil. This can be demonstrated in the case of a book trader, who in 1682 was seriously injured in his suicide attempt and died a few days later. Shortly after the deed he asked a pastor why God had not answered his prayers and protected him from the devil when he was tempted to take his life. To him the urge to commit suicide appeared as a power struggle between godly and demonic forces, for which deep faith and prayer were helpful countermeasures. The book trader, who had employed this strategy in the face of self-destructive urges sent by the devil, had requested the active intervention of God and wondered why this technique had failed. God had heard his prayer, answered the pastor, for in the end he did not allow the devil to complete his work, but instead snatched away his hand and gave the book trader time to do penance.[14]

This interpretation, based on simple but ingenious logic, demonstrates the contemporary position on forgiveness of sins in such cases. Since suicide was treated as a deadly sin, damnation in the afterlife seemed a consequence impossible to avoid. In this case, the fact that the book trader survived his suicide attempt was a clear sign of God's grace: he had the chance to do penance as a remorseful sinner before dying, so that he might be purified and go directly after his now Christian death into the kingdom of God.

The spiritual-theological aspect of the book trader's suicide attempt was only one side of his experience; he also suffered from physical symptoms. To a physician, he had complained about a number of ills. He could not sleep and struggled constantly against anxiety. Often during the day and night small flames flickered before his eyes; a foul smelling mist arose in his head; he suffered from constant pain in his head and stomach and was tormented by nightmares. Other than this, he felt "perfectly fine" physically and psychologically.[15] The book trader's perception of his body corresponded closely to the seventeenth-century stereotype of melancholy, the symptoms of which included sleeplessness, headaches, visions of flames, buzzing in the ears, constipation, stomach pains, and anxiety. According to the contemporary belief in the humoral pathological model of body fluids, melancholy was triggered by a warm and dry mist that rose from the stomach to the head and there stimulated deceptive fantasies, although those affected believed that their cognitive abilities were fully intact.[16] As a book trader he was presumably aware of the current literature on melancholy and transferred these phenomena to his own body. That is, he perceived his body entirely according to the specific terms that were culturally formed for him. Only when he deciphered his physical distress using the prevailing cultural code for melancholy did he understand his problem.

How can one explain the interaction between melancholy as physical illness and melancholy as demonic seduction? These apparently contradictory concepts were both part of a contemporary cultural code. The conception of melancholy was based on the ancient fluid model of the body. External factors, such as changes in climate or injuries that penetrated the body, led to an imbalance of fluids, a surplus of black bile in the body that triggered the illness. Medicine and theology were united as follows: the vapor from the bile rose to the head and made the brain susceptible to delusions, including the desire to take one's life. Consequently, the individual's suicidal tendencies were constructed as stemming from the illness of melancholy itself or from the devil's exploiting the weakness of a melancholic person for his own purposes.[17] In both cases the affected human body was passive and served merely as the battleground for external forces. Thus self-destructive wishes were found in the body and spirit of an individual but were caused by mechanisms beyond the individual's control.

Sometimes contemporaries interpreted demonic influences in gender-specific ways, as demonstrated in the case of a thirty-three-year-old widow who murdered both her children in 1664 and then failed to kill herself only because neighbors intervened. During her detainment she did not appear to be conscious of these events. The widow claimed that the children stood with her in a room while Satan waited outside the door to take them. Later she chafed as she described how the devil sat on her shoulder and distressed her.[18] A suppressed reaction to the shock of her deed? Or did she employ the stereotype that women were more prone to diabolical temptations than men in order to consciously deflect blame away from her before God and judicial authorities? In early modern and modern times, the murder of one's own children is normally associated with cruelty, aggressiveness, a lack of feeling, and cold-bloodedness, characteristics that are contrary to the image of women as caretakers and mothers. Also, the aggressiveness and supposed coldness of the act appeared as a dangerous violation of early modern gender norms—women who behaved more like men threatened the order of society. With cultural interpretive models, this threat could be tracked and reintegrated into societal order. When women violated boundaries of acceptable behavior, people around them often responded by trying to put such women back into their proper female realm, or by making others responsible for their behavior. This widow did both without the help of others. During the course of the trial, she ascribed her actions not only to diabolical powers but also to the female realm of emotions, associated with her role as mother and wife: she cited anguish over her husband's death, feelings of guilt over the death of another child, and financial problems as the reasons behind her decision to kill herself and her children.[19] The contrast between these matter-of-fact explanations and her immediate reaction after the murder of her children and the attempt on her own life are noteworthy. In doing so, she operated within the culturally accepted boundaries of behavior for women whose emotional well-being was connected to the realm of a successful family life.[20] Under the immediate shock of realizing what she had done, the widow was unable or unwilling to attribute her actions to herself, for no code of female conduct existed for such aggressive, brutal behavior. At this moment the devil became the agent, and personal responsibility played no role. Later the widow provided the court with an explanation that placed the deed in an acceptable domain for her and society: external circumstances like the death of two family members and a financial crisis brought her into conflict with the correct exercise of her female role and made her susceptible to a demonically induced act and thus removed her individual guilt.

The power of the devil remained central to perceptional models of suicide until about the end of the seventeenth century, after which a transition began to set in. The body fluid model, with its belief that melancholy resulted from a surplus of black bile in the body, remained an accepted part of the explanation throughout the eighteenth century, as did the perception of suicidal tendencies and melancholy as passive experiences. But while the theological and medical-scientific perception and explanation were equally integrated in this model in the 1600s, during the second half of the eighteenth century the emphasis shifted toward the latter, as explanations became increasingly based on pathological melancholy. After about 1700 the association of suicidal behavior with demonic forces declined, and during the second half of the eighteenth century demonic forces permanently disappeared from the perceptions of suicidal behavior. Suicidal wishes were more and more viewed as the result of a physical or psychological illness.

The new emphasis on medical explanations can be seen in the case of a gardener's apprentice, who in 1759 attempted to kill himself with a knife. Afterward he explained his condition to a doctor in terms of a melancholy that "overcame" him ("*ihm zugestoßen sei*"), to which he was "predisposed" ("*aus Disposition*"). The cause of this was "hidden hemorrhoids" that would violently break out from time to time.[21] The gardener's apprentice saw himself as a victim of a possibly inherited illness, and thus free of personal guilt. Religious or supernatural forces played no role. The youth implicitly declined responsibility for his actions by blaming them on his illness which, though part of his bodily constitution, he portrayed as something outside his body, something that "overcame" him and over which he had no control.

In a similar manner a woman who had made numerous suicide attempts and self-inflicted injuries described her condition to a doctor in 1795. Things were going quite well, she explained, since she could eat, drink, sleep, and work. Yet occasionally her head would become "heavy and foolish" ("*schwer und närrisch*") and she would suffer from a severe attack of headache, "at which time everything began spinning around, and she had twisted ideas" ("*wobei denn alles mit ihr*

Figure 4. William Hogarth, *The Suicide of the Countess,* from *Marriage à la Mode,* plate VI, 1745. Reproduced with the permission of the National Gallery, London.

herumginge und sie allerhand verkehrte Ideen hätte").[22] Although this woman did not explicitly refer to a melancholic illness, she clearly did hold sickness responsible for her self-destructive behavior. For her, the urge to injure herself was something that came from outside of her that was beyond her control, placing her in an unsound mental state. This interpretation was in unison with the enlightened medical position of the day. In both these examples the self-destructive intentions were described as something that overcame them, something understood by contemporary medical theorists as rage, a variant of melancholy, which was also attributed to an imbalance in body fluids. At times suicidal inclinations worked in the form of a "fixed idea" on the fantasy of victims and caused them to attempt to injure either themselves or others.[23]

Some men and women who tried to commit suicide ascribed their desire to die solely to their own individual psychic constitution. They made certain events or circumstances in their lives responsible for their feelings without resorting to theological or medical explanations. Significantly, cases such as this did not occur until the second half of the eighteenth century.[24] For these people, the wish to die almost always developed from interpersonal conflict involving marriage or partnership. To a degree, they took responsibility for their suicidal wishes but described the feelings they underwent while actually trying to kill themselves as out-of-body experiences, as if outside forces, not the self, acted at this point.

In 1762, for example, neighbors intervened to prevent a former soldier from hanging himself from a tree. The man was living with his betrothed, a widow, and her small child in a cottage, and they were supposed to get married soon. On this particular day, the child had become unruly and started screaming. This irritated the man, who angrily announced that once they were married, he would use a cane to silence the child. This announcement outraged his bride-to-be so much that she immediately canceled all marriage plans and announced that now he would never become the father of her child, a drastic reaction that provoked a drastic response. The former soldier was so deeply shocked by the shattered marriage plans that he grabbed a piece of rope, stormed out the door and into the woods in order to hang himself. Some of the neighbors chased after him, however, and convinced him to return to the cottage.[25]

Later the man described his behavior. The announcement to cancel all marriage plans "had set him beside himself."[26] He had not been aware of how he felt, and in such a state the thought crossed his mind that he should commit suicide. The former soldier added that in this state of mind he had not been able to recognize the neighbors who had followed and prevented him from hanging himself, although, as he stressed, they were well known to him otherwise. This is one of the rare sources in which the survivor of a suicide attempt was actually able to describe the development of his feelings and what ultimately caused the attempt on his life. The rejection by his bride caused such a forceful and traumatic emotional shock to the man that he felt compelled to speak of being outside of himself or detached from his normal identity. In this condition in which the veteran was no longer in control of himself, one can again see the passive state so characteristic in the self-perception of many early modern suicides. The image of a divided body is a well-known phenomenon. It is interpreted as a reflex of developing hostility toward the self, and is a key in understanding self-destructive behavior.[27] Sigmund Freud saw the division of the body into two imaginary parts as a symbol that the hatred aimed at someone else—in this case at the veteran's bride—is projected onto the self instead, causing the wish to die. Instead of killing the hated person, the affected person kills himself or herself.[28]

Another case of someone who acknowledged personal problems as the starting point of suicidal desires involved a young woman who in 1802 explained that she had attempted suicide because of disappointed expectations in love and marriage. She had recently married and felt that neither her emotional nor her financial needs were met by her husband. In addition, the woman was plagued by guilt over an illegitimate child that she had conceived with another man and secretly brought into the world the previous year. (The child had died during birth.) On the day of her suicide, she planned to confide in her parents but returned from her visit without telling them. Her husband found her weeping on the floor of the cottage. Instead of asking why she was so sad, he tried to cheer her up with jokes, but did not succeed. Instead the young woman became upset and threw a barrel cover through a windowpane, after which the husband struck her. This was too much for the woman. She ran out of the cottage and threw herself into a nearby mill creek, but was rescued from drowning by her father-in-law. In the protocol the young woman described what she was feeling just before she attempted to drown herself as follows: "The pain and a sudden, indescribable feeling made her gasp for air, and in this frightened state she sprang into the mill creek, without knowing what was happening in her head."[29] This case provides another rare glimpse into the physical and psychological feelings that led to a death wish. As with the former soldier, the newly married woman's suicide attempt seems to have been an impulsive reaction to a long-standing conflict that had reached a breaking point. However, the woman did not feel herself divided in two or "beside herself." Instead she described an inner force leading to a state of unconsciousness, a blackout: the vehemence of her feelings cut off her breathing—not an atypical sensation.[30] To her there seemed only one recourse to escape this unbearable, forced condition: commit suicide. Being overcome with a feeling that threatened her very existence was such a horrible experience—a literally *unthinkable* one—that in retrospect it appeared to have suddenly blotted out all consciousness of her actions, an experience she shared with the former soldier.

In these two cases, a mixture of passive endurance and active involvement of the individual seems to have formed the experiences of suicide attempts. Separation from the self caused by some compulsive force occurred with both the former soldier and the young woman. A force triggered something in the woman, doing something *to her.* This suggests that although she acknowledged an active part in carrying out the suicide attempt, she felt that at that crucial moment she was not acting like herself but rather as someone who was overcome by an external impulse or, at most, reacted to such an impulse. Other examples confirm this point of view. Certain anxieties about the future became "increasingly strong and irresistible," explained an older homeless man in 1788 after his attempted suicide, and "in the end so *overpowered* him" that he tried to kill himself.[31] He too recognized that his fears were triggered by external, yet personal circumstances that he himself had brought on. (He was unmarried, old, suffered from pain, and worried about the future.) According to his description, during his suicide attempt, these feelings took on an independent character: they became an active agent that he passively experienced. From his point of view, the anxieties that had plagued him had nothing to do with any aspect of a melancholic illness.

Religious Melancholy

A variant of melancholy appeared throughout the eighteenth century that was closely connected to new religious developments. Some men and women came to believe that they were incapable of meeting the demands of leading a good, Christian life. They felt that no matter how hard they tried, their individual faith would never please God. Consequently, these people were very concerned about their personal salvation. This development appears to be connected to the spread of Pietism in Lutheran northern Germany during the eighteenth century, with its emphasis on individual self-reflection on guilt and sin, living a godly life, and emotional, individual conversion experiences.[32] Apparently the pressure to have a proper conversion and live the right way was more than some men and women could bear. These "religious melancholics" felt that they were so sinful that they could not die a Christian death and see God in the hereafter.

Medical theorists explained religious melancholy like every other form of melancholy by employing the body fluids model, and many theologians seem to have agreed. According to this interpretation, the blood of melancholics was full of bad fluids, leading them to feel that God had forsaken them. Because of this, self-denunciation became a common phenomenon.[33] According to the logic of the medical theorists, there was nothing illogical in a suicide caused by religious melancholy, and this was compatible with contemporary Pietist thought as well. Some Pietists, for example, believed that melancholy was a "healing" doubtfulness through which an individual could become aware of his or her own sinfulness.[34] The connection between religiously approved melancholy and suicide remained taboo, but in cases where circumstances forced Pietists to recognize an association between the two they adopted the medical explanation. In discussing suicide in his autobiography, the former Leipzig preacher Adam Bernd (1676–1748) explained why religious melancholics often felt drawn to the very thing they most feared because of its sinfulness. The physical circumstances of melancholy influenced the sensitive nerves and stimulated anxious ideas and images within the mind of the victim. This involuntary imagination (*imaginatio involuntaria*) could take on such an intensive, forceful state that reality and fantasy could no longer be distinguished. Thus deep within the conscience of religious melancholics loomed the specter of what they feared most: suicide. It was hardly possible for them to escape the suggestive character of this seemingly real vision. In the end this led them to carry out with a complete lack of will the very deed that had so tormented their thoughts.[35] In the new cultural code that shaped suicidal behavior, there was no trace of the traditional influence of the devil, but rather of the convergence of new medical explanations and new or different religious views.

Religious melancholics and the influence of Pietism can be seen in the rural areas of Schleswig and Holstein as well, but here the new medical explanations were not important.[36] People did not see themselves as victims of an illness amplified or brought to a conclusion by religious melancholy, and they did not suffer from the typical physical symptoms of a melancholic sickness. Further, they assigned demonic influences a subliminal role, or at least did not explicitly name them, as they had done earlier. Instead they connected their feelings to personal religious failings. These Pietists viewed God as a strict, punishing judge whose measuring stick for achieving salvation lay unattainably high because of the abundance of individual guilt and sin. But if suicide reputedly led to eternal damnation and believers' principal concern was salvation, how could religious anxiety push a believer to suicide? From the believers' perspective, the issue presumably involved choosing between leading a life that would progressively accumulate more and more sins, or committing the mortal sin of suicide. Apparently some preferred the sinfulness associated with suicide, convinced that it weighed less than all the other sins they would have amassed had they stayed alive. The sensations of people suffering from religious melancholy were directly contrary to the purported passivity of the many suicides described previously who saw themselves the victims of outside forces. Their death wish sprung from their reading of a cultural code that was heavily influenced by Pietism, which emphasized personal failure and led them to believe that the only proper thing to do was to commit suicide. Thus they actively and willingly carried out this act.

The influence of Pietism and active religious elements are clearly recognizable in the case of the young son of a farmer, who in 1752 believed that he had sinned and provoked God's wrath on his entire family. In order to avert this wrath, he attempted to use his own suicide to reconcile with God. As he later explained to his neighbors, it all began when his brother lost a foot and the young farmer was pleased because this meant he could then inherit the family farm. Shortly thereafter all the farms in the area suffered crop damage from bad weather, and the young farmer and his family were particularly hard hit. He told a neighbor that he was certain that the good Lord had punished him and his parents because of his sins. Because of him they were no longer happy and everything was going wrong. Everyone in the neighborhood tried to convince him that this was not so. The pastor asked the young farmer if he did not believe that Christ had already paid for his sins. He answered yes, but that this did not change anything—he was still terribly sad.[37]

The view of the young farmer was not atypical, nor was it entirely attributable to new developments in Pietism. There was a long tradition of believing that human behavior could cause supernatural phenomena, and belief in divine intervention to provide a sign or to punish sinners remained a part of Lutheran church discipline in this era.[38] In this case, occurrences in nature played a significant role in ecclesiastical theories concerning divine punishment. Sensitized by church doctrine presented from the pulpit, the young farmer knew how to discern signs of God's punishment, and his guilty conscience led him to believe that his own actions had caused them. The question now was how could he be reconciled again with God? First he attempted to do penance by serving time in jail, but no one would take his wish to be locked up seriously. When the farm continued to encounter economic difficulties, he concluded that his family would be better off if he were dead. A number of times he expressed this thought to others. For example, at a later hearing a neighbor stated that the young farmer had told him that "he wanted the good Lord to take him from this world, since he was no longer of use to it."[39] Obviously believing that no normal form of penance would alleviate God's punishment of his family, the young farmer hanged himself in the barn of his parents.[40]

Interestingly, the considerable number of individuals of the later eighteenth century who viewed their self-inflicted deaths as a form of sacrifice were all males. Penance and concern over one's own sinfulness, together with the belief that only a blood sacrifice could atone for that sin, never played a significant role in female suicide cases.[41] Contrary to the cases described previously, religious melancholics did not feel pushed by some external force but rather accepted individual responsibility for their physical and spiritual condition, which led them to believe that only their own deaths could alleviate contemporary woes. Thus an interesting reversal took place: while passive "sufferers" from suicidal desires had sought to deny responsibility for something considered taboo, religiously motivated suicides accepted individual responsibility for the deed. Be that as it may, contemporary medical theorists and theologians saw external forces at work in such cases and considered religiously motivated suicides the result of debilitating delusions that placed the victims in a passive, unsound mental condition.

Suicidal Murders

Another form of suicide related to those caused by religious melancholy was suicidal murder. This referred to suicidal people who intentionally murdered someone because they wanted to die by capital punishment, which they believed allowed them to avoid the eschatological consequences of suicide. Usually it was impossible to ask for forgiveness for the sin of suicide because there was no time to confess, show regret, be forgiven, and then die an "honorable" death with the knowledge that God would grant them mercy. The strange logic of suicidal murder cases could resolve this problem. This is demonstrated by a servant who killed a boy in 1752 for no apparent reason. He explained that he was thinking of committing suicide, concluded that this would be a terrible sin, and decided that, "there can be no mercy without the shedding of blood, and in order to receive that mercy, he had to shed blood, so that in turn his blood could be shed, because his sins were so great that he had to atone for them."[42]

The servant employed a Biblical view of sin, forgiveness, and sacrifice similar to what the previously discussed young farmer had done. According to the Old Testament, the wages of sin is death, and those who have sinned and distanced themselves from God can come close to him again only by offering a blood sacrifice. For this purpose the throat of an animal (usually a lamb) was cut, and its blood dispersed on an altar (Leviticus 4:1–35, 5:1–13). This view continued in the New Testament, but it was Jesus, the Lamb of God, who bore the sins of the world and gave his blood to atone for those sins (John 1:29; Matthew 26:28). The servant followed this logic, though for him only a human sacrifice offered the assurance that he would be executed. To please God, he had to shed blood by murdering someone and consequently his own blood would have to be shed at the place of execution as penance. Only in this way could he be sure that he could do penance while still on earth, which to him was required in order to be forgiven for his sins. Thus he had the chance to die as a "poor sinner"—and he wanted to die anyway—because he would have time to show remorse and be comforted by a pastor before his execution. In this way the servant could be sure of dying a "good" Christian death, something that he never could have achieved by committing suicide.

Other potential suicides in the Duchies of Schleswig and Holstein pursued this goal as well, especially in the mid-eighteenth century. Not all of them were inspired by Old Testament understandings of sin and blood sacrifice, and their greatest concerns did not always stem from religious issues of accumulated sin and forgiveness. They were consistently obsessed, however, with the sinfulness of one single deed: their planned suicide. Cases like this occurred in northern Germany until the late eighteenth century, by which time the laws concerning suicide were rarely enforced. So serious was the problem of suicidal murder that in 1767 a new law was passed that denied the death penalty to suicidal people who had committed murder with the goal of being sentenced to death; they were to receive life imprisonment instead.[43] Suicidal murders represented an extreme case in which the knowledge of the religious consequences of suicide led to a coldly calculated, active strategy by people who were fully conscious of their actions.

Conclusion

Religiously motivated suicides and suicidal murderers actively sought their own deaths, whereas the sizeable majority of suicidal males and females in early modern Germany passively ascribed the wish to die to external forces. Regardless of the reason victims favored in explaining their experiences and self-perceptions— the devil, illness, personal religious failures, personal conflicts, or melancholy— they did not perceive themselves as the agents behind their self-destructive actions. Instead something appeared to have been done to them over which they believed they had no control. Many reportedly suffered blackouts at the very moment they tried to carry out the suicide or had some out-of-body experience. Two different but related factors were critical for this understanding of self-inflicted death: first, the culturally determined possibility to name and communicate suicidal fantasies and their related physical and psychic symptoms; second, societal and individual perception of suicide as a criminal offense.

In almost every suicide case mentioned, a certain cultural code or understanding of melancholy shaped the individual's perception of his or her body. Hidden within the term "melancholy" lay a number of differentiated meanings and expressions. Although it was possible for suicides to recognize and understand the physical and emotional conditions of depression, grief, pain, and the like, they were silent about what this could lead to. There is no evidence that people consciously conceptualized a connection between known physical and emotional conditions and the development and implementation of the desire to commit suicide. The connection was generally not discussed. A farmer's wife who clearly formulated for herself and others the desire to die and finally carried out the deed in 1801 is one of the few who did. After several failed suicide attempts she declared again and again to her family that she would have been "happy" if she "had lost her life."[44] Most could no longer remember or describe their feelings or even all of their actions, much less the connection between their physical and spiritual condition and the decision to kill themselves. The former soldier allegedly did not realize what condition he was in and did not recognize the neighbors who ran after him to stop him, even though, as he emphasized, "they had otherwise been well known to him."[45] In 1793 a cobbler explained after his attempted suicide that he could "not remember the sensation at all" that immediately preceded his accident.[46] The disappointed young woman in the case from 1802, described previously, lost her orientation and emphasized that she did not know where she was. Were these merely strategically planned ruses intended to deceive the authorities in order to escape the legal consequences of attempted suicide? A critical reading of the documents must take this possibility into account, but this interpretation would ignore a known psychological phenomenon. After confrontation with an onerous and terrifying event, loss of memory, blackout, and obliviousness can be a normal symptom of a state of shock that can follow and might function as a means of "purifying" or ridding the mind of some unbearable experience.

The blackout served as a way to deal with a culturally determined taboo and could allow individuals to protect themselves from its consequences. Suicide was so reprehensible that individuals who made attempts on their lives may have experienced a mental block surrounding their suicidal actions. The death wish was something for which there was no understood expression. It was something that had to remain diffuse and distant in the conscious mind, no matter how much it existed in the subconscious. In this manner the connection between the melancholic condition and the death wish was suppressed. If one survived the suicide attempt, then this event had to remain unthinkable and imperceptible in order to be able to endure the aftermath. The taboo made it impossible for most people to accept responsibility for the deed as something that their inner self had *actively* perpetrated. They could not see themselves as responsible for the act, but instead understood that the devil, an illness, or some unnamed force had exercised its power on them. Although the evidence cited here comes almost entirely from the testimony of those who survived suicide attempts, the view of suicide as something passive was almost universally shared. Relatives and friends giving testimony for completed suicides in the eighteenth century recalled statements that were very similar to those offered by survivors of suicide attempts.[47] People in early modern German society viewed suicide as a threat because it reflected an awareness that individuals could voluntarily remove themselves from that society by killing themselves. To avoid understanding this as some radical expression of the individual will, they blamed it instead on something else, some external factor. This was a protective process of repression, a kind of catharsis in the face of the ultimate act of self-determination and interference with God's will. Thus the open perception and designation of physical and spiritual conditions remained within the realm of melancholy, but this could not legitimately be connected to suicide.[48] This phenomenon clearly reveals the body as a socially and culturally constructed work and the problems associated with this, which Jakob Tanner has aptly described as the unbridgeable gap between the silence of the real body and the discourse of the symbolically constituted body.[49]

The passive component and the taboo among male and female suicides also show that the view of suicide as a deadly sin, as a criminal offense, and a threatening act of magic survived for a long time in rural areas of northern Germany.[50] In these areas belief in the sinister nature and frightening consequences of suicide remained powerful, even though they became anachronistic as the decriminalization and medicalization of suicide proceeded throughout the eighteenth century both in theoretical debate and in judicial practice.

Although the reconstructed self-perception of most victims did not and could not show it, the individual perceptional taboo of suicide also signaled that people were definitely conscious of the fundamental religious and legal consequences that resulted from this act. On the day of her suicide attempt in 1802, the young woman mentioned previously explained that "an oppressive feeling weighed on her breast like a stone. She regretted everything she had done. God knew that she could not comprehend the criminal nature of her behavior, and she loathed every thought that could induce her to commit suicide."[51] This testimony indicates she had been quite conscious of the possible consequences of her deed, and the swiftness of her reaction shows that she was aware of the reprehensible nature of suicide. In this case strategic considerations may have played a role, since the woman quickly showed remorse and suggested that she was in an unsound mental state.

The legal consequences may have been less a cause for concern than the religious, for in the end most potential suicides calculated that they would die. Because suicide usually did not leave time for perpetrators to express remorse for this serious sin and receive penance, achieving salvation was clearly problematic. Death by one's own hand also raised the difficult question of a proper Christian death. The examples of suicidal murders in the mid-eighteenth century suggest that the reluctance to commit suicide could not have merely reflected a vague awareness of the reprehensible nature of the deed in a religious sense; rather, it reflected a concrete awareness of a problem that had to be resolved. Religiously motivated suicides chose death by committing a horrible sin rather than leading a life that they thought could only result in the long accumulation of possibly even graver sins. Both suicidal murders and suicides committed for religious reasons actively tackled the religious consequences of suicide or of a sinful life, while suicidal people who attributed their actions to the devil, an illness, or personal circumstances confronted the same problem by perceiving themselves under the force of outside powers for which they could hardly be responsible themselves.

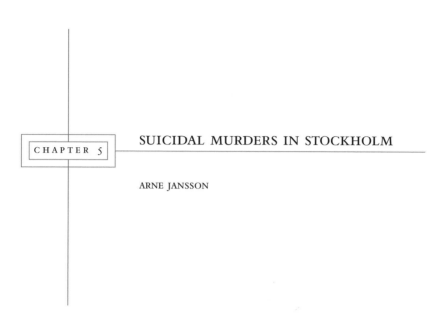

ARNE JANSSON

SUICIDAL MURDERS IN STOCKHOLM

Before beginning my research on violent deaths in early modern Stockholm, I had expected to read about sordid tales of premeditated murders, blood feuds, crimes of passion inspired by adultery or unrequited love, and so on. The homicides I actually discovered proved to be of a very different nature. Most common were cases of manslaughter, unplanned killings that were often the results of drunken brawls between individuals who were not well acquainted with each other. The next most common form of violent death was suicide. But I was quite surprised to discover a most unusual form of homicide: the suicidal murder, killing another person with the sole intent of then being sentenced to death and executed.

A typical example of such a case was that of Barbro Persdotter, a young woman who had come to Stockholm from the countryside. In 1668, Barbro was an inmate of the Danviken hospital because of an "infirmity of the face," perhaps leprosy. Barbro developed a love interest in a certain Mats Johansson, and both parties expressed a strong desire to marry. Mats himself suffered a major physical disability, having lost both his legs, and Barbro's relatives and the hospital's overseer both opposed the marriage to this handicapped man. Disappointed, Mats withdrew from the betrothal, leaving Barbro bitter and humiliated. Unable to bear this reversal, Barbro went to the home of a friend, an iron carrier, which was the site where the wedding was supposed to take place. There she slit the throat of the iron carrier's three-year-old child in order to be sentenced to death. The judges of Stockholm's Municipal Court were quite embarrassed with her blatant attempt to be executed, especially since they had handled a very similar case the previous year. They concluded:

> We have taken into consideration this atrocious case and tyrannical deed against an innocent child, who had never done anything against [Barbro]. It was found that she committed this act out of wicked intent, solely to leave this world, in imitation of Gertrud Joensdotter, who in the same way committed such a frightful deed in June of last year. It was found desirable to prevent this sin from taking hold and becoming rampant. Nonetheless, we concluded that we could not deviate from the law and accordingly resolved that she must die according to God's law and worldly law, and [Barbro Persdotter] is hereby sentenced to death.[1]

Though wanting to prevent future similar cases of suicidal murder and reluctant to impose capital punishment, which was precisely what Barbro wanted, the judges apparently considered alternative forms of punishment but ultimately felt bound by law to impose capital punishment.

If the jilted Barbro could no longer bear living, why did she not just take her own life rather than killing an innocent child in order to be executed? This behavior, which may appear bizarre to us, was apparently motivated by the fear of damnation. As is well known, ever since patristic times, Christian thinkers singled out suicide as a particularly heinous crime. In choosing the moment of their deaths, suicides were usurping God's powers and were not submitting to His will. Moreover, people who took their own lives did not have time to repent of their sins, whereas a murderer could show remorse, receive pastoral consolation, and ultimately hope for divine forgiveness when facing execution. Records reveal a total sixty-two such cases, but surely many more existed for which there are no extant records. This chapter examines early modern Stockholm's experiences with suicidal murder and other forms of indirect suicide, a phenomenon that, though not unknown elsewhere, was most common in Scandinavia and northern Germany.

Early Modern Stockholm and Sweden

The seventeenth and early eighteenth century marked the apogee of Swedish power. This was a period of political expansion, especially during the reigns of Gustavus II Adolphus (1611–1632), a great military leader best remembered for his key role in the Thirty Years War, and of Charles X Gustavus (1654–1660). Finland had been under Swedish suzerainty ever since the Middle Ages, and by 1660 the Swedish Kingdom extended to include much of the Baltic and Pomerania, the bishopric of Bremen, and provinces that had previously been under Danish dominion: Skåne, Halland, and Blekinge in the south and Bohuslän on the west coast. During this era, the Swedes developed well organized instruments of governmental administration, including an efficient system of justice. Higher education was improved, allowing the legal and administrative professions to thrive as never before. Ever more under the dominion of the crown, the church dutifully served the state, and strict Lutheran orthodoxy was enforced throughout the kingdom. Toleration of religious diversity was limited, and the crown strove to control what was printed throughout the country. During this era, domestic political relations were relatively calm, perhaps in part because even the peasants were represented as an estate in the parliament or *Riksdag*. The Great Northern War, 1700–1721, brought an end to Sweden's political prominence. After the unsuccessful campaign of Charles XII (1697–1718) against Peter the Great, Sweden lost most of its Baltic possessions to Russia and returned to being a second-rate power.[2]

During this era, Sweden, especially Stockholm, also experienced important demographic growth. The population of the realm, including Finland and possessions on the other side of the Baltic, was approximately 1.1 million in 1625 and 1.5 million in 1721. Thus Sweden remained a rather sparsely populated kingdom compared with countries to the south. Swedish crop yields were low because of the severe climate, especially during the "Little Ice Age" which lasted from the end of the sixteenth to the middle of the seventeenth century.

As Swedish power increased so did the importance of Stockholm within the realm. The capital grew from about 6,000–9,000 inhabitants at the beginning of the seventeenth century to approximately 54,000–60,000 at the end, though the city lost about 15,000 people to a plague epidemic in 1710–1711. The city's substantial population growth was due to extensive immigration from all parts of Sweden and Finland and even from other countries. Throughout the early modern period, Stockholm always had a large number of residents who were born outside of Sweden.[3]

Not only did Stockholm's population increase considerably during this period, the city also became much more impressive architecturally. Sixteenth-century Stockholm was small, poor, and about as rural as it was urban. By contrast, the much larger city of the mid-seventeenth century was adorned with the beautiful palaces of many noble families. In the 1600s, the crown, heavily dominating city administration, scrupulously oversaw the details of urban planning for its capital.

The most important sources for this investigation are court records from early modern Stockholm. Criminal cases involving civilians were normally tried at the Stockholm Municipal Court, the *rådhusrätten*. Lesser offences, disputes, and the examination of witnesses could be delegated to lower courts, the *kämnärsrätterna*, each of which had jurisdiction over a particular district within the city. The Municipal Court could not pass final sentences for serious crimes, such as murder and suicide, but rather had to refer their recommended decisions to the High Court, the *Svea hovrätt,* to be confirmed. Records from the lower courts are on the whole well preserved, but those of the *Svea hovrätt* regrettably are not. Until about 1700 a plaintiff had to press charges against the accused in criminal cases, but thereafter such charges were more commonly brought by a public prosecutor.

Swedish penal law stated unequivocally that both murder, the more serious form of homicide, and manslaughter should be punished by death, but during the seventeenth century those convicted of manslaughter were often sentenced only to fines and damages. According to written law, the bodies of suicides were to be taken into the woods and burned, except in cases of madness, in which case the victims were to be buried outside the cemetery. Secular judicial authorities, not clergymen, determined the fate of the bodies of suicides. In practice, in Stockholm the hangman was responsible for the disposal of the suicide's corpse, which he ordinarily buried in the gallows field, in spite of the dictates of written law. The judicial treatment of suicides was roughly in line with practices elsewhere in medieval and early modern Europe. Although court records often do not mention the desecration of the corpses of suicides, in one case the executioner was explicitly said to have hanged the corpse from the gallows, something that was fairly common in premodern Europe.[4] The fact that the suicide's body was handed over to the executioner showed that suicides in Sweden, as elsewhere, at the very least were denied honorable burials. By contrast, the confiscation of the property of suicide victims—often imposed elsewhere in premodern Europe—was apparently unknown in contemporary Sweden.

Frequency of Direct Suicides and Suicidal Murders

Table 5.1 shows the number of direct suicides and suicidal murders, both completed and attempted, found in the court records and other sources. The sixty-two cases of suicidal murder include nine cases in which assailants tried but failed to kill their victims. To what extent do these figures depict the real numbers of direct and indirect suicide? The actual number of direct suicides cannot be known. Self-inflicted deaths were considered dishonorable, and people had a vested interest in covering up their relatives' suicides. Still, ample evidence suggests a real increase in suicides beginning in the late seventeenth century. When registers are satisfactorily preserved, the number of recorded suicidal murders is a reliable measure of the real number of such indirect suicides. By definition, perpetrators of these murders wanted to be caught and confessed their crimes. Seven

TABLE 5.1.
Direct and indirect suicides in Stockholm, 1600–1773

Years	Suicides	Suicidal murders	Sum	Per year	Suicide rate per 100,000
1600–09	2	0	2	0.2	2.2–3.2
1610–19	2	0	2	0.2	2.2–2.5
1620–27	2	1	3	0.4	2.8–4.7
1636–49	1	1	2	0.1	0.3–0.8
1650–59	1	1	2	0.2	0.5–0.6
1660–69	1	2	3	0.3	0.6–0.9
1670–79	7	3	10	1.0	1.9–2.4
1680–89	17	5	22	2.2	4.0–4.4
1690–99	21	8	29	2.9	4.8–5.3
1700–09	18	13	31	3.1	5.6–6.3
1710–19	21	13	34	3.4	7.8–8.6

Sources: Arne Jansson, *From Swords to Sorrow: Homicide and Murder in Early Modern Stockholm* (Stockholm, 1998) 25; table 7 on page 26, based on Appendix 3, list of suicide cases, 177–78; table 8 on page 50, based on Appendix 2, list of homicide cases, 170–76. City Archives of Stockholm, Krim prot 1696 28/8, 1161–62, 1698 7/5, 486–94; 1706 22/12, 518, 29/12, 498; 1715 20/5, 514, 12/12 621; Protokoll från Norra förstadens kämnärsrätt (Minutes from the District Court of Northern Stockholm) 1698 21/4, 1134–36; Kriminalprotokoll från Stadens kämnärsrätt (Minutes from criminal cases of the District Court of Central Stockholm) 1737, 14/5, 785. Population estimates for the suicide rates are taken from Sven Lilja, "Stockholms befolkningsutveckling före 1800," *Historisk tidskrift* 3 (1995): 328.

suicidal murders have been found for the years 1720–1749 and eight for the years 1750–1773, but the actual number of suicidal murders was surely considerably higher since many sources are lacking for these periods. The suicide rates listed in the right column include the suicidal murders; the two figures for these rates are based on different population estimates that have been made for Stockholm.[5]

Table 5.1 shows clearly that the number of suicidal murders increased beginning in the late 1600s. They also increased considerably in relation to cases of manslaughter. For 1600–1649, we find records of only two suicidal murders compared to 138 cases of manslaughter. By contrast, the two decades of 1700–1719 witnessed thirty-five cases of manslaughter and twenty-six suicidal murders (including five cases in which the would-be homicide victim survived). Combined with cases of direct suicide, these suicidal murders—examples of which have also been found elsewhere in early modern Sweden, Denmark, and Germany[6]—show that an increasing number of Stockholmers wished to put an end to their days. Moreover, since the suicidal murders were motivated more by the desire to die than to kill, we can say that growing numbers of people in Stockholm ultimately directed their aggression more against themselves than against others.[7]

Why the sudden increase in suicides and suicidal murders? Could social changes have played a role in dramatic growth in suicidal behavior which began in the late 1600s? Emile Durkheim and other sociologists have associated a growing penchant for suicide with urbanization and modernization that purportedly weakened the strong ties of family, community, and religion in traditional rural society, all of which strongly integrated the individual into society and, con-comitantly, offered considerable protection against suicide. Perhaps the Stock-holmers who demonstrated suicidal behavior suffered from social isolation, a characteristic often viewed as fundamentally important in contributing to high suicide rates.[8]

Stockholm's direct suicides unfortunately provide very little information on the social conditions in which the victims lived immediately prior to their un-timely deaths. In handling cases of suicide, judicial authorities were concerned with the issue of burial. They were therefore quite interested in determining if the death was a homicide, accident, or suicide. If they concluded that the death was self-inflicted, judges also tried to determine if any mitigating circumstances, such as mental illness, might justify not handing the corpse over to the hangman. Beyond certain issues of mental stability, however, the records shed little light on the people who took their lives in Stockholm in the late seventeenth and early eighteenth centuries.[9]

The records, however, shed much more light on the lives of suicidal murder-ers than on those of direct suicides. Each suicidal murder apparently provoked feelings of shock and indignation among the court members, leading them to investigate the backgrounds of the perpetrators of these heinous crimes.

Characteristics of Suicidal Murder

The various investigations show that the suicidal murder of Barbro Persdotter, mentioned previously, was typical of indirect suicides in a number of respects. To begin with, Barbro killed a child, and fifty-two out of sixty-two victims of sui-cidal murder were children. Why children? One reason was simply practical: chil-dren generally were easier to subdue than adults. But another reason seemed even more important: popular belief held that a child was considered innocent and thus not in danger of going anywhere but to heaven after death. A child sup-posedly did not need to go through a process of repentance and gain absolution for his or her sins. Killing an adult, by contrast, made one guilty of not giving that person an opportunity to repent, a very wicked deed. Occasionally the per-petrators killed their own children, but usually the victims were the children of others, since, as we shall see, most suicidal murderers were single women who were not mothers.

Stabbing, the method Barbro employed to dispatch the iron carrier's son, was the most common method used by suicidal murderers. Others bludgeoned or strangled their victims, whereas suicidal murderers rarely used firearms. Drowning became more common after about 1700. A female servant, Catharina Thomasdotter, used this method in killing a nine-year-old boy in 1706. As he sank in the water, she exclaimed, "Dear child, right now your soul is with God, as you have no sins"[10]—an example of the popular conviction that children, because of their innocence, were assured of going to heaven.

Most important, Barbro's action was typical insofar as suicidal murder was for the most part a female crime. Of the sixty-five people convicted of murdering or attempting to kill a person in order to procure a death sentence, fully fifty-three were women (in three cases, two people together tried to kill another in order that they both be sentenced to death).

The court records provide ample evidence that the women and men guilty of these indirect suicides tended to suffer from varying degrees of social isolation. Many sociologists affirm that marriage provides protection from social isolation and is a source of regulation: before considering suicide, married people must consider the impact of their actions on their spouses. Accordingly, marriage is said to offer a shield against suicide, and parenthood reputedly imparts even greater immunity to suicide—the fear of what will happen to one's children is supposedly a strong deterrent to taking one's life, especially for women.[11] By contrast, of Stockholm's fifty-three female suicidal murderers, only seven were married, three of whom were separated from their husbands at the time they committed murder. In short, the evidence on marital and parental status suggests that social isolation, a factor long associated with suicide, was rife among suicidal murderers.

Decreasing Social Integration

The life led by suicidal murderers was in fact consistently one of loneliness and isolation. Typical was the situation of Christina Johansdotter, who killed a child in 1740 in order to be executed and put out of her misery. Christina lived alone as a lodger, had no relatives, no steady job, and seldom socialized with anyone or went to church.[12] It was understandably easier for feelings of the meaninglessness of life to pervade the thoughts of such an isolated person than of someone with a family, a steady job, and a sense of belonging to an occupational, political, or religious group. As we shall see, the number of persons leading isolated lives, more or less like Christina's, increased considerably in Stockholm beginning in the seventeenth century.

Other evidence suggests that weakening family ties contributed to the growing numbers of suicides and suicidal murders in Stockholm. In the seventeenth century, the city's strong population growth and the municipal authorities' mandates concerning urban planning together effected important changes in traditional forms of contact. Immigrants to the city, whether Swedes or foreigners, surely encountered greater difficulties in becoming established in the city and this was likely exacerbated by the fact that the immigrant portion of the city's population was growing. The predominance of immigrants in certain professions was quite noteworthy. In 1644, for example, out of about five hundred young men listed for conscription into the navy, only eighteen were born in Stockholm.[13] Not having the protection that kin could offer, growing numbers of immigrants were more vulnerable to social isolation and suicide.

During the period under study, Stockholm also witnessed significant diversification in its labor force. The military forces expanded considerably, as did the numbers of people who were employed in the administration of the state and the city. These changes in turn helped stimulate the development of many new professions and crafts, including manufacturing in some large-scale enterprises. Among these were tobacco-processing, tanning, glassblowing, and—especially important and extensive—the manufacture of clothing at Barnängen in the southern part of Stockholm. These economic developments resulted in a more mobile labor market and a weakening of the formerly close relationships among masters, journeymen, and apprentices within the crafts. Earlier, a master's son usually followed his father's footsteps, learning his father's trade and eventually taking over his workshop. A study of Stockholm's carpenters shows, however, that in the second half of the seventeenth century, only two out of forty sons of carpenters became carpenters themselves.[14] Other artisanal crafts showed a similar tendency, as growing numbers of young men in Stockholm found other careers more attractive than working in their fathers' workshops.

As the economic ties between the generations weakened, sons and daughters showed greater independence in forming marriages. As sons were less likely to work in their fathers' shops, parents wielded less economic leverage that could influence their children's choice of mates. Significantly, Stockholm of the late seventeenth and early eighteenth centuries witnessed increasing numbers of legal disputes between parents and their children over the latter's formation of marriages. Quite simply, the ties between generations were becoming somewhat looser. The greater independence that Stockholmers enjoyed compared to their parents came at a price: they received less economic and, more important, moral support from parents and kin, leaving them more vulnerable to suicidal inclinations.

For many women in early modern Stockholm, marriage was never an option and economic prospects were bleak. For long stretches of the early modern period, women far outnumbered men in Sweden's capital. To a considerable extent, this resulted from the absence of large numbers of men during times of war. Since many men perished in the wars, the gender imbalance in Stockholm endured for years. The most extreme imbalance dated from 1715–1716 when there were as many as 1,443 women per thousand men in the Swedish capital. Given this imbalance, many women never married, and widows seldom could find new husbands.[15] These demographic realities were accompanied by a decline in the economic position of women during the course of the seventeenth century. The competition among women for work resulted in a decline in wages so great that many risked falling below subsistence level.[16] And traditional misogynous views tended to strengthen rather than decline. A severe law against sexual crimes was passed in 1608 and vigorously enforced, and women were increasingly regarded as suspected temptresses.[17]

Another demographic factor that may have played a minor role involved the average age of the population of Stockholm. As the pace of population growth slowed toward the end of the seventeenth century, Stockholm probably witnessed a slight increase in the average age of its residents. Sociological studies from many modern Western countries have consistently shown that suicide rates are higher among older people than among younger folk.[18] Older people are more apt to be afflicted with painful and incurable illnesses or to suffer from bouts of melancholy, and the elderly often have fewer contacts with others, resulting in greater social isolation.[19]

Changing Attitudes toward the Church

The evidence from Stockholm also suggests that the social ties provided by the church were weakening by the late 1600s. In the 1520s Protestantism began to gain ground in Sweden, which eventually became a thoroughly Lutheran state. Luther and his followers placed much emphasis on the personal knowledge of Scripture and stressed the importance of the direct link between God and the individual believer. Some, such as Durkheim, have suggested that Protestantism has been more individualistic than Catholicism, providing fewer communal ties and therefore offering less protection against suicide.[20] Be that as it may, Stockholmers appeared little prone to suicidal proclivities prior to the late 1600s.

Although, theologically speaking, Stockholm's pastors of the late seventeenth century differed little from their predecessors, they served larger congregations than ever before. The city's rapid population growth of the seventeenth century caused an increase in the number of persons in each congregation—existing congregations were not divided, nor were new congregations created to accommodate the growing number of residents. In the 1670s the largest parishes of Stockholm had more than 3,000 parishioners per clergyman, while corresponding figures for some rural parishes in different parts of Sweden ranged from 250 and 900 people per pastor. Stockholm's pastors were spreading themselves very thin to serve these large congregations, spending a great deal of time merely performing baptisms, marriages, and funerals for the expanding ranks of their congregations.[21] The positive side for the pastors was that these rituals all included fees, thus providing Stockholm's clergy with unprecedented affluence. But the cumbersome size of the congregations caused a certain weakening of the sense of religious community in Stockholm beginning in the mid-seventeenth century.

The weakening of communal religious ties was also seen in the tendency of first nobles and later wealthy burghers to prefer private to public ceremonies for marriages, baptisms, and burials. Moreover, the clergy increasingly even granted requests to administer communion and give sermons in private to the elite members of their congregations. More broadly, by the late 1600s, the percentage of people who attended church and took communion regularly was down considerably from earlier decades. This void was partially filled by Pietism; beginning about 1670, increasing numbers of Swedes were attracted to Pietism, with its emphasis on the emotions and on the individual's personal devotion to God. Moreover, literacy increased sharply in Stockholm in the late seventeenth and early eighteenth centuries.[22] Durkheim and others have associated higher educational levels with a greater proclivity for suicide, asserting that traditional beliefs, including those pertaining to religion, are weaker among the better educated. Consequently, increasing literacy can go hand in hand with growing "moral individualism," meaning that religion provides less of a brake on suicidal inclinations.[23] Simply put, the evidence is overwhelming that by the late seventeenth century, the religious bonds of the community had greatly weakened in Stockholm.

All told, there is ample evidence to indicate that the ties offered by the family, church, and community were decreasing in late-seventeenth-century Stockholm. Increased individualism could result in more social isolation and in increasing numbers of direct and indirect suicides.

Attitudes toward Suicide

As in other European countries, suicide was viewed as an abominable sin in early modern Sweden. Suicides brought dishonor to their families and to the guilds or other societies to which they belonged. A well-known case from 1663 bears testimony to the popular and official abhorrence of suicide. Having discovered that one of his female servants had hanged herself, Samuel Hammarinus, vicar of the St. Klara parish in Stockholm, cut down the hanging body. Hammarinus, a clergyman well respected in the chapter, had first asked some of his other servants to cut the rope, but they all refused, declaring that they would not perform the hangman's work. For having sullied the office of clergyman by cutting down the body of a suicide, Hammarinus was ordered removed from his clerical office. In his defense, Hammarinus pleaded his ignorance of the law forbidding such action, observing that his action was in no way forbidden by the Bible and that the suicide victim was mentally unstable. His pleas were to no avail, however. The royal council, during the regency of the minor king Charles XI, ordered that he be removed from office. Both royal officials and Hammarinus's servants shared a strong taboo against touching the bodies of those who took their lives.[24]

This tenacious view that suicide was an utterly abominable sin—worse than the murder of another—can be seen in the confessions before the courts of those who committed suicidal murders in the seventeenth and eighteenth centuries.[25] Some of the suicidal murderers explicitly said that they had contemplated suicide, but chose instead to kill someone else to avoid jeopardizing the salvation of their souls and landing in hell. They asserted they could confess and repent of murders, however awful they may be, and be forgiven by God for them. It was believed that someone who took his or her own life did not have the opportunity to show remorse for this sin and so was consigned to hell. When the court asked Christina Johansdotter what had driven her to commit murder, she answered that she had been agitated for many years and that six months ago she decided to shorten her life. She said that she was sure that "if she committed an atrocious deed on herself, she would be damned forever, but if she could be allowed to die for somebody else, she would be sure of eternal bliss as well as anybody else."[26] The suicidal murderer Paul Wulff wrote in his memorial to the court that he was convinced he would be united with God since he had not committed the murder for money or love and had not acted at the urging of anyone else.[27] During her trial, Margareta Jakobsdotter Höök expressed confidence that God would forgive her sins when she prayed.[28]

It is of course very difficult for us to comprehend the mindset behind suicidal murders. Not only the crime but even the subsequent repentance of the sin was premeditated. Did suicidal murderers really believe that God would look favorably on such repentance? Such a belief would seem to suggest that the outer expression of repentance itself was enough, regardless of whether true remorse came from the heart.

None of the suicidal murderers showed signs of real regret. When clergymen tried to get Christina Johansdotter to express regret for the murder she had committed, she responded with derisive laughter. The court reported that, when interrogated, Christina freely acknowledged her actions without showing a trace of guilt or anxiety about having killed a young child. When explicitly asked if she felt she had done "something bad" and if she were not more agitated in spirit than before, Christina answered that "it was bad that she had caused Mallenius and his wife sorrow by killing their little child. Nonetheless her mind was more satisfied after she had been able to make the decision [to bring an end to her own life] which had hitherto worried her so much."[29] Only in very few cases do the legal minutes mention whether the perpetrator felt any remorse. Some rationalized that their actions amounted to freeing their victims from a miserable existence. When asked, both Beata Demin and Elsa Persdotter explained that they wanted to save themselves and the children they had murdered from a life of destitution.[30] Paul Wulff defended his choice of victim by referring to the sickliness of the child in question.[31] Lena Jönsdotter refused to answer and only declared that she wanted to die.[32]

The large number of suicidal murders indicated that the popular abhorrence of suicide was even greater than that found among the judicial and religious leaders of Sweden. Michael MacDonald's description of popular attitudes in early modern England—"Fear and hatred of self-killing long remained a foundation-stone in the edifice of folk psychology, and it could not be removed without reconstruction of the whole structure of popular thought"[33]—can be readily applied to contemporary Sweden.

According to the popular mores of this era in Sweden, the world was permeated by supernatural forces. The many trials for witchcraft in Sweden in the mid-seventeenth century bore witness to the firm conviction that the devil and demons, in conjunction with maleficent witches, were actively causing harm in this world. The devil, appearing in a wide variety of physical forms, and his demons were able to tempt people to take their lives, if the evil machinations of witches and demons were not counteracted with prayers, amulets, or holy ointments. Swedes used the term *Skam* to refer both to "disgrace" and to the "devil," who was believed to help people fulfill the last details of their suicides. It was enough to put a noose around one's neck, and the devil then tightened it; if one tried to drown oneself, the devil helped hold the drowning person under water.[34]

As elsewhere in early modern Europe, suicides were considered "sleepless souls" who might haunt the living after their own deaths. A suicide was believed to walk again, and these sometimes vengeful ghosts were more feared than others, having no rest in their graves, hovering between heaven and earth until the day of judgment. Accordingly, people did not want the corpses of suicides buried on their land. Popular belief mandated that the corpses of suicides be interred at night along with their personal belongings. The threshold of a house where a suicide had been committed was to be cleansed with gunpowder. All these practices stemmed from the popular fear of suicide and of the ghosts of those who took their lives. Burial at night was intended to make it more difficult for suicides to find their way back to haunt survivors, and putting their belongings in the grave with them was intended to remove an incentive to return to the places they had formerly inhabited. Cleansing the threshold reflected the belief that a home in which a suicide had been committed was considered defiled—scour-

Figure 5. Johan Tobias Sergel, *Overcome by Despair,* drawing, 1795. Reproduced with the permission of the Nationalmuseum, Stockholm.

ing it with gunpowder also might hinder the sleepless soul from recognizing the site where he had taken his life.[35] Like the clergy, the common laity in Sweden strongly disapproved of people who left this world of their own volition, thus rebelling against the divine order of things and usurping privileges reserved to God alone. In short, many Stockholmers of the late seventeenth and early eighteenth century were absolutely convinced that self-inflicted death was a much greater sin than killing another person.

Moreover, a common theme found in sermons and popular religious literature of this era was the disparaging of earthly life and the glorification of death and the afterlife. Death was celebrated as "a joy without turning back." Referring to the heavenly afterlife, the author of a prayer in a popular devotional manual wrote, "All that we see there is none other than beauty; all that we taste is none other than sweetness; all that we hear is none other than music; all that we smell is none other than balsam; all that we take in our hands is as soft as flowers." In sharp contrast, this world was portrayed as a dirty, foul-smelling jail.[36] The widespread abomination of suicide was thus coupled with a certain longing for death.

Motives for Suicidal Murder

Many of those who killed in order to be killed seemed pushed more by the desire to leave this world than pulled by the desire to go to heaven. For many suicidal murderers, unsatisfactory social networks, isolation, and loneliness were paired with poverty, humiliation, crime and prostitution, melancholy, anxiety, and hopelessness. Some already were prisoners for life when they committed murder. Lisken Jakobsdotter was serving a life sentence for having had illicit relations with three married men and for having already attempted to murder a child. Among her fellow inmates was Christina Jönsdotter, a dear friend whom Lisken said she loved as much as her own soul. One day in 1727, the two women were sitting together and chatting in the house of correction. Lisken asked Christina if she would be faithful to her, and the latter replied that she would be faithful "in death." They gave each other their hands and at once grabbed a knife and stabbed to death the four-year-old child of a fellow-prisoner.[37]

In an earlier conversation with the prison chaplain, Lisken Jakobsdotter had threatened to commit suicidal murder and predicted that after the deed she would "be taken out with clergymen and a procession."[38] With this, she was referring to the common practice of solemn executions, in which the condemned, dressed in black or white mourning clothes with ribbons, was carried to the place of execution outside town in a beautiful cart drawn by three or four horses and accompanied by two or more clergymen. Lisken knew that many people would follow her on her last journey and that her life and her crime would be common topics of conversation around tankards and clothes baskets in Stockholm for a good while. Clearly, Lisken was desperately seeking in death the attention that she had not received in life.

A similar yearning for attention was evident in those who openly committed murder to protest against their plight, crying out that society has been unfair to them. They bemoaned various forms of mistreatment, such as being starved, raped, tortured in the house of correction, humiliated, and ridiculed. Perhaps they felt that there was no other way to get anyone to listen. Often these accusations were directed against the whole society, but in some cases the perpetrators avowed that they sought to take revenge against a particular individual. In 1667 Gertrud Joensdotter freely confessed that she slit the throat of a seven-year-old boy, not related to her or her fiancé, in order to make the latter repent for having accused her of loose living and sorcery.[39]

Gertrud viewed the accusations as wrongly impugning her reputation, and the loss of honor in one way or another was a frequent motive for suicidal murder. Maria Elisabet Runbom was a poor, sick widow. In dire straits, she found herself compelled to sell the copper pan in which she prepared concoctions composed of ants, which she sold as medicine against rheumatism. Deprived of her livelihood, Maria Elisabet became most upset when she got wind of a rumor that she was living loosely. Distraught that her friends, believing the rumor, were reluctant to support her in her distress, Maria Elisabet stabbed her one-year-old daughter to death in 1744, reputedly inspired to do so by the devil. The devil was also said to have encouraged Elisabet Devall to murder the baby of a poor woman in 1767. Like Maria Elisabet Runbom, Elisabet was a poor woman who felt her honor had been besmirched—she was charged in court of infidelity to her husband, who had been away at sea for three years.[40]

Some suicidal murders were impulsive deeds, triggered by some very frustrating event, while others were carefully planned in advance. An example of the former was the suicidal murder of Anna Thomasdotter, another poor woman who was fined for having illicit sexual intercourse and sentenced to a few days in the house of correction for having lied to the court in 1698. She had accused another woman of taking a jewel dishonestly, but the court rejected her claim and sentenced her to a heavy fine. The night after the trial, reputedly inspired by the Evil One, Anna suddenly despaired and strangled her child, whose father had recently died.[41] In contrast, Christina Johansdotter had seen an execution a month before her own deed in 1740. She could think of nothing better for herself and thereafter searched more or less systematically for opportunities to come close to a child who would be a suitable victim.[42]

At times a minor dispute apparently triggered the deed. Elisabet Larsdotter, the widow of a soldier, sold her house in 1706, receiving the formal purchase price but not the extra or "discretionary" payment that had been promised by the buyer. She confessed that the home buyer's apparent refusal to do so had made her melancholic and sleepless, causing her to contemplate killing somebody in order to be sentenced to death herself. After a quarrel, Elisabet struck Ursila, a neighbor who worked as a servant, in the head with an axe. Although Elisabet intended to kill the woman, Ursila survived the attack. During the trial, the home buyer explained that he had withheld the discretionary surcharge only because he was waiting for the formal confirmation of the purchase by city authorities.[43] It is thus plausible that a simple misunderstanding was at the root of her emotional malaise and violent attack. True, it is quite possible that Elisabet's melancholy had physiological causes, such as low levels of serotonin or dopamine in her nervous system. It is conceivable that, unaware of the "real" origins of depression, Elisabet attributed her melancholy to an apparent cause, as dictated by the cultural mores prevailing in Stockholm of the early 1700s.[44] Then again, outside events, such as the personal reversals experienced by Elisabet, can have a direct impact on one's chemical balance.

Some individuals had long histories of melancholy before committing suicidal murder. A case in point was the above mentioned Paul Wulff, a German goldsmith about thirty years old, who had been seriously depressed all his life and had tried to strangle himself with a shoelace as early as the age of seven. Paul's mother, whose husband had abandoned her and their six small children, punished the boy with hard blows for that attempt but did nothing to alleviate his morbid melancholy. After another suicide attempt at eleven—he jumped from a high tower—Paul was apprenticed to a goldsmith. As a journeyman he made a third suicide attempt but recovered and left his native Germany for Stockholm about 1645. His weariness of life was as strong as ever, and he rejoiced at the prospect of dying when he took seriously ill there. After recovering in spite of himself in 1651, he again resolved to take his life, getting a pistol and bringing it to his chest. Concern about the salvation of his soul, however, prevented him from pulling the trigger. He therefore opted for suicidal murder, asking a female acquaintance to go out and buy food for him. In her absence, he shot her child. At trial, Wulff claimed that he chose the victim because the child was sickly and that the mother wanted to be free of the child, just as his own mother had longed for his death. Paul Wulff submitted to the court a kind of autobiography written in his own hand, a long, well-written document in which he depicted his sufferings in detail. The afflictions he described were entirely mental, with virtually no mention of mundane misfortunes or bodily pains, other than his frustration at not having succumbed to the grave illness. Wulff began and ended this treatise with a request for an autopsy, explaining that this would give all honest parents an example of how they could get help for their children while they were still in their youth. This suggests that he believed that a physical cause would be found, an early example of a medical explanation for his unbearable depression. As in cases from eighteenth-century northern Germany, this may have been a way of claiming relief from moral—but certainly not legal—personal responsibility.[45] Convinced that his soul was saved, Paul Wulff went to his execution with a light heart, happily singing religious songs.[46]

Alternative Forms of Indirect Suicide

Killing another person was not the only means of procuring a death sentence in early modern Stockholm, and some suicidal people sought capital punishment by other means. Another method of committing indirect suicide was to confess falsely to murder rather than actually killing someone. Some women tried to convince the court that they had murdered a newborn infant and annihilated the corpse; others avowed that that they had killed an orphaned child whom nobody would miss. In the seventeenth century, the prevailing theory held that a confession by the perpetrator was the very best type of evidence in court, and persons wishing to be condemned to death exploited this tenet. But the courts became more reluctant to convict someone of murder based solely on his or her confession; lacking a *corpus delicti,* judges proved to be increasingly skeptical in regard to such confessions. In 1696, for example, Brita Andersdotter confessed to killing her newborn child. With no other evidence that this child had even existed, the court of appeals doubted her confession. Wishing to die, Brita lost patience in custody and cut the throat of the child of a fellow prisoner with whom she had quarreled, crying out, "There you have it, you devil. They haven't wanted to believe me before, so now they can look and believe." After committing this crime, she thanked God that she would soon escape her miserable existence.[47]

Confessing to the crime of bestiality might lend itself more readily to conviction than feigning a murder. Having sex with an animal, such as a cow or mare, did not produce any *corpus delicti,* and at least six or seven hundred people, mostly peasants and soldiers, were executed for this crime in Sweden in the seventeenth and eighteenth centuries. Nowhere else in Europe were convictions of bestiality more common than in Sweden. The high frequency of this crime has been assumed to be the result of the interaction between the aggressive control efforts on the part of the authorities and popular disgust with bestiality. A considerable number of men, however, freely confessed to bestiality without having been accused. Some of these confessions were made out of remorse for deeds that were actually committed, but many confessions were surely made as a means of indirect suicide. Having no witnesses, the courts had no way of distinguishing real from feigned cases of bestiality. But confessing to a crime that one has not committed came to be popularly known as "lying oneself out of life," and judges became increasingly skeptical of such unsolicited confessions.[48]

A final possible means of indirect suicide involved recklessly seeking fights or exposing oneself to dangers on the battlefield.[49] There were some cases in early modern Stockholm of men trying to pick a fight, seemingly with the intent of being killed.[50] While at war, several men in the army of Charles XII were convinced that the king was consciously seeking death in making rash moves when faced with defeat in Russia in 1709.[51] Likewise, his father Charles XI—young, inexperienced, and doubting the competence of his generals—under severe military pressure and almost desperate, once uttered that he demanded nothing but death.[52] In the battle of Lund in southern Sweden against Denmark in 1676, he gave evidence of suicidal rashness by riding right through the lines of the Danish cavalry in order to establish contact with a surrendering force on the other side.[53] A few years later, he uttered similar words when suffering from a severe illness, suggesting that he really did have a death wish. Such examples of suicidal rashness in military actions were probably not unique.

Disappearance of Suicidal Murders

By the end of the eighteenth century, indirect suicides had almost disappeared, causing one to wonder why suicidal murders declined. In light of the previous epidemic of suicidal murders in early modern Stockholm, one may well wonder why the courts ever imposed death sentences on the perpetrators, in effect fulfilling the wishes of these suicidal assassins. A sentence of life imprisonment, for example, might seem a more appropriate (and even more painful) punishment. Several legal documents show why judicial authorities did not consider a life sentence an option. The Swedish statute of 1662 against duels decreed that God demanded that a homicide be atoned for by the death of the perpetrator; failing to do so would result in God's punishing the whole society with the plague or some similar disaster.[54] Swedish and Danish authorities therefore tried at first to prevent suicidal murders by other means—statutes were issued in 1741 and 1749 respectively, prescribing that executions should not be solemn, as they had been, but rather simple and, more important, dishonoring. The Danish statute also enjoined that the murderer be tortured before execution, a procedure that a Swedish statute of 1754 also recommended.[55] The hope, of course, was that the prospect of the intense physical suffering before execution would serve as a deterrent to suicidal murders.

The decline of suicidal murders during the course of the eighteenth century, however, apparently owed little to such preventive measures. More important was the eventual abolition of capital punishment for suicidal murder. In 1767 statutes in both Germany and in Denmark abolished capital punishment for this misdeed in favor of life imprisonment.[56] In Sweden the same became the rule through a precedent-setting case in 1787.[57] The declining use of capital punishment was apparently an important factor behind the sharp decline in the number of suicidal murders toward the end of the eighteenth century.

Also important were some significant changes in mentality evident in Sweden and elsewhere. The Enlightenment apparently helped reduce the fear of God's wrath among many believers; as more people questioned whether eternal damnation awaited all suicides, an important deterrent to taking one's own life weakened. Eighteenth-century Europeans also showed increasing tolerance toward suicides as victims of mental illness, personal reversals, and the like.

More intriguing than the disappearance of these suicidal murders is the question of why they existed in the first place. Most notably, why did the far northern regions of Europe show a special penchant for such indirect suicides? One factor was surely that of imitation. After committing murder, Christina Johansdotter, for example, had confessed that she was following the example of others in seeking the death penalty for herself. In the years under study, one can speak of clusters of cases of suicidal murder. There were three cases in 1689, five in 1706, and nine in 1709–1710, all of which suggest that imitation was a contributing factor in Stockholm's plethora of indirect suicides.

But where did the idea of killing in order to be killed originate? Although its origins remain hidden, we do know that in Denmark a widespread "whimsical religious doctrine" was believed to have influenced suicidal murderers in that country in the 1700s. This belief held that the safest way to eternal bliss was to die in a violent way, but not by suicide. We do not know who originated this belief or what, if any, other ideas were associated with it.[58] It seems plausible, however, that the reduced confidence in Stockholm's state church, with its increasingly remote and greedy pastors, could facilitate the spread of underground religious ideas and movements. The growing popularity of Pietism, for example, showed that many Swedes were looking for spiritual fulfillment outside the state church.

More fundamentally, the anomie associated with the dramatic growth of the city of Stockholm made many people more vulnerable, as the long-established ties provided by kin, community, and religion weakened. This vulnerability coexisted with the strong traditional Judeo-Christian fears of damnation which deterred many people from taking their own lives. The growing numbers of isolated people, the time-honored fear of hell, the strong expectation of the death penalty for murder, and the well-publicized examples of suicidal murder combined to produce large numbers of indirect suicides in early modern Stockholm.

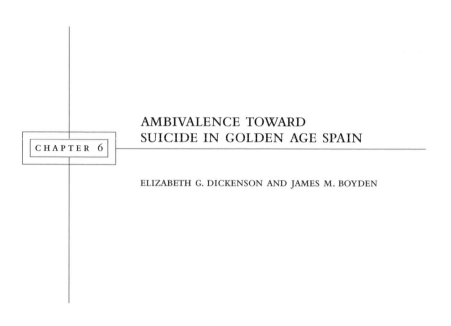

ELIZABETH G. DICKENSON AND JAMES M. BOYDEN

Approaching the history of suicide in early modern Spain poses a daunting challenge. To date, the subject has received scant attention from Hispanist scholars of the period. Very little is known about the incidence or the common methods of suicide or about the application in specific cases of legal sanctions directed against the bodies or estates of suicides. No general studies exist—certainly nothing at all comparable to the extensive works of Michael MacDonald and Terence Murphy concerning England or of Jeffrey Watt on Geneva. Indeed the subject of suicide occupies less than four pages in Fernando Martínez Gil's authoritative social history of death and dying in early modern Spain.[1]

In this realm as in many others, Spanish behaviors and attitudes in the early modern centuries bore the imprint of the Iberian Peninsula's peculiar medieval history. Spain's religious pluralism, unique in Western Europe, was aptly seen in prevailing attitudes toward suicide. In addition to classical and Christian ideas concerning self-murder that were common to the civilizations of the West, traces of alternative Jewish and Islamic traditions can sometimes be glimpsed within early modern Spanish culture, despite the repressive efforts that accelerated within the dominant Christian community in the late fifteenth century and led to the extirpation of most apparent vestiges of religious pluralism.

Although Christian values were imposed with a vengeance on Spaniards whose allegiance to orthodoxy came under suspicion, the culture of the *siglo de oro* (Golden Age) was hardly monolithic in adherence to the norms upheld by the Church. Honor was a preeminent passion of many early modern Spaniards, not only among nobles but even peasants who were Old Christians—reflecting racial prejudices, the term "Old Christians" referred to those whose ancestors had been Christian for centuries, thereby excluding and denigrating converts from Judaism or Islam and their descendants. According to one scholar, by the seventeenth century the code of honor allegedly "no longer bore any relation to Christian morality."[2] Though this statement is somewhat hyperbolic, there is no question that Spanish conceptions of honorable behavior encompassed arrogant demeanor, harsh speech, and forms of violence and sexual conduct not easily reconciled with a Christian ethical code. Attitudes toward suicide displayed the same contradictions and ambiguities. This essay makes a first step toward a history of suicide in early modern Spain by focusing on episodes and developments that illuminate the evolution of normative strictures against self-inflicted death and their interplay with alternative attitudes about or valuations of suicidal behavior.

Isabel de los Olivos y López: Suicide as Heterodoxy

On 7 May 1513, Isabel de los Olivos y López, a twenty-five-year-old married woman, committed suicide in the home of Melchior de Saavedra by deliberately throwing herself into a well in his courtyard. Although eyewitness testimony both before and after her death confirmed that she was under a physician's care and mentally distraught, the ecclesiastical authorities of the Inquisition tribunal of Ciudad Real concluded that this was a suicide and that Isabel should be "punished" accordingly.[3]

In the previous year, Isabel had been the subject of an Inquisition trial. A *conversa*—*conversos* were Jewish or Muslim converts to Christianity, though the label *morisco* was more commonly applied to converts from Islam—raised and educated at Córdoba, Isabel had come to Ciudad Real to marry in 1502, when, as she testified, she was around the age of fourteen. In May 1512 a *criada* (serving woman, perhaps a slave) in the home of Juan Ramírez, Isabel's brother-in-law, reported to the Inquisition authorities in Ciudad Real that Isabel and others had been keeping the Jewish Sabbath in Juan's home.[4] Her suspicions had been aroused by the fact that on Friday nights and Saturdays they put on clean clothes, did no work, lit candles with new wicks, and read from a book. Isabel later testified that she did not know which book this was, because, being partially deaf, she could not hear it being read. In August 1512, the inquisitors of Ciudad Real formally charged Isabel de los Olivos y López with heresy and apostasy in the practice of the Jewish religion, outlawed in Spain since 1492.[5] In her *proceso* (trial), conducted in Toledo by the functionaries of the Holy Office, Isabel was accused and convicted of Jewish practices, which included observing the Jewish Sabbath, eating meat on Fridays, and wearing clothes on Friday nights and Saturdays that were clean and better than the clothes she wore other days of the week. She admitted to lighting candles with new wicks on Friday nights, to bowing her head when Jewish books were read and Jewish prayers uttered. She was accused of and confessed to following the law of Moses, the tradition in which she had been raised and educated from childhood.[6]

The inquisitors came to regard Isabel as a crucial witness in an important related case. They were intensely curious about the meetings that had been held in cellars and other rooms of the various residences of Juan Ramírez in Ciudad Real and about who attended or knew of them. These venues were of particular interest since in a roundabout way they linked the Judaizing cell in Ciudad Real to an extremely prominent figure in the kingdom, Cardinal Francisco Ximenes de Cisneros, Archbishop of Toledo since 1495 and Inquisitor General from 1507. Juan Ramírez served His Eminence in a position of trust and responsibility as majordomo. This high profile case—touching the Franciscan Cardinal Cisneros—was forcefully prosecuted by the inquisitors of Ciudad Real, some of whom were Dominicans. Under torture in Toledo's inquisitorial prison, Isabel's husband, Diego Sánchez de Madrid, implicated Isabel and other family members.[7]

Isabel's *fiscal* (legal adviser) persuaded her to confess to everything that was asked of her and to implicate those whose names were put to her, not excluding her closest relatives and associates. Isabel heard her husband being tortured. She was shown the legs of a woman who had undergone torture and was advised to avoid a similar fate. Isabel did what the inquisitors asked, accusing family members and friends of participating in the weekend gatherings led by Juan Ramírez in his houses. In the end she cooperated completely, even providing a complete inventory of her earthly possessions for confiscation.

For a time after her confession and the conclusion of her *proceso* on 30 October 1512, Isabel remained quietly behind the bars of the prison in Toledo. But her case files indicate that at some point between November 1512 and May 1513, Isabel's conscience and her voice reasserted themselves, greatly embarrassing and inconveniencing her tormentors. Exhibiting unmistakable signs of derangement (*locura*) and despair, she began loudly to lament her false testimony and to protest against the coercion exerted by the inquisitors. Testimony from her jailers and from other women who were incarcerated and implicated with Isabel indicates that she began to neglect the care of her clothes and person: Isabel was described as appearing disheveled and sleepless, raking her face with her nails and refusing food and water. The inquisitors placed her under a physician's care, and she was force-fed by her male jailers, who themselves complained that they could not sleep at night because of Isabel's loud lamentations. Her shouts and cries could also be heard during the day throughout the prison and even in the hall of the *audiencia* (court).[8]

In May 1513, the inquisitors ordered her gagged and removed secretly from the prison where she had been held for almost a year to the home elsewhere in the city of Melchior de Saavedra, the *alcaide* (chief jailer). There she was to be kept in isolation for medical treatment and observation. Did they simply wish to remove a disruptive prisoner from the general population, or might this have been the inquisitorial version of a suicide watch? Saavedra later testified that after calmly proclaiming her innocence and that of the individuals whom she had implicated, Isabel inquired about the safety and well-being of her husband and children. She then ate, drank, and slept. The next morning Isabel committed suicide by throwing herself into the well in the courtyard of Saavedra's home.[9]

Although she had been placed under the care of a physician, in Isabel's day there was no widespread conviction that medical expertise was relevant to madness, and the determination of mental competence was not reserved to physicians.[10] During the centuries when leprosy was becoming a medical category, insanity remained ill-defined and was often construed as a spiritual disorder, even though—as with leprosy—it was a label whose legal consequences could be of the utmost significance to an individual or his family. The civil law concerning the property forfeiture required of suicides could be circumvented, for example, were it successfully argued that illness had caused temporary madness. Issues of mental competence, however, more often required the expert testimony of a priest or canon lawyer than of a physician. Isabel's inquisitors were willing to concede her deficient mental state in order to have her removed from the prison and *audiencia* hall but, as we shall see, were emphatically unwilling to accord her any further charity *in extremis*.

Isabel's choice of a method for self-destruction was breathtaking, both in its simplicity and in its utter disregard for Christian authority, and the extent of her scorn hardly went unremarked. The documentary record conveys the outrage with which the inquisitors pronounced Isabel excommunicate and damned her memory (*in memoria damnada*). They went to the length of ordering the exhumation of her bones, which were to be broken in pieces and then "relaxed" to the secular authorities. *El brazo seglar*—in the person of the public executioner—burned Isabel's shattered bones, thus eradicating all physical evidence of her existence. Subsequently, the inquisitors deprived her heirs in the male and female lines of their rights to her property and barred her descendants in perpetuity from holding any ecclesiastical or public office. Isabel's descendants were also barred from a number of private occupations, including those of pharmacist and attorney. They were forbidden to receive honors of any kind whatsoever, to own or to ride horses, to carry arms, or to own any precious metals, gems, or rich fabrics, all in perpetuity.[11] It is impossible to know for certain, but it seems likely that Isabel's cooperation with the inquisitors would have led to a sentence of penance—and perhaps corporal punishment or a term of imprisonment—

and reconciliation. Her suicide, however, greatly compounded her culpability in the eyes of the authorities, propelling her into the posthumous status of a relapsed and intransigent heretic, subject to the most draconian perpetual penalties.

Despite the strenuous efforts of the Holy Office, however, the suicide of Isabel de los Olivos y López did not result in her complete eradication from historical memory. The record of the very Inquisition trial which sought to erase her name forever survives to provide us with eyewitness testimony of her ordeal, derangement, and death. This documentation offers a poignant insight into women's experiences as victims of the early Inquisition in Spain. It also illustrates the unique mix of legal and cultural traditions that distinguished Iberian jurisprudence from that of other western European countries. Isabel's case bears the marks of canon law used by the inquisitors to condemn her as a heretic and apostate, if not before her suicide, then certainly afterward. It also reflects the strictures of civil law derived from ancient Rome, which denied the heirs of suicides the right to inherit their property—as Machiel Bosman has shown in chapter 1 of this volume, in early modern Europe this was especially true for criminals who took their lives.

Most interesting are the elements of this sentence that were unique to Spain. The extreme penalties imposed in perpetuity on the heirs of a suicide were, to our knowledge, unknown in any place or time outside early modern Iberia. The inquisitors did not articulate why they placed these severe restrictions on Isabel's descendants, but they were surely related to her Jewish ancestry and her reputed Judaizing. Spain, whose population was perhaps more obsessed than any other people with the concept of "honor," witnessed in the fifteenth century the rise of the principle of *limpieza de sangre* (purity of blood), which emphasized racial purity and considered all *conversos* tainted by their Jewish or Muslim origins. Although the Inquisition was often critical of *limpieza* rules, Tomás de Torquemada, the first Inquisitor General, issued an Instruction in 1484 which perpetually forbade the descendants of *conversos* who had been penanced by the Inquisition to hold civil or ecclesiastical offices, receive any honors, or exercise a number of professions, including those of attorney, notary, merchant, and accountant. Although some Old Christians favored banning all *conversos* from these influential offices and professions for purely racialist reasons, Torquemada was targeting only the descendants of those guilty of heresy or apostasy and sentenced by the Inquisition to serious penances. It is safe to assume that the eternal penalties imposed on Isabel's descendants—which, like many statutes of *limpieza,* were probably not rigorously enforced—were based less on her self-murder than on her alleged apostasy, the sin with which the Spanish Inquisition was initially most concerned. In the eyes of the inquisitors, her sin of suicide amounted to both the full fruition and the definitive proof of apostasy and heresy.[12]

Isabel's case may have been shaped by her Jewish heritage in another important way. Jewish legal traditions may help explain her decision to kill herself. Though hardly monolithic, Jewish law concerning suicide in its general historical tendency differed from the punitive Western European legal traditions, providing instead that suicide should be dealt with compassionately, and calling for censure only in very specific cases where full mental capacity, deliberation, and immediate execution of the act could be demonstrated. In Jewish law and tradition, those who killed themselves to avoid further sin or to atone for misdeeds, could be labeled martyrs and honored for their courage.[13] Isabel de los Olivos y López may have chosen self-destruction to exercise what she perceived as a righteous option under Jewish law to kill herself in order to avoid further sin or to expiate the heavy sins she had already committed. Whether or not her coerced confessions had been truthful, Isabel could scarcely avoid regretting their consequences for her relatives and circle of friends and acquaintances. At least one other woman, implicated by Isabel's testimony, would burn as a heretic on 7 September 1513. Isabel surely felt a heavy burden of sin and remorse and perhaps sought death as both penalty and sacrifice for her offenses. Even if her derangement rendered her incapable of exercising such judgment, Jewish law would most likely have dealt with her more leniently than either civil or canon law, because of her mental state and the circumstances which gave rise to it.

While we cannot penetrate all the mysteries of her motives, it seems inescapable that Isabel's suicide comprised an act of protest against the Holy Office and the persecution brought to bear on herself, her family and friends, and her people by a Christian elite. Of course such protests, individual or communal, and silenced only—and forever—by the grave, did not necessarily convey their intended messages to authorities who chose to envision self-destruction within an ongoing pantomime of Christ's Passion and Judas Iscariot's suicide.[14]

Traditional Attitudes about Suicide and Their Development

Distinctions between suicide and voluntary martyrdom had sometimes been used deliberately to define, differentiate, and ultimately, to profess religious faith in medieval and early modern Spain. In the most famous instance, the Mozarabic priests Perfectus and Eulogius led the so-called martyrs of Córdoba in protesting Muslim political and religious supremacy in ninth-century al-Andalus. Prompted by Islamic authorities, a council of bishops issued a lukewarm censure of the deliberate courting of martyrdom in 852, but without condemning those who had already chosen the course of defiance and death.[15] Moreover, as David Nirenberg has shown, the distinction between Christian and Jew in late medieval Spain was often most sharply drawn each year during Holy Week. Arguably the most striking contrast in the Passion rituals of the season was that between the

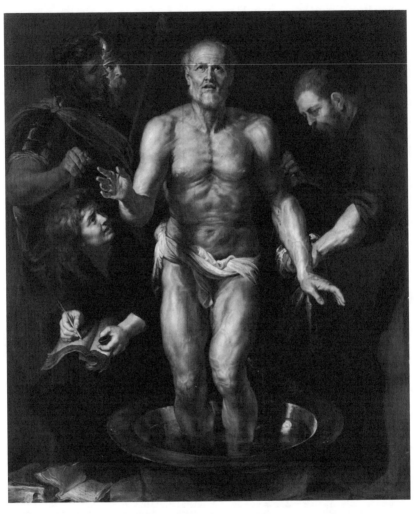

Figure 6. Peter Paul Rubens, *The Death of Seneca,* 1608. Reproduced with the permission of the Bayerische Staatsgemäldesammlungen, Alte Pinakothek, Munich.

voluntary self-sacrifice of Jesus Christ—emblematic of charity—and the suicide of Judas Iscariot, sometimes envisioned quite literally as the source of Jewish corruption and avarice: "when Judas hanged himself, his guts poured forth their excrement and polluted the land of Judea (and hence the Jews)."[16]

But however important distinctions between suicide and voluntary martyrdom may have been in medieval religious struggles, the right to take one's own life had not always been defined by religious doctrine or affiliation. In the ancient world, the legitimacy of suicide was determined by law, by social class, and often perhaps by gender. Sometimes self-destruction was upheld as noble or rational: Seneca, a native of Iberia, famously wrote in the first century AD that the man who awaited his doom inertly was overly fond of life, just as the man who drained his bottle was too fond of its contents.[17]

Early patristic writers, however, rejected such arguments justifying suicide and attempted to draw clear distinctions between, on the one hand, martyrdom arising from persecution and, on the other, willful self-destruction through provocative behavior or excessive asceticism. The Church father Jerome (c. 347–420), for example, rebuked Paula for her public display of grief at the funeral of her daughter, Blaesilla, who had died following rigorous fasting. Jerome feared the Romans might view her demise as evidence that Christians encouraged believers to seek death voluntarily; he accordingly sought to dissociate Christianity from this courting of death that bordered on suicide.[18] In *The City of God,* Augustine of Hippo argued against voluntary martyrdom. Like many of his classical precursors, Augustine employed a female example, that of Lucretia, who committed suicide after having been raped.[19] In *Against Gaudentius,* Augustine denounced the Donatist bishop who wielded the suicides of some of his followers as a political tool against Roman bishops in North Africa. Augustine defined voluntary self-destruction and its advocates as heretical.[20] For centuries afterward, Augustine's was the predominant Christian moral and theological doctrine concerning suicide. It was adopted in Iberia at the Council of Braga, held in May 563 in Galicia, where the Catholic bishops mandated, "No commemoration of suicides was to be made at the sacrifice of the Mass, nor should the bodies of suicides be buried with Psalms."[21] The same prohibitions were to be observed in regard to criminals executed for their crimes.

The views of Augustine and his followers effectively criminalized suicide, a development which would eventually be echoed in the civil law of Christian states. As we have seen in chapter 1 of this volume, since the first century AD, Roman law held that suicide by a criminal was itself a crime, a deed that was deemed an act of cowardice rather than courage. The property of the criminal who committed suicide was accordingly forfeit under Roman law.[22] In Iberia, the seventh-century *Lex Visigothorum* continued in this tradition, further stipulating, "No physician shall assist any prisoner to suicide, lest the course of justice be thwarted by it."[23] Meanwhile the contemporary churchman Isidore of Seville, in his *Etymologies* (book 8, chap. 2), addressed the issue within the religious context of sin by defining hope and despair as polar opposites. Hope was a crucial element of religion and of faith (*id est fides, spes, caritas*), and thus despair could not be an element of either (*unde et e contrario desperatio*). In an alphabetical listing in book 10 (at 72), Isidore defined the *desperatus* as one who was vulgarly described as "an evil and lost soul who was utterly without hope" (*malus ac perditus nec iam ullius prosperae spei*).[24] Other ecclesiastical condemnations followed Isidore's; for example, the Sixteenth Council of Toledo in 693 declared, "If anyone has attempted to commit suicide, and has been prevented, he is to be excluded for two months from all fellowship with Catholics and from the holy communion."[25]

In Spain, by the thirteenth century law codes had come to address suicide at greater length, most notably in the *Siete Partidas* of Alfonso X of Castile. In Partida VII, the introduction to title 27 defines *desesperados* as persons who, having lost hope and succumbed to the sin of despair, can never aspire to God's mercy. In this title, suicides are placed within a spectrum of deviants that encompasses Jews, Moors, apostates, heretics, and those who insult the Virgin. The provisions of title 27 detail five types of *desesperados:* those who despair to the point of death over crimes they have committed, or because of pain or disease, insanity or rage, the loss of honor or property. The fifth category of *desesperados* includes persons who assisted the suicides of others for reward. Still echoing Roman law, title 27 distinguishes between the suicides of criminals and noncriminals. Individuals who aided another to commit suicide, presumably for reward, were specifically vilified as criminals guilty of homicide.[26]

In another work attributed to Alfonso X, the consequences of suicide are tempered by Christian mercy and forgiveness. Alfonso's *Cantigas de Santa María* include three instances of suicide. In Cantiga 2, a woman who had fornicated with her uncle attempted suicide by swallowing spiders. On appeal to the Virgin for mercy, however, the woman was forgiven her sins and restored to health. Cantiga 26 illustrates the story of a pilgrim who committed fornication and then, encouraged by the devil disguised as Santiago, died as a result of remorseful self-castration. The pilgrim was restored to life—and presumably wholeness—by the Virgin, because he had been deceived by the devil. In the third example, from Cantiga 84, the wife of a knight committed suicide for love of her husband, who had told her that he was seeing another woman. Predictably, the woman the knight was seeing in his nocturnal devotions turned out to be the Virgin. Once the misunderstanding was unraveled, the wife of the pious knight was restored to life.[27]

While thirteenth-century Castilian literature and art depicted voluntary death in a variety of ways, the criminalization of suicide was manifest in a fourteenth-century law of Enrique III, which stipulated that the property of suicides should

be forfeit to the crown.[28] Although the late medieval laws of Alfonso X and Enrique III were restated and expanded in the legal compilations of the early modern centuries, they were not superseded until the early nineteenth century, when
the forfeiture provision was removed. Assistance to suicide, however, remains prohibited in the Spanish criminal code to the present day.[29]

Religion, Honor, and Ambivalence about Suicide

A great deal stands to be learned from exploring the intersections—and more
importantly the discrepancies—among widely upheld value systems in the early
modern Iberian world. Most noteworthy are the ways that core Christian values
and precepts—found in sermons, clerical injunctions, and in secular law—conflicted with influential models of honorable behavior. These sorts of conflicts,
and the very nature of honor itself, were subjected to intense scrutiny, and perhaps nowhere more searchingly than in the contemporary theater. The drama-
tists of the period, from Lope de Vega to the most obscure playwrights, seemed
never to tire of dramatizing situations that counterpose contrasting values, and
they often rendered ambivalent verdicts on the behavioral choices of pride versus humility, arrogance versus resignation, conquest versus submission, and like
dichotomies. Suicide could be said to stand at an odd junction of the dominant
value systems within early modern Iberia. Whereas it had notoriously been esteemed by classical thinkers as an honorable exit from impossible dilemmas,
Christian critics strove from the outset to dismiss associations between suicide
and honor. This may be seen, for example, in Augustine's assertion in *The City of
God* (1. 22) "that suicide can never be prompted by magnanimity."

If the basic social history of suicide has been ignored in Iberian historiogra-
phy, the situation is no better with respect to cultural attitudes toward suicide. Of
course, normative statements are not hard to find. As elsewhere in Europe, Spanish sermon collections contain abundant exemplars in which despair and suicide
are denounced as comprising the final perfidy of Judas Iscariot. In civil law, too,
despair was seen as the crucial sin that led to self-murder. As we have seen, according to the thirteenth-century code of the *Siete Partidas*—whose strictures
concerning suicide remained in effect throughout the early modern centuries—
"despair is a sin which God never pardons in those who commit it, for although
men err . . . [in numerous ways], providing only they retain hope, they can secure the mercy of God, but one who dies in despair can never obtain it."[30] Self-
murder was not only a mortal sin but a civil crime: the codes imposed penalties
of the confiscation of goods of suicides, provisions that were reiterated strongly
in the reign of Enrique III and maintained on the books thereafter.[31]

Theologians and writers of confessional manuals also took up the topic of despair and self-murder. Most stood squarely within the Augustinian or neo-Augustinian tradition, with its blanket condemnation of self-homicide, except when authorized by divine command.[32] "Judas sinned more in succumbing to despair," asserted one moralist, "than the Jews did in crucifying Jesus Christ."[33] The topic engaged the attention of Francisco de Vitoria (c. 1480–1546), the great Dominican scholar of the University of Salamanca, who went somewhat beyond the Augustinian position to address specific concerns of his own time. Vitoria lectured at length on this topic in 1529 and 1530. His analysis combined a powerful theological explication of the illicitude of suicide with some sketchy but suggestive remarks in which Vitoria recognized the possibility of exceptions to the general ban on voluntary self-destruction.[34] For instance, he examined the case of a shipwreck survivor who surrenders a plank or a place in the lifeboat to a companion, knowing that he condemns himself to death by doing so. Vitoria quoted Lactantius to the effect that he would rather die voluntarily than kill willfully, and concluded: "Doubtless, then, to give one's life for one's friends seems a folly to the world; but it is wisdom before God."[35] Significantly, though, Vitoria offered no exoneration for suicide in the name of honor. Having surveyed a set of biblical texts that might be read to suggest otherwise, Vitoria concluded forcefully that, "it is not licit to give one's life for the sake of fame or glory, and that not only do those who slay themselves for this cause commit mortal sin, but so also do those who place their lives in grave danger for no other cause than human glory." The great Dominican did not exempt even pagans from this judgment, despite the argument that they believed such actions virtuous, and, ignorant of the truth of Christianity, knew no better.[36]

But if authoritative voices in church and state were effectively unanimous in condemning suicide, considerable evidence suggests that social attitudes were more complex. Though strictly speaking the law saw no exoneration in madness, it was recognized that suicide could be the product of the uncontrollable urges of insanity and that such a diminished capacity reduced culpability. An early seventeenth-century dictionary, defining *desesperarse,* listed the dire penalties—on earth and in heaven—levied against suicides, but noted, "This is not believed [to apply] to those who committed the act without sound judgment, such as madmen or lunatics."[37] But beyond such humane impulses toward pity and compassion, evidence in the historical record suggests that some forms of suicidal behavior were in fact evaluated positively, admired, and even held up for emulation.

Distinguishing the unpardonable sin of voluntary or willful death from the eternal glory of martyrdom had of course been the burden of much influential Christian writing on the topic. Augustine had recognized one exception to his general ban on courting one's own death: when a person so acted in response to divine orders. This doctrine, however, was not a particularly useful tool for separating legitimate martyrs from sinners inviting death for their own rather than God's glory. This issue had arisen repeatedly in the era of Muslim rule within the Peninsula—most notably in the ninth-century episode of the martyrs of Córdoba—and again became a lively issue across Europe because of the religious divisions of the sixteenth century.[38] No less celebrated a Christian than Teresa of Avila broached the topic in a revealing fashion in her *Vida,* drafted in the 1560s. Writing of her early awakening to spirituality, Teresa recalled that she had been attracted to the tales of sainted martyrs, thinking "that they had bought their entry into God's presence very cheaply." Looking back decades later, she regarded her youthful dreams of martyrdom as having been self-interested, propelled by her desire to attain the joys of heaven. Here then, and in keeping with the apologetic purpose of her autobiography, Teresa clearly recognized that personal glory was not a sufficient motive for courting death. But her next passage, again characteristically, may be read in a somewhat contradictory sense. "I used to discuss with my brother," she wrote, "ways and means of becoming martyrs, and we agreed to go together to the land of the Moors . . . so that we might be beheaded there. I believe," she continued, "that our Lord had given us courage enough even at that tender age, if only we could have seen a way."[39] Here Teresa seemed to address the theological justification for martyrdom, perhaps implying that this God-given courage was equivalent to the divine command that could convert an otherwise reprehensible act of self-destruction into true martyrdom. In the next generation, the devout noblewoman Luisa de Carvajal y Mendoza solemnly vowed to "pursue, to whatever extent possible, all avenues of martyrdom which are not repugnant to the law of God." The legalistic disclaimer in the final clause skirted the difficulty at the heart of the issue, and Carvajal's quest for martyrdom—enacted in England, where she lived and proselytized for Catholicism from 1605 until her death in 1614—enjoyed at least tacit validation from ecclesiastical and secular authorities. Jesuits sponsored her vow and the journey to England, while the Spanish ambassador extended his protection in London and powerful figures at the court of Philip III maintained a sympathetic correspondence with her.[40]

Teresa's recollections on this score may comprise a tantalizing contemporary rumination on the justifiable motives of martyrdom and the complexity of separating a quest for personal fame and glory from the service of God, but neither they nor Luisa de Carvajal's vow and provocative actions transgressed the bounds of contemporary orthodoxy. When contemporaries examined some sorts of secular suicide, however, discrepancies between normative values, on the one hand, and cultural evaluations of behavior, on the other, became much more sharply delineated. An example: the choice of death over dishonor was an ancient topic, and in one particular form it emerged repeatedly in sixteenth-century Iberia. In these narratives, soldiers or ministers of state confronted with royal displeasure saved honor—and, implicitly, rendered a final service to the state—by seeking death. A striking case was that of the Portuguese nobleman Rodrigo de Sousa de Carvalho, governor of Tangier in Morocco for King Sebastian (himself widely— if hardly unanimously—admired in later years for his suicidal crusade in North Africa). Reprimanded for military ineffectiveness by the king in 1572, Sousa sought out a skirmish with Moors and threw himself deliberately and heedlessly into a fight against an overwhelming force. Predictably, he was hacked to bits.[41] Similarly, Cardinal Diego de Espinosa may have found in death solace for the displeasure of his master, Philip II. As befitted his clerical station, however, Espinosa did not seek a soldier's death in battle, but instead died rapidly and mysteriously at home.[42]

Perhaps the most striking instance of the celebration of suicidal behavior in early modern Spanish culture emerges in treatments of the theme of the siege of Numantia in historical and dramatic writings during the sixteenth and seventeenth centuries. While the historical basis of this story—the prolonged Roman siege and eventual destruction of the fortified Celtiberian town of Numantia (near modern Soria) during the second century BC—had long been known from the accounts of Latin historians, this ancient episode gained extraordinary currency in Spain during the reign of Philip II. Four major treatments of Numantia, each exercising clear influences on succeeding versions, appeared between 1573 and 1630. They were: 1) the continuation by Ambrosio de Morales of the *Corónica general* of Spain, published in 1573; 2) *La destrucción de Numancia*, a play written by Miguel de Cervantes Saavedra in the early 1580s; 3) the Jesuit Juan de Mariana's *Historia general de España,* published in Latin in 1580 and in Castilian in 1601; and 4) two linked dramas by Francisco de Rojas Zorrilla, *Numancia cercada* and *Numancia destruida,* written around 1630.[43]

Variations among these retellings of the siege are numerous and interesting, but all relate (more or less approvingly) the fate of the Numantians—the town's defenders killed themselves (men, women, and children) rather than surrender to the Roman army. Each author also treats the end of Numantia as a central episode in the historical formation of Spain and the Spanish character. Two principal characteristics of the Numantian situation are depicted as quintessentially Spanish in these works. The positive trait is the compulsion to choose death over dishonor, which even foreigners appear to have regarded as a particular predilection of Spaniards.[44] The less attractive trait is the Spanish tendency toward local particularism and regional disunity: the final siege could not be broken because neighboring cities refused to cooperate with Numantia against the Romans. Understandably, but alone among these authors, the Jesuit Mariana placed greater emphasis on the perils of disunity than on the glorious example of Numantian suicide.[45]

As might be expected, the richest of these accounts of Numantia is Cervantes's play, which bears extended analysis not just as a finely-crafted drama, but also on several historical counts.[46] Of special relevance here is the gloss of the story that Cervantes provides through the intervention of a series of allegorical figures, whose dialogues and soliloquies interrupt and analyze the action of the play. The first intervention comes in act 1. Once it has become clear that the Numantians cannot break the Roman siege, a figure representing Spain appears and appeals to the (also personified) River Duero, which abuts Numantia on one side, to rise up and sweep away the besiegers. Duero responds that this is impossible because the Romans have sealed off the river between dikes. Duero nonetheless goes on to console Spain, saying that the deeds of the Numantians will live in glory for all future ages. Also, the river prophesies, the tables will turn on the Romans in magnificent days to come, when Spain under the great king Philip II will dominate Italy and the world. In this colloquy, Cervantes unequivocally traces the genealogy of modern Spain to Numantia, and it is difficult to escape the conclusion that he meant to present an act of mass suicide as a primal scene of the nation's birth.[47]

The next significant allegorical intervention occurs at the end of the play. The personification of Fame takes the stage after the lone surviving Numantian, the boy Bariato, throws himself from a high tower to his death, thus cheating the Roman commander Scipio of the last captive who might have been displayed to prove his triumph over Numantia. In a final speech, Fame eulogizes Bariato and all the brave Numantians, promises that her voice will keep their names alive forever, and "foretells the valour that the Spanish breed / Will in the coming centuries inherit / From ancestors and fathers of such merit."[48]

Cervantes took up this theme near the zenith of Spanish power in the age of Philip II, whereas Francisco de Rojas Zorrilla's Numantian plays date some fifty years later from a period of dwindling national fortunes during the reign of Philip IV and seem correspondingly gloomier. The later playwright's identification with the beleaguered Numantians is more direct: where Cervantes had denoted the defenders as "Numantinos," for Rojas the protagonists of *Numancia destruida* are "españoles" pure and simple.[49] Most interesting is the dream scene near the end of *Numancia destruida,* where Rojas explicitly equates suicide with military victory, and individual self-immolation with national survival. As the hero Retógenes dozes, figures of Numantia and of Rome, weapons drawn, appear to him in a dream sequence that foreshadows the end of the siege. Rome marvels at the continued defiance of overmatched Numantia, who responds by denouncing the Romans as cowards afraid to engage in a pitched battle.

The stakes in the contest as delineated by Rojas are fame or oblivion. To Rome's cry of "die, you peasant," Numantia responds that "I will have died content when your memory is blotted from the earth!" Subsequently, Rome returns to this theme, threatening to "deliver your name [of Numantia] to Oblivion."

This dire threat causes the sleeping Retógenes to stir and lament the harsh fate of Numantia. But he too defies the mighty foe: "Try it, Rome! But be warned: Give me my death that the *patria* may live!" Here Rome loses patience and puts forth an ultimatum: "If you would not lament mortal wounds / Bend your neck before my divine valor!" In response, Numantia hurls defiance, proclaiming victory through self-destruction:

> Neither the Quirinal nor the Aventine Hill shall witness
> My dishonor in the triumphal chariots,
> And since I expect no remedy to such manifold evils
> This dagger shall open my adamantine breast,
> And with eternal glory I shall myself have triumphed!
> (*Strikes self with the dagger.*)[50]

In Cervantes's *Destrucción de Numancia,* then, contemporary Spanish valor is explicitly likened to the Numantian choice of self-destruction over defeat and dishonor, a choice which moreover would lead in the fullness of time to the Spanish preponderance of the late sixteenth century. For Rojas, the poetic justice of such a historical reversal could not be expected—"What covetous fate, what harsh decree of providence has brought you, Numantia, to such a pass?" laments his hero[51]—and suicide is exalted quite straightforwardly as an exit from desperate straits to everlasting fame. Cervantes in fact goes even further, arguably flouting orthodoxy when he has Scipio Africanus eulogize Bariato in these terms: "Well then, boy, carry off the winnings, and also the glory that heaven prepares for you."[52] In these plays, we are very far from the authoritative pronouncements of Francisco de Vitoria, that seeking death in pursuit of fame or the preservation of honor is a grave and unforgivable sin. Simultaneously the heirs of Numantia and the most powerful sons of the Church of Rome, Spaniards of the Hapsburg age moved within a culture that, not least when the subject was suicide, celebrated and upheld divergent and irreconcilable models of behavior.

Final Thoughts

The evidence from the *siglo de oro* shows that Spaniards were profoundly ambivalent in regard to suicide. On the one hand, throughout this period they continued to associate taking one's life with despair: suicide, the crime of Judas Iscariot, seemed inextricably linked to *desesperación,* and self-murderers (or their abettors) were *desesperados.*[53] The ultimate act of despair provoked extreme reactions in survivors. In the Numantian plays, Scipio witnesses the final suicides with a mixture of awe and frustration. "Oh! Never have I seen so memorable a deed," blurts Cervantes's Roman. "By casting yourself down, you [Bariato] have triumphed over him whose fortunes, once cresting, have now fallen even further."[54] For Rojas Zorrilla, Scipio's frustration gives way to an impotent vengeance:

> But since I'm carrying neither slaves, nor gold,
> Nor even silver back to Rome,
> Raze these walls to the ground,
> Grind these houses into the dust
> From which they sprang,
> So that no memory shall remain
> Of a city that, by my men
> Besieged, has defeated me.[55]

Similarly, we may gauge the fury that suicide (combined with heresy and apostasy) provoked in the inquisitors of Ciudad Real by the draconian sentence they posthumously imposed on Isabel de los Olivos y López. Like Scipio thwarted before Numantia, the Holy Office resolved to eradicate all traces of the *desesperada* whose self-destruction served to mock its authority. Despite the prevalence of confident assertions that suicides would find incomparable punishment in the afterlife—"worst of all is that they're going to keep company with Judas" for all eternity[56]—the act of self-murder often elicited what appears an unreasoning rage and the compulsion to visit temporal indignities on the perpetrator. Although it is not clear that the penalty was regularly applied, some local ordinances in Castile provided that "when the crime [of suicide] succeeded, the corpse was to be exposed publicly, 'in a shameful place,' so as to damn the memory of the deceased."[57]

Clearly, however, the emotional valence of despair could vary depending on the observer or the context. The suicidal desperation of a criminal or heretic compounded his offense and intensified the punitive wrath of the authorities, while suicidal behavior could confer honor if undertaken to avoid disgrace or in defiance of religious persecution or of an overwhelming enemy force. In the latter cases, perhaps *desesperación* could assume the coloring of *desengaño,* the clearsighted disillusion and resignation to fate that was exalted by contemporary authors as a precondition to a good Christian death. "Here he put aside the hopes of life," wrote Quevedo, in perhaps the most poetic description of this acceptance of mortality, "and commenced to dwell with the *desengaños.*"[58] From this unsentimental clarity about human destiny it was perhaps no more than a few steps along the path of stoicism to a celebration of the nobility of suicide in the face of insurmountable odds.

CHAPTER 7

HONFIBÚ

Nationhood, Manhood, and the Culture of Self-Sacrifice in Hungary

DAVID LEDERER

The martyrdom of Socrates,
Stern Cato's earnest loyalties,
The sacred dust of Zrínyi great—
These are but wanton jests of fate.

Ferenc Kölcsey, *Vanitatum Vanitas*

Suicide in Hungary a Historical Problem

To the outsider, Hungary stands out from other European cultures in two salient ways: its language and its very high reported suicide rate.[1] First and foremost, the language, Magyar—a Finno-Ugric tongue with Altaic roots—linguistically separates Hungarians from Indo-Europeans. Its etymological roots lie buried under successive layers of migrations and conquests that have characterized Hungary's history since late antiquity. In the Middle Ages, the region known today as Hungary was conquered by the Huns, Avars, and Charlemagne, among others, before the arrival in the ninth century of the Magyars (as Hungarians still refer to themselves). The Magyars harried their German neighbors until suffering a devastating defeat at Lechfeld in 955. A religious coup occurred shortly thereafter, when St. Stephan converted the Magyar Arpad dynasty to Christianity in 1001. The Arpads struggled to control the nobility during the Mongol incursions of the thirteenth century until the death of their last male heir, Andreas III, in 1301. Seven years later, the Pope succeeded in placing Charles Robert of the Neapolitan Angevins on the throne. Over the next two centuries, marriage alliances with the Luxembourgs and Hapsburgs drew Hungary into the Imperial sphere of influence. Then, Budapest fell to the Ottoman Turks under Sulieman the Magnificent after the terrible military disaster at Mohács in 1527. One hundred fifty bitter years of Turkish occupation finally ended with the siege of Budapest in 1686 and the subsequent Peace of Karlowitz in 1699, enabling the Hapsburgs to reassert their dynastic claims effectively. Their rule was no less bitterly opposed during the nationalist revolution of 1848. Thereafter, Hungary was elevated to quasi-equal status in 1867 under the dual monarchy. Still nominally part of the Danubian empire ruled from Vienna until the end of the First World War, Hungary finally became an independent republic in 1919, only to be occupied by the Nazis in 1944 and, thereafter, by Soviet troops at the conclusion of the Second World War. After an abortive uprising in 1956, Hungary remained under Moscow's domination until it became the first Warsaw Pact country to break free after the collapse of the USSR. Although each successive wave of conquerors enriched the language with expressions from Persian, Mongolian, Slavic, German, Latin, and especially Turkish, the Hungarian language has nevertheless acted as a fundamental bond of cultural and, from the nineteenth century, nationalist unity. The Hungarian language has an idiomatic expression for the desperate plight of the homeland: *honfibú,* literally meaning patriotic sorrow.

Like its language, Hungary's reported suicide rate is unfortunately another unique aspect of its national culture. Throughout the twentieth century, it ranked among the world's highest rates of reported suicide, consistently topping the charts. As is obvious from Table 7.1, statistics give the impression of a traditionally high incidence of suicide in Hungary.[2] Theoretically, standard sociological categories are generally employed to explain these statistics.[3] Alternately, the suicidal tradition is sometimes depicted as an essential characteristic of Hungarian culture. In ethnolinguistic terms, its origins are sought among obscure myths and clues, analogous to Carlo Ginzburg's search for the common roots of communalism and pantheism in Indo-European cultures.[4]

This investigation combines elements of both theories, but presupposes the necessity of locating suicide in its specific historical context. Furthermore, it presumes that perceptions of suicide are modified not only by historical circumstances, but by the very retelling of history. In this sense, historical story telling sets out signposts that demarcate cultures as autonomous self-conscious entities, providing flags around which people rally in good times and bad. Tales about suicidal self-sacrifice have a long tradition in Hungary, serving for centuries as a cultural totem in changing contexts.[5] Perceptions of suicide in medieval and early modern Hungary are an especially relevant key to the creation of Hungarian national identity as a masculine ethos in the nineteenth century.

Commenting on the situation in his homeland, one social critic, Paul Lendvai, offers us a statement pregnant with interpretive connotations. In 1988, citing

TABLE 7.1.
Comparative suicide rates in European countries, 1921–2001
(Annual rate per 100,000 people)

Country	1921–1930	1931–1940	1960	1970	1986	1992	1999–2001 (male/female)
Hungary	30.0	32.0	26.0	34.6	45.3	38.6	47.1/13
Austria	31.8	40.0	23.1	24.2	28.3	21.3	27.3/9.8
Britain	12.3	13.0	11.2	8.0	8.6*	8.0	11.8/3.3
France	19.1	20.2	15.9	15.4	22.7	21.8	26.1/9.4
Germany	25.9	28.6	18.8	21.2	31.1**	16.7	20.2/7.3
Sweden	14.5	16.4	17.4	22.3	18.5	15.6	19.7/8,0
Switzerland	25.3	25.8	19.0	18.4	22.8	N/A	26.5/10

Sources: Ede Böszörményi, *Az öngyilkosságok múltja és jelene* (Budapest, 1991), 64; Központi Statisztikai Hivatal, *Demográfiai Évkönyu 1996 Magyarország Nepesedéje* (Budapest, 1998), 252; Edgar Borgatta & Marie Borgatta (eds.), *Encyclopedia of Sociology* 4 (New York, 1992), 2116; *United Nations Demographic Yearbook 48* (New York, 1996), 806–47. The most recent statistics of the World Health Organization (2003, consulted 12 February 2004) are available on-line at: http://www.who.int/mental_health/prevention/suicide/suiciderates/en/
* England and Wales
** Average of East (19.0) and West Germany (43.1)
N/A — Not available

Hungary as the nation with the world's then-highest suicide and parasuicide (attempted suicide) rate, he aptly commented, "It is almost like saying that the entire population of a medium-sized Hungarian town is living in a kind of psychic death-row."[6] In the way of an explanation, he added, "Like alcoholism, suicide is probably part of the Hungarian national character and social behaviour. Thus, for example, every year between three and seven persons take their own lives in the town of Balatonszarszo on the Balaton lake by way of imitating the celebrated poet Attila Joszef, who threw himself in front of a goods train in 1937."[7] Similarly, in the face of the overwhelming statistical evidence, the cultural historian Tamás Zonda rhetorically questions whether Hungary might therefore be considered a suicidal nation with a depressive and excessively pessimistic national character.[8] In response, he suggests that any social inclination towards depression and pessimism is not necessarily an essential Hungarian trait, but is instead indicative of

> a rather realistically perceived, sad and hard historical experience. . . . This nation has withstood all this for more than a thousand years, even though all its revolutions and all its wars of independence were crushed. . . . Turkish, Austrian, and Russian forces have been attempting, for the last 550 years, to wipe out, or integrate, or Germanize, or Russianize Hungary, to destroy its identity, to question its European status. . . . After this much pain, humiliation, subjugation, and unjust punishment, having seen the indifference of the West, this attitude is not all that surprising.[9]

Statistically, however, high reported rates of suicide were not always the rule in Hungary. In his study of Catholic and Protestant church registers from Hód-mezővásárhely and Csongrad, Ede Böszörményi identified only four suicides among 24,000 total deaths from 1750 to 1800, about 1 per 100,000 deaths over a fifty-year period. This low figure doubled (seven suicides among 23,000 deaths) for the shorter period of 1801–1825.[10] In the years 1826 to 1850, the total jumped to twenty-eight suicides for 33,000 deaths. Reported suicides continued to spiral to the end of the nineteenth century as overall mortality rates declined (see Table 7.2), the only constants throughout being higher rates among Protestants than Catholics and among men than women.[11] Although both of these constants conform to standard European patterns, rates among men in Hungary are unusually high—three times higher than those among women.[12]

Furthermore, despite Böszörményi's claims that rising rates coincided with the emotional stresses of political modernization and the anomie of industrialization, Lendvai offers important contradictions to the social crisis theory. Specifically, he cites rates well above the national average in the less-industrialized Csongrad district studied by Böszörményi and a drop in rates at the height of the Stalinist terror.[13] Historically, national-level statistics from the nineteenth century confirm that, although suicide rates in Hungary remained lower than many European nations (with the notable exception of Britain, which it had surpassed by 1881), they still witnessed a continuous and dramatic increase.[14] For example, the journal *Hetilap* placed rates in Pest from 1835–1845 at one suicide per 10,109 people, ranking it lower than either Paris (1 / 1,665) or New York City (1 / 7,797).[15] Nevertheless, from 1851 to 1900, countrywide rates increased nearly fivefold. In historical terms, then, we can identify a major shift in suicide statistics in the mid-nineteenth century. The actual cause behind the sharp rise in suicide statistics—whether representing an absolute increase, reflecting a heightened awareness, or merely indicating better record keeping—is unclear. The fact remains that the increase is first perceptible around the time of the failed revolution of 1848.

Suicide, long perceived as a major *social* malaise in Hungary, has not been considered as a potentially *historical* problem until quite recently. Of the two major contributors to this debate, Böszörményi views the problem largely in demo-

TABLE 7.2.
Suicide and death in Hódmezövásárhely, later nineteenth century

Church registers	1851–1860	1861–1870	1871–1880	1881–1890	1891–1900
Suicides	22	109	206	236	288
Deaths	12,236	14,617	17,423	15,247	14,462

Source: Böszörményi, "Hódmezovásárhelyi öngyilkosságok," *Történeti statisztikai tanulmányok: Központi Statisztikai Hivatal Könyvtáre, Magyar Országos Levéltar* 3 (1977): 237–304.

graphic terms with reference to classic (Durkheimian) sociological categories, while Zonda's focus on culture is refreshing. This investigation builds on his analytical framework in two ways. On the one hand, traditional historical methods, as employed by Zonda, enable comparisons between Hungary and its neighbors in Western and Central Europe. Methodologically, this entails an analysis of suicide as a felony through the examination of normative criminal codes, as well as popular attitudes toward suicide and related phenomena during the early modern period. Although the historical development of criminal law in Hungary closely paralleled its evolution in the Holy Roman Empire, no evidence suggests that suicide was ever demonized or persecuted in Hungary with the same attendant cruelty or to the same extent as in Western Europe. Hence, a culturally demonstrable variance occurs between Western legal norms, which penetrated Hungarian culture, and Western attitudes and practices toward suicide, which apparently did not.

Here, my conclusions are at variance with Zonda's stance on suicide as initially alien to Hungarian culture. He suggests that the increase in suicide was primarily the result of Westernization in general and German influences in particular.[16] Nonetheless (as he, too, correctly notes), German influence in religion (and, as we shall see, in law) began in the early sixteenth century. Significantly, as Richard Aczel points out, by the late-eighteenth century a distinctive Hungarian literature had emerged as "a modern, autonomous and self-conscious discourse."[17] Only after the Hungarian literati thoroughly rejected foreign ideals during the populist movement (best represented in the works of Petőfi and Vörösmarty) did reported rates of suicide commence their dramatic rise. Above all, it was a fatalistic preoccupation of Hungarian poets with the "death of the nation" (Szózat) as a literary and historical motif—which depicted the Hungarians united in a brave and relentless struggle for survival against foreign powers—that coincided with the tragic events of 1848 and Hungary's rise to preeminence in suicidality.[18]

On the other hand, a survey of legends depicted in art and literature from the late Middle Ages to the twentieth century raises disturbing questions about the influence of community in the formation of a fatalistic tradition. Again, Zonda's orthodox claims about alien Western individualism and liberalism miss several more subtle issues. Here, I suggest that History (with a capital 'H') can be deadly.[19] In his introduction to the centennial edition of Thomas G. Masaryk's (the first president of Czechoslovakia) famous 1881 study of suicide, the Hungarian J. C. Nyíri notes that "whilst the level of suicide in a culture is independent of short-term political changes, a social structure which permits a high suicide rate is nevertheless a result of definite, long-term historical and political developments" and, according to Masaryk's thesis, "philosophy and literature are just as much manifestations of the pathological state of society as is the increased disposition to mental illness and suicide."[20] For Nyíri, the specific implication is that, "It is quite possible that the historical experiences of the residual popula-tions of the areas devastated by the Turkish occupation, combined with the weak-ness of the internal forces of the society constituted by the influx of German-speaking immigrants, contributed to the relative emotional poverty and coldness in the subculture of the southeastern plainlands."[21] Although the suggestion that an influx of immigrants contributed to higher rates of suicide in Hungary, Nyíri's claims in no way substantiate Zonda's about the influx of German cul-ture. Instead, he points to a breakdown of social cohesion and "spiritual anarchy" in a state of "semi-education" as a "common source of both philosophy and suicide."[22]

Again, my premise here is somewhat different, rather less philosophical and more pedagogical. The unique history of Hungarian relationships with foreign invaders explains why a strong self-sacrificial tendency persisted there long after this tradition declined in other parts of Western Europe. Initially, the early mod-ern ethos of self-sacrifice was purely aristocratic and spread only gradually as a system of elementary and secondary schools was set up in Protestant areas dur-ing the golden age of Hungarian culture under Turkish occupation.[23] However, romantics and populists subsequently reinterpreted their past in the nineteenth century, when this ethos was incorporated into a cultural ideal of nationhood and manhood manifest in art, poetry, and literature. As historical figures entered the pantheon of Hungarian nationalism at that time, the collection of particular legends helped create a new sense of imagined community among rival ethnic groups. In their confrontation with both their past and present, liberal bourgeois historians, poets, and artists invented a resilient shared tradition of self-sacrifice which transcended class and ethnic boundaries and still pervades Hungarian culture, from scholars to soldiers to ordinary people. As part of a communal con-sciousness originally aimed at group preservation, this historiographic interpre-tation has played an ironic role in lowering the individual threshold of inhibition for self-destructive behavior in a society where the good of the many was pri-oritized over the good of the individual for reasons of collective self-survival. Optimistically however, given present conditions, I would argue that the histor-ical problem of suicide in Hungary is a social atavism and part of the solution lies in changing popular perceptions of history.

The Crime of Self-Murder in Comparative Perspective

Like the English term "suicide," the Hungarian expression *öngyilkosság* (arising from language reforms around 1800), is a modern compound construct literally meaning self- (*ön*) murder (*gyilkosság*); prior to 1800, the more neutral expression "self-destruction" had been used.[24] Of interest, the earliest Hungarian criminal prohibitions against suicide are not found in Magyar, but in the German-language civic code of Ofen (*Ofener Stadtrecht*), established by the German citizenry and overlords of Buda in the late fifteenth century. Article 261, titled "Where one should bury those who kill themselves," contains penalties for suicide that were standard fare throughout the Holy Roman Empire: "He who kills himself is not worthy to be buried anywhere else than under the gibbet, and his possessions should fall to no one, neither little or much, other than to his wife, his children, or his relations."[25]

As the first civic law code in Hungary, the Ofener statutes underscore the early influence of eastward migrations from German-speaking lands (in this case, Swabia) since the eleventh century. This particular juridical import, and with it the legal proscriptions against suicide, served as a model for numerous other Hungarian civic law codes in the early modern period. Thus, article 261 explains why standard legal procedures for dealing with suicide in late medieval and early modern Germany permeated Hungarian law even before the elaboration of Hapsburg dynastic claims. Procedures in article 261 concentrated on the disposal of the corpse and the estate. Burial of a self-murderer under the gallows was common throughout Western Europe, as were many other degrading funerary rituals.[26] In terms of the disposition of the estate, the casual gender presumption is worthy of note (that is, that suicides would be male), since married women were not prohibited from disposing of heritable (dotal) property. That the authorities were denied any rights of confiscation and that all possessions fell to the legal heirs is yet another validation of the Germanic origins of the article. In some areas of Western Europe, such as England, Flanders, and parts of France, confiscation was practiced with terrible regularity against self-murderers who were suspected criminals and noncriminals alike.[27] As one moved eastward through Central Europe, the situation changed.[28] In the Empire, an early law code from Saxony (*Sachsenspiegel*) forbade confiscation in the thirteenth century and, by 1532, the Imperial penal code of Charles V (*Carolina*) explicitly opposed confiscation in all instances of suicide, excepting suspected and condemned criminals.[29] In northwestern Schleswig-Holstein, confiscations were practiced, but became rare through the course of the seventeenth and early eighteenth centuries.[30] In southeastern Bavaria on the other hand, the terms and conditions of the *Carolina* had already been sanctioned as early as 1508, were repeated in mandates on territorial policy (*Landesfreiheiten*) in 1514, 1516, and 1553, and were codified into territorial law in 1616 (*Codex Maximilianeum*).[31] In Austria, the dynastic lands of the Hapsburgs, the more lenient prohibitions of the *Carolina* prevailed as well.

On the law books, attitudes toward suicide in Hungary followed the Imperial tradition and were fully secularized only by the Josephine legal reforms of the

1780s. Taking the hiatus of the Turkish occupation between 1527 and 1699 into account, we need refer only to the eighteenth-century corpus of Hungarian municipal statutes to see how little legal norms changed from the medieval civic code of Ofen. In 1721, for example, a county statute for Baranzamezge stipulated that persons who hanged themselves were to be removed and dishonorably interred by the executioner at a cost of 10 florins, but no confiscation was authorized.[32] In 1764, the Gömörmegyei statutes still ordered the bodies of self-murderers to be burned, a ritual purification also applied to suspected witches.[33] Mathyis Bodo's standard criminal code of 1751 (De Jurisprudentia criminalis) discusses more thorough procedures for magistrates investigating suicides under the rubric De Morte sibi ipsi illata (concerning self-inflicted death).[34] Again, burning by the executioner was given as the preferred method of disposal and no provisions were made for confiscations other than in criminal cases. More extensive references were made to the insanity defense and other mitigating circumstances, such as special provisions for pregnant women, who were considered prone to suicidal tendencies.[35] In the latter case, the magistrate was to have a physician or surgeon attempt to save the child: "Moreover, they are obliged to open the pregnant woman who has most maliciously killed herself, as quickly as possible, and remove the foetus, so that by this means, the child might be saved. Even if the child be taken out dead, no loss of honor will follow from this. And in such a case, the child, being exempted in this way, is to be buried not with the mother but in a secluded place."[36] Thus, the deceased child was buried separately since, although unbaptized, it was innocent of the deed and not subject to the same form of dishonorable burial as the mother. Despite legalistic affectations of leniency in certain circumstances, Bodo's De Jurisprudentia was no complete legal secularization of suicide, as it continued to differentiate between "defects of a sane mind" (ex defectu sanae mentis) and "impious desperation" (ex malitiosa voluntate, & impia desperatione)—a categorization with significant religious overtones—in its decision on the final resting place.[37] Enlightened change in juridical procedure first came to Hungary with the adoption of Joseph II's criminal code of 1787, which fully decriminalized self-murder, declaring all legally suspected suicides non compos mentis (not sound of mind). By 1792, anyone who either assisted a suicide or did not try to hinder one was liable for punishment, and this legislation was relaxed only after 1843, after which time bystanders were subject to prosecution only if the suicide died within thirty days of the act.[38] Far from peculiar, the Hungarians' experience of suicide, in purely legal terms, was identical to that of their German-speaking neighbors.

In terms of actual practice and popular beliefs, there is little evidence about the enforcement of these laws, as archival records of prosecutions for suicide in late medieval and early modern Hungary are conspicuously lacking. This not only reflects the absence of a central bureaucracy during the Turkish occupation, but also appears to represent a lack of interest in persecuting the crime in early modern Hungary. Apart from the church registers examined by Böszörményi, cases do not appear regularly in administrative records until after the Josephine reforms.[39] These later records consist solely of autopsy reports and decisions in disputed cases of death by misadventure. By that time, no bodies were subject to dishonorable burials, indicating that, by 1800, the Josephine criminal reforms were firmly in place in the bureaucracy and the decriminalization of suicide had occurred largely without resistance. In practice, there is a complete absence of the type of complaints against secularization, either from members of the ruling elite or the common people, as one sometimes finds in the Empire. Investigations conducted in the municipal archives in both Buda and Debrecen revealed no cases of actual criminal prosecution conducted against suspected self-murderers in the early modern period.[40]

The absence of prosecutions makes it difficult to gauge popular attitudes toward suicide in early modern Hungary. Unfortunately, the subject is also conspicuously absent from standard indices of Hungarian folkloric motifs as well. Although tales of revenants and ghost stories abound, no evidence suggests any connection with traditional Western beliefs concerning the return of self-murderers from the dead to haunt the living, suggesting that these popular beliefs were less relevant in premodern Hungarian folk culture.[41] It is, however, possible to extrapolate scattered clues from attitudes toward related phenomena. Recent research has shown how popular notions about witchcraft, the devil, dishonorable burials, and suicide were linked. However, Hungary had as many differences as similarities to Western European beliefs and practices. Witches were clearly persecuted in Hungary, but significant trials commenced at a much later date, and there is disagreement over evidence for large-scale witch persecutions on the level of parts of Western Europe.[42] A clear substratum of belief in nocturnal journeys, ecstasies, white magic, and fertility cults existed, but, as in the case of suicide, an unusually high proportion of the accused were men, as with Rosa, a male "devil" burned at the stake for having "sold the clouds to the Turks," that is, engaging in weather magic in the eighteenth century.[43] In German-speaking lands, these same types of weather-related folk beliefs were closely associated with the corpses of suicides interred in communal cemeteries. In Germany, suicides represented a potential metaphysical danger to communities. Through their association with Satan, who tempted them to the deed, desperate self-murderers threatened to profane cemeteries. This invited celestial wrath in the form of hail and storms which damaged crops, leading early modern communities in Germany openly to revolt and refuse them burial in hallowed ground.[44] Nonetheless, although evidence of beliefs in weather-related magic exists in Hungary, none corroborates a connection of these beliefs with suicide, even if Hungarians were normally very particular about their choice of a final resting place. For example, during a terrible plague in Debrecen from 1739 to 1742, riots occurred when the magistrates attempted to enforce a policy of quick burials in mass graves without proper ceremonies, leading to a spate of clandestine burials in private backyards.[45] The only palpable evidence for a connection of suicide to witchcraft is tangential. In Debrecen, a witch was suspected of driving a man to suicide, but his suicide was passed over without further mention or prosecution.[46] In terms of popular practices and metaphysical and magical beliefs, the best we can say is that the initial normative legal clarity of a cultural parallel between Hungary and Western Europe, including the Empire, breaks down at the popular level. Is it possible that a greater social toleration of suicide existed in early modern Hungary and, if so, what could explain it?

A Cultural Mohács

If the comparative implications of legal norms and popular attitudes leave us with more questions than answers, then the cultural history of legendary self-sacrifices in late medieval and early modern Hungary is less perplexing. Legends of desperate and, at times, apparently futile acts of personal self-sacrifice are numerous and have been woven into the national consciousness to a far greater degree than in Western Europe. Since the inclusion of self-sacrifice entails a broadening of the definition for suicide, some theoretical discussion of martyrdom seems in order. As the events of September 11, 2001 evidence, there is a thin line between martyrdom and suicide that is culturally relative. Mircea Eliade's *Encyclopedia of Religion* is instructive: the opening paragraph from the article "Suicide" immediately refers back to the entry on "Martyrdom," corroborating the blurred distinction.[47] In the latter, it is suggested that heroic martyrs unite a people, invoking a higher, purifying vengeance against a dominant adversary, generally depicted as cruel and murderous. According to Max Weber, the heroic martyr imbues economic and political struggles with sacred meaning, creating an "ethic of the absolute ends, with little attention to the cost."[48] The martyr mobilizes political action directed toward this-worldly as well as other-worldly ends. He or she becomes a banner for a self-determining society which takes political control over its own destiny through an appropriation of their sacrifice as a cultural symbol.[49] These criteria certainly apply to depictions of the Turkish Wars in Hungary. The heroically motivated suicide is an ambivalent symbol, especially in Western Christian cultures, with contradictory traditions of condemning suicide while commending martyrdom.[50] Obviously, not all martyrs are suicides, but there is a considerable gray area of action between legitimate risk taking, on the one hand, and exposing oneself to unnecessary risks or confidently facing the prospect of certain and futile death, on the other. While there are strong indications that the image of the suicidal martyr was on the decline in Western Europe under the hegemony of the late medieval Church, the presence of the Turkish threat gave it renewed vitality in Hungary. This was not the devil-may-care *desengaño* of the conquistadors and Golden Age Spanish literature, nor the ultimate expression of neostoicist *ataraxia,* the psychological freedom from all emotional disturbances, but rather a manifestation of defiant hopelessness.

Heroic martyrdom in Hungary during the late medieval and early modern periods has many famous examples. One of the earliest legends is that of Deszö (see Figure 7). After the struggles following the extinction of the Arpad dynasty in 1301, Charles Robert of Anjou succeeded to the throne in 1308 with papal support, defeating the baronial parties of Wenceslas of Bohemia and Otto of Bavaria. During a subsequent campaign against the Wallachian ruler, Besarab, Charles Robert was trapped in one of the Carpathian mountain passes. He and the bulk of his army were saved when Deszö donned the king's clothing, armor, and weapons to willingly fall into an ambush set for Charles without any hope for survival.[51] A second famous self-sacrifice is that of Dugovics Titusz (see Figure 8). He was part of the Hungarian relief column during the abortive Turkish siege of Belgrade in 1456, an action that became a legend in its own time by stalling the Turkish advance through the Balkans for decades after the fall of Constantinople. During the siege, Titusz led a counterattack on a breach in the wall. He then snatched the Turkish flag and, in order to remove it from the citadel and rally his troops, he threw himself from the wall with the flag to certain death. Here, in a painting by Sándor Wagnor of 1859, the casting down of the Turkish flag is replaced by the symbolic raising of the modern Hungarian colors. However, it was foremost the occupation of Hungary by the Turks after the military disaster at Mohács in 1527 which occasioned the majority of such tales of self-sacrifice. In 1542, for example, Count Riditz shielded Duke Moritz of Saxony with his body at a battle near Pest until the latter could be saved by imperial troops from otherwise certain death, a story still remembered in an eighteenth-century book on suicide.[52] Another dramatic and influential incident is celebrated by the painting, *The Women of Eger* (see Figure 9). Although not an actual heroic martyrdom, per se, the tale of the siege of Eger is especially interesting as a gender construct designed to invoke the machismo inherent in the self-sacrificial tradition as an admonition to Hungarian men. In 1552, the Ottomans were following up their victory at Mohács when a 2,500−man garrison at Eger under István Dobó blocked their advance. The numerically superior Ottomans besieged Eger for five weeks and, after bitter fighting, were repulsed in their first major defeat of the campaign. In 1553, Sebestyen Tinódi composed a commem-

Figure 7. Molnaár Jósef, *The Brave Dezső Sacrifices Himself for King Charles Robert,* 1855. Reproduced with the permission of the Hungarian National Gallery, Budapest.

Figure 8. Wágner Sándor, *Dugovics Titusz's Self-Sacrifice,* 1859. Reproduced with the permission of the Hungarian National Gallery, Budapest.

Figure 9. Székely Bertalan, *The Women of Eger,* 1867. Reproduced with the permission of the Hungarian National Gallery, Budapest.

orative poem to celebrate the victory. Here, he describes the valiant efforts of the women of Eger in defense of their home:

> To the breech at Prison Bastion, Dobó sped;
> His page had a gilded helmet on his head,
> Which was soon shot off; the page fell dead.
> Dobó's hand and foot in the fight were wounded.
>
> He called on his men to stand the battle's shock,
> Ordered women-folk to carry up the rocks,
> And, for those worn out by fighting, large wine crocks,
> To support them in battle's fierce deadlock.
>
> Hurling boulders, these women proved brave and bold.
> Petö had brave people, too, in his stronghold.
> Ali Pasha's flag embroidered all in gold,
> Buda's gelded, Pasha's flag fell ours to hold.[53]

Tinódi's admonition to the noblemen of Hungary subsequently echoed in a panegyric celebrating the battle at Szigetvár. The battle is depicted in the most famous Hungarian legend of all times, the epic of Count Miklós Zrínyi. Another Miklós Zrínyi, great grandson of the original hero, composed the eulogy to his grandfather in 1646 as *The Peril of Sziget*. The younger Zrínyi was heavily influenced by Tinódi's verse, as well as the neostoicism of a family friend, the humanist Archbishop of Gran Péter Pázmány, who arranged for him to study with the Jesuits in Graz, Vienna, and Nagyszombat.[54] His own emotional account recalls the Ottoman march on Vienna under the personal command of Sultan Sulieman, halted at the fortifications of Szigetvár in a siege lasting over a month. When the situation became critical and no reinforcements were forthcoming, the hopelessly outnumbered Hungarian commander (Ban) Zrínyi hurled himself at the Turkish army in a final desperate sortie on September 8, 1566. Although Zrínyi and his men faced certain annihilation, Suleiman was also mortally wounded and the Turks had to break off their advance on Vienna. Here follows the younger Zrínyi's depiction of his grandfather's speech before throwing himself at his invincible adversary:

> Looking back, the Ban sees in the distance,
> How the Turkish sabres mow down his men,
> Quickly he turns to find his flock
> In order to announce to those still surviving:
>
> "Our lives, heroes, are dedicated
> To honor the one who died for us on the cross.

It is our heroic duty, bravely and with joy
To suffer death for him and our salvation!

Clearly, I see God's Kingdom high above . . .
Clearly, I can see the great son of Eloim,
I recognize the Angel beside God's throne,
Who holds the untarnished crown eternal!"

He also recounts the Ban's self-sacrifice and subsequent apotheosis:

The enemy feared to approach Zrínyi;
But the Ban was hit by the fire of the Janissaries
And two bullets struck his breast and forehead
And he sank to the ground among the other heroes.

Legions of angels soared down to him,
Singing songs of highest praise to his honor,
Gabriel and a host of twenty others swing low
To the Ban, to carry him to bright heights.

Every angel took a hero's soul with him,
So that each might shine in heaven above;
So harmonious was the song of angels,
That I am now moved to end my praise.[55]

The direct ascension of the elder Zrínyi and his heroes to paradise (in essence a popular canonization) is a first in Hungarian legends of heroic martyrs and, in the seventeenth century, has a curious ring of the pre-Christian, Germanic elements of the medieval *Nibelungenlied,* not to mention the Islamic concept of *shahada* (a profession of faith through martyrdom in a holy war). There is certainly debate as to whether he is represented as a Christian hero (*athleta Christi*) or national hero.[56] The younger Zrínyi, himself an eyewitness to the brutality of the Turkish Wars, also devoted his life to the struggle against the invaders of his homeland. His literary works celebrated an aristocratic ethic of self-sacrifice in that struggle.[57] He summed up the state of affairs in his last and greatest prose work, *The Remedy for the Turkish Opium* (1661). He warned the Hungarian noble factions that they could expect no assistance from outsiders, but should instead enlist the support of the common people and the peasantry in their fight for freedom from external domination.[58] Zrínyi concluded with a bitterly determined and, once again, unmistakably gendered call to arms to shake the nobility from their infighting, opportunism, and apathy: "See, I am calling, see, I am shouting, hear me, Hungarians! Here is the danger, here the consuming fire. . . . We, the descendants of the glorious Magyar race, must go to our deaths if need be for our wives, our children, and our country."[59] The younger Zrínyi himself was killed by a wild boar while hunting in 1664 and his death was mourned throughout Europe. Coincidentally, his brother, Peter Zrínyi, who is also officially revered as a national martyr, was executed in Vienna ten years later.[60] He had participated in a failed uprising against the Hapsburgs, who hoped to bargain away yet unoccupied portions of Hungary to the Turks in return for assurances of a respite for Vienna. Immediately thereafter, the Hapsburgs used the incident as a pretext to suspend the Hungarian constitution, turning the remaining autonomous portions of Hungary into a buffer zone.

Civic chronicles illustrate how this legendary ethos of self-sacrificial heroism translated into political action. They also indicate the extent to which the population had adapted (under duress) to certain Ottoman customs, in this case hostage-taking and ransom.[61] In 1660, for example, one chronicler records how a group of Ottomans led by Pasha Seidi surrounded Debrecen, which was undefended, demanding a large tribute—at first 30,000, then 60,000, and finally 300,000 Thalers.[62] The town had been plundered several times already and was in no position to meet even the first demand. As a result, the Ottomans took hostages from among the leading male citizens, as per their standard procedure. When the town council recommended offering all they had in ransom, one councilor, István Biczó, who later became mayor, suggested withholding at least enough provisions to survive the coming months, "at the cost of three or four councilors' lives," that is, he reckoned with retribution for failure to meet the demands.[63] Biczó himself led the delegation to the Pasha with the lesser amount, but he was rejected, whereupon he commented, "it would have been better for me to die in the Ottoman camp" and later repeated, "it would have been better for me to have been killed by the Ottomans."[64] When the Turks publicly humiliated him and other members of the council, he lamented that "they would rather be killed by the Ottomans" than to suffer the humiliation.[65] One year later, another mayor of the town was summarily executed by the Pasha after the council delivered him false information on the movements of nearby Imperial troops.[66]

The Populist Legend of Self-Sacrifice

Even after the expulsion of the Turks at the end of the seventeenth century, these legends remained fresh in the minds of Hungarians during the subsequent Hapsburg occupation. At the beginning of the nineteenth century, when Hungary was caught up in the nationalist and populist movements, the greatest literary and artistic figures of the day returned to these legends in their quest for national autonomy and the creation of a new cultural identity. Their ideals are reflected in works of art celebrating the legendary self-sacrifices of their late medieval and early modern ancestors. Several nineteenth-century artistic representations were already intentionally employed here, albeit anachronistically, to convey a populist interpretation of late medieval and early modern events more familiar to modern Hungarians. Poets and painters were particularly consumed with a romantic sense of their past and it was through their eyes that perceptions of heroic legends entered into the popular national consciousness for the first time. For example, the poet Ferenc Köscsey recalled the deeds of Zrínyi and the heroes of the Turkish occupation in thinly veiled comparisons to the current Hapsburg occupation, as a veritable torrent of *Zriniana* achieved status as a literary genre in its own right.[67] In his own *Song of Zrínyi* and *Zrínyi's Second Song,* Köscsey expressed despair over the fate of his country and offered a vision of Hungary as a nation historically struggling under the constant threat of extinction.[68] In another telling comparison cited at the onset of this essay, Köscsey fatalistically referred to Socrates' consumption of hemlock as martyrdom and placed Zrínyi's own martyrdom alongside the classical suicides of that Athenian and of Cato of Utica, also commemorated by the Romans as a martyr. The romantic notion of national despair even acquired a name: *honfibú,* an idiomatic expression meaning patriotic sorrow, first entered the language at this time. After the failed revolution of 1848, it represented a fatalistic view of history as cyclic and circular prevalent among Hungarian intellectuals, especially prominent in the poetry of Mihály Vörösmarty.[69]

The greatest of all Hungarian populists, Sándor Petőfi, extolled the independence movement in his own poetry. Petőfi, born in 1823 of humble Slavic parents, was a leading figure in the creation of a national ethic of self-sacrifice in a romantic literary movement which embraced the "pure" language of the common people.[70] Unlike other European romantics, although he extolled the virtues of landscapes, nature, and the people and was active in the preservation of folk songs and motifs, he emphasized a specific form of Hungarian communality. His subsequent imitators (known as *petőfieskedők*) also proselytized the spirit of *honfibú* through this popular literary style, making it accessible to the average citizen and immediate to their personal experiences. In 1848–1849, after one hundred and fifty years of Austrian occupation, the Hungarians rose up in another desperate attempt to throw off the yoke of external domination. A self-professed adherent of radical Jacobinism, Petőfi himself volunteered immediately for the *Honvéd* (originally referring to a traditional medieval militia) and died when Russian forces six times its size massacred the citizen army in 1849. Among the evocative titles of his most famous revolutionary works were *Onward to the Holy War, A Sea Has Wakened Up,* and the most politically significant poem in modern Hungarian history, *The National Song*—the first product of the uncensored revolutionary press, which he recited publicly on the eve of the revolution on March 15, 1848.[71] He was buried in a mass grave, but had predicted his own self-sacrifice in a short aphoristic poem, a national appellation to all Hungarians destined to outlive him and earn for him an international (and somewhat misleading) reputation among European romantics as an individualist:

> Love and Liberty
> Are all the world for me!
> For love I'd sacrifice
> My life on every day,
> For freedom I would give
> My very love away![72]

As political tensions mounted from the 1840s with the rise of a strong nationalist movement in Hungary, so too did reports of suicides—a curious phenomenon. As we have seen, while the actual rate of recorded suicides remained relatively low in the eighteenth century, Hungarian bureaucrats took a keen interest in recording accurate statistics in the 1830s and 1840s. If these statistics accurately reflect the rates, then a massive explosion of suicides must have occurred around the time of the failed revolution of 1848, just as the fatalism of *honfibú* was inscribed as a bourgeois ethos on the new national consciousness during the repressive regime of the Hapsburg-appointed minister, Alexander Bach. Even if the apparent increase in suicides that began in the mid-nineteenth century can be attributed partly or even wholly to better records or more thorough investigations, the shared culture of self-sacrifice still explains why reported rates were higher in Hungary than in other countries. The emphasis on the group at the expense of the individual removed incentives of survivors to cover up a suicide and lessen the reluctance of officials to classify a death as self-inflicted. Ultimately, the fascination of populist poets with historical self-sacrifice in the face of insurmountable odds left an indelible mark on Hungarian society, embedding the pessimism and fatalism of *honfibú* in its linguistic, literary, and iconographic heritage.

Symbols celebrating self-sacrifice are still highly visible throughout Hungary. One poignant example is a bronze relief inlaid in the wall of the Servite Church in Pest (see Figure 10—note the commemorative wreath bearing the Hungarian national tricolor, which celebrates the 1956 uprising). The plaque, commissioned in the 1920s, represents a Hungarian Hussar from the army of the dual monarchy fighting in the Great War. Mortally wounded, he leans precariously from his saddle only to be scooped up into the outstretched arm of Jesus, who reaches down from the cross and delivers the fallen warrior directly into heaven. This modern icon of selfless martyrdom and apotheosis is hauntingly reminiscent of Zrínyi's sacrifice four centuries prior. In 1956, Hungary witnessed yet an-

Figure 10. Istók János, Plaque Commemorating the Wilhelm Hussar Regiment, 1930, Servite Church, Martinelli tér, Pest. Photograph by David Lederer.

other in its long history of desperate uprisings against insurmountable odds which ended, like all past struggles, in bloodshed and failure. A monument to this tragic event can be found today in the central cemetery of Budapest, where the bodies of protesters were disposed of anonymously. In 1989–1990, as communism collapsed in Hungary, the bodies of leaders of the uprising, such as those of Imre Nagy and Pal Maléter, were exhumed and reburied. The remains of countless others who could not be identified were carefully gathered piece-by-piece and laid to rest near a bronze plaque, which bears the inscription *"Gloria victis"* — glory to the victims, the inversion of the ancient Roman saying, *"Vae victis"* — pain to the victims.[73] The precise effects of communism on rates of suicide are difficult to gauge. While precision record-keeping by the Demographic Research Institute of the Central Statistical Office achieved the status of a hard science under the socialist dictatorship, high suicide statistics remained a nagging contradiction to the ideal of a worker's paradise. Perhaps this is hardly surprising when one considers that the Hungarian populist tradition was revived in pragmatic alliance with the People's Republic even as bourgeois nationalism gave way to socialist equality under Soviet occupation.[74] Although suicide rates dropped slightly in reaction to the Stalinist terror, they soon returned to their former heights.

After an initial jump during the social upheaval of the perestroika era, more recent statistics indicate that suicide rates are on the course of a gradual decline in Hungary; a welcome trend, perhaps signaling either the real arrival of Western individualism in Hungarian society, a new-found sense of international security as Hungary stands poised to take its place in the European Union, or a popular willingness to break with the past and embrace globalization. Perhaps Hungarians have indeed hoisted a new flag to rally around. Still, rates remain extraordinarily high relative to the rest of the world, both in absolute terms and in the gender ratio of male to female suicides. Sociological factors alone, such as poverty and alcoholism, can only go so far in explaining this phenomenon, for Hungary is hardly unique in these concerns.

The purpose of this essay has been to examine the historical problem of suicide as another relevant factor. The stories and legends of heroic self-sacrifice originated in the medieval and early modern periods, initially representing a male ethos for aristocratic warriors. They were transformed by romantics into an equally male national ethos disseminated by bourgeois populists in the fatalistic spirit of *honfibú* through poetry and art. This romantic ethos of nineteenth-century Hungary was decidedly communalistic rather than individualistic. By the twentieth century, it had become an important symbol of the Hungarian cultural tradition. One could locate the origins of this tradition in the common linguistic denominator, or in the obscurities of an Altaic Ur-culture, or in its reawakening as a moral force against the Turkish invasions, or in an Ottomanization of the Hungarian population during two centuries of occupation, or simply in an anthropological reaction, a functional defense mechanism aimed at group self-preservation through the sacrifice of the individual. Whatever myth of origin one chooses, this tradition is an enduring perception of Hungarian history.

I experienced this personally during a presentation of interim findings to a group of university students in Debrecen in 1998. Throughout my detailed presentation of medieval and early modern legends, the students were perceptibly amused by my self-assurance at having uncovered something new. When I asked a colleague why, he reminded me that there was no need for a pedant to explain these ancient legends to Hungarians; they all learned them at their mothers' breasts. However, a subsequent question put to the group at the conclusion of the lecture was greeted by a different reaction. When asked how many knew of someone close to them who had committed suicide, the raising of all-too-numerous hands evinced noticeable discomfort and rekindled their interest in the plausibility of the connection. Their reactions, in turn, convinced me of its potential significance, thereby prompting the present essay. Obviously, an historical understanding alone is no panacea for high rates of suicide, but the historical problem of suicide in Hungary seems to offer at least one instance where historians can and should lend a hand, despite their customary reluctance for proactive posturing. For, as this analysis ultimately suggests, perceptions of history can be very deadly indeed.

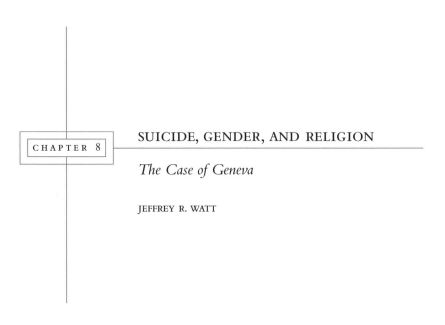

SUICIDE, GENDER, AND RELIGION

The Case of Geneva

JEFFREY R. WATT

An independent state from 1536 to 1798, the Republic of Geneva was a vitally important arena for both the Protestant Reformation and the Enlightenment. These two radically different cultural movements inform the traditional belief that early modern Europe witnessed developments toward secularism and rationalism, as religion's influence on culture gradually declined. Nowhere should this be more apparent than in the attitudes toward and the frequency of suicide. While Christian thinkers since the patristic period aggressively condemned "self-murder," many sociological studies portray suicide as rife in modern Western societies, a phenomenon sometimes blamed on declining religious values.[1] Using Geneva as a case-study, this chapter analyzes suicide and its relationship to changing religious mores, paying special attention to whether there existed a suicide gender gap typical of modern Western societies, where men consistently kill themselves in much greater numbers than women.[2]

This chapter includes a close examination of the frequency of suicide, an analysis that probably cannot be duplicated for any other area of premodern Europe. Legal records and death registers for other early modern polities are generally too spotty and inconsistent to undertake a social history of suicide.[3] This study's statistical element is possible because it concentrates on one small state whose archival sources are incredibly rich and most accessible thanks to a vast series of indices and inventories. Considered a crime, suicide was subject to criminal proceedings, and these investigations provide detailed accounts of the circumstances surrounding these untimely deaths. The Auditeurs or police officers in charge of these inquests were interested not only in determining whether a death was self-inflicted but also in establishing the motives for taking one's life.[4] Though some of these criminal investigations have been lost for the sixteenth and seventeenth centuries, they are fully extant for the 1700s. Also important are the registers of the Small Council, which, serving as the chief tribunal, heard the Auditeurs' reports and passed sentences. I have consulted the Council's records, fully extant for the life of the Republic, for every death that could possibly have been self-inflicted. Finally, Geneva's rich death records are vitally important. For every death in the city of Geneva, a surgeon examined the body and recorded the name, age, profession, and political status of the deceased; the date, hour, and place of death; and, most important for this study, a brief description of the cause of death. Well over 100,000 deaths are recorded from 1549, the date of the first extant register, through the demise of the Republic in 1798. These death records have few lacunae—none after 1616—and provide most reliable evidence on the total number of unnatural deaths and make a statistical study of suicide possible.

It is important to note that this study is not based on official statistics on suicide similar to those examined by Emile Durkheim, the giant who still towers above all others in the sociological study of suicide.[5] Critics avow that official statistics are unreliable, insisting that some coroners are much more likely than others to declare certain deaths self-inflicted, a view that Genevan records tend to corroborate.[6] In fact, my conclusions are not necessarily those of early modern officials. During these two hundred fifty years, some magistrates were quite reticent, in spite of overwhelming evidence, to declare a death self-inflicted. An excellent example involved a young man who died in April 1704 after some bitter disputes with his mother. The body was found hanging by the neck with a rope in a second-story room that was locked from the inside and in which there was no sign of a struggle. Although magistrates deemed the evidence inconclusive, I have labeled this death a suicide.[7]

Using commonsense criteria in analyzing these various sources for the years 1536–1798, I have identified 404 deaths, among the total of 3,668 unnatural deaths, that were beyond a reasonable doubt suicides.[8] The quantity of unnatural death cases is large enough to provide some meaningful statistical analysis, but small enough to allow a very close examination of all the individual cases. Most striking is that though suicide was rare through the seventeenth century, Geneva experienced an explosion in suicides after 1750—almost three fourths of suicides (288 of 404) occurred after 1750, reaching a crescendo in 1781–1798 when 160 Genevans took their lives. The Republic's modest population growth cannot explain the more than fivefold increase in suicides from the first to the second half of the eighteenth century. The figures for the 1780s and 1790s correspond to a high annual suicide rate (per 100,000 inhabitants) of 34.4 while that for the first half of the century was 5.2.[9] These suicide rates of course should not be taken to indicate the absolute frequency with which Genevans took their lives but rather as a barometer to demonstrate the dramatic upswing in suicides in the late 1700s. For comparative purposes, in 1990 official figures put the suicide rate at 12.6 for the United States, 21 for France (the highest rate among the seven largest industrialized powers), and 7.4 for the United Kingdom.[10]

This increase cannot be dismissed as simply the result of more accurate record keeping or more aggressive investigations in the late eighteenth century. The criminal procedures were the same as those established in Reformation Geneva, and records are fully extant from the mid-seventeenth century. Moreover, contemporaries certainly perceived that suicide was becoming more common in Geneva. Members of the Small Council expressed alarm already in 1758, as did the Consistory, a type of morals court, in 1774.[11] Voltaire wrote in a letter in 1767 that Genevans were more melancholic than the English and, he believed, that there were proportionally more suicides in Geneva than in London.[12] In May 1773, Pierre-Michel Hennin, the French Resident in Geneva, wrote to his compatriot, the Duke of Aiguillon, that suicide was actually admired in Geneva and that more suicides occurred in that city than anywhere else. In a reply, Aiguillon concurred, blaming Genevans' penchant for suicide on their pride and idleness.[13] If we are to believe the accounts of contemporaries, other areas of Europe experienced an increase in self-inflicted deaths in the late eighteenth century.[14]

Geneva's increase also cannot be attributed to the important changes in the judicial treatment of suicide that occurred during the course of the early modern period. In Reformation Geneva, as elsewhere, magistrates could be quite harsh in dealing with suicides, not only denying them funerary honors but often confiscating their goods and desecrating their corpses by having them dragged through the streets on a hurdle or impaled and left exposed. Apart from a handful of isolated cases, however, sentences that went beyond the denial of funerary honors fell into disuse in the mid-seventeenth century. If the previous corporal and financial penalties had effectively deterred the suicidal from taking their lives or incited survivors to cover up family members' self-inflicted deaths, then the increase in suicides should have begun decades earlier than it actually did. It is also important to note that the late eighteenth century witnessed increases not only in suicides but also in homicides, accidents, and even questionable unnatural deaths. These last three, however, rose at a much more modest rate than the increase in suicides. Had trends in suicide rates gone in the opposite direction from these forms of unnatural deaths, then one might well suspect whether some deaths, which were really self-inflicted, might formerly have been listed as accidents or homicides but were now more likely to be declared suicides. The fact that all types of unnatural deaths were on the rise after 1750 militates against a decline in cover-ups. Moreover, the success of cover-ups would have been highly unlikely in Geneva's tight-knit, closely regulated society.[15]

Interestingly, the era that marked the explosion in suicides in Geneva also saw the birth of a significant gender gap, so typical of modern Western societies, in self-inflicted deaths. For the entire early modern period, men outnumbered women among suicides by over two to one (275 men and 129 women). For the two centuries up to 1750, however, males comprised just 56 percent of suicides, and men outnumbered women among suicides by only 28 to 26 in the first half of the eighteenth century.[16] After 1750, by contrast, men comprised about three-fourths the suicides (210 of 288). When the suicide rate reached its peak in the 1780s and 1790s, years that were plagued by economic and political crises, men represented 122 of 160 self-inflicted deaths.

What changes may have accounted for either the explosion in voluntary deaths or the change in the male/female ratio for suicides? Sociological studies have offered a host of explanations for the gender gap, some of which are quite unsatisfactory. Durkheim claimed to reject all nonsocial factors—such as those pertaining to race, climate, biology—in determining variations in suicide rates. In explaining the different rates between men and women, however, he apparently embraced biological determinism: "Women's sexual needs have less of a mental character because, generally speaking, her mental life is less developed. These needs are more closely related to the needs of the organism, following rather than leading them, and consequently find in them an efficient restraint. Being a more instinctive creature than man, woman has only to follow her instincts to find calmness and peace."[17] Today, no scholar seriously believes that women are less prone to kill themselves because they are more dominated by biological instincts than are men.

Among other possible factors, perhaps the method chosen to take one's life might have an impact on different suicide rates for men and women. Studies on modern suicide show that while men are apt to choose very lethal methods, such as shooting themselves, women are more likely to take poison or try to drown themselves, methods which are less likely to be fatal.[18] The evidence from Geneva suggests that greater access to firearms was indeed a factor in both the huge growth in self-inflicted deaths and in the widening gender gap in suicides in the late eighteenth century. Death records reveal that 400 people died from gunshot wounds in Geneva during times of peace from the sixteenth through the eighteenth centuries. Of these, 180 (45 percent) died after 1750, 112 of whom (almost two-thirds) were clearly suicides. By comparison only 148 people had died in Geneva from gunshot wounds—be they the victims of murders, accidents, or suicides—in the previous century (1651–1750), a period for which there are no lacunae in the death records. Significantly all 112 of these post-1750 suicides were men. Indeed only one woman took her life by shooting herself during the entire early modern period, a reflection in part of men's greater familiarity with firearms.

Firearms were surely more available in the late eighteenth century than ever before. Men who were citizens, only about a fifth of the males residing in Geneva, were required to maintain arms to ensure the security of the Republic. Postmortem inventories regularly indicate that men possessed muskets or rifles, which they passed on to their sons. While the old arms were inherited, newer, more efficient weapons were being made. Genevans' demand for arms was sufficient to support seven full-time gunsmiths in 1788, a time when the city and dependent territories numbered fewer than 30,000 souls.[19] Largely out of fear of armed uprisings by noncitizens, eighteenth-century Genevan authorities made serious efforts to control the ownership of weapons, issuing about forty edicts against the unauthorized possession of firearms, swords, and daggers.[20] The fact that authorities of the late eighteenth century repeatedly passed such mandates suggests that firearms were more of a problem as they became more prevalent. More important, the large number of deaths by gunshot in the late 1700s shows that magistrates had little success in keeping unauthorized arms out of the hands of the residents of Geneva.

Still, firearms alone can explain neither the explosion nor the widening gender gap in suicides. After 1750, 176 individuals ended their lives using some method other than firearms, a figure that easily surpasses the total number of recorded suicides (116), including those involving firearms, for the previous two centuries. Moreover, after 1750, men still outnumbered women among suicides by a substantial margin (98 to 78), even if we exclude all suicides by firearms.

Suicidologists have suggested that social mores concerning masculinity and femininity help explain why more men kill themselves. According to Jean Baechler, the social image of the male is characterized by "an exaggeration of strength and a denial of dependence." This latter characteristic may impede men who are depressed from seeking consolation from others. Men may deem showing their emotions as unmanly and thus have no safety valve for their frustrations, ultimately finding solace only through death. Moreover, Baechler argues that aggressiveness—be it against oneself or others—is the province of males, based on education, social custom, and physiology.[21]

These explanations may indeed be partly valid for Geneva in the late 1700s. Though very detailed, the postmortem investigations do not provide enough information to generalize whether men were more prone than women to suppress their fears and frustrations until they reached the breaking point. But if this were a principal cause of the difference in suicide rates, one still must explain why Genevan males and females killed themselves in equal numbers in the first half of the eighteenth century. No evidence suggests that social mores governing gender roles changed noticeably in Geneva during the course of the 1700s. Similarly, if physiology were a key determining factor behind male aggression, how can one explain the parity between male and female suicides before 1750?[22]

Another argument for the suicide gender gap is that women have tradition-ally been more fully absorbed into the family and benefit more from the immu-nity that the family allegedly offers. Social scientists have long recognized that strong emotional support from one's family is one of the best prophylactics against suicide. Marriage may serve as a means of integration and thus protec-tion from social isolation, commonly cited as a cause of suicide, and as a source of regulation: before contemplating suicide, a married person must consider the impact on the spouse. Many sociologists argue that parenthood doubles the im-munity to suicide offered by marriage, especially for women: concerns for one's children reportedly deter mothers more than fathers from taking their lives.[23]

The evidence from Geneva shows that single people were in fact overrepre-sented and married people underrepresented among suicides. This trend held true, however, for both men and women, as women comprised about a third of all suicides and about a third of those who were married. Moreover, the findings from Geneva contradict the contention that parenthood offered more immunity to suicide than marriage for both women and men. If motherhood actually de-terred suicide, then one should find many childless women among married sui-cides. In reality, after 1750, married women with children were slightly more likely to kill themselves than married women without children. Although fathers were more numerous than mothers among suicides, women comprised almost exactly the same proportion of those who left legitimate children as of suicides in general.

A stereotype has also existed that men generally kill themselves because of mundane reversals, such as financial problems, while female suicide is more of-ten motivated by emotional reasons, such as unrequited love. According to this reasoning, male suicide generally results from the dangers inherent in men's re-sponsibilities and roles, while females take their lives when they deviate from their culturally assigned roles of wives and mothers.[24] In early modern Geneva, how-ever, men made up the large majority, roughly equal to their share of suicides in general, of those suicides that were allegedly motivated by problems related to the family. Men comprised 69.3 percent of the eighty-eight suicides that were motivated by the death of a loved one, romantic misadventure, marital break-down, generational conflicts, and other issues related to the family. In short, ev-idence on the marital and parental status of suicides does not suffice to explain the gender gap in the late 1700s.[25]

Just as suicides increase during economic depressions in modern Western so-cieties,[26] so the explosion in suicides and the contemporary widening gender gap were strongly affected by the economic crisis that plagued Geneva in the last two decades of the eighteenth century. Evidence from Geneva indicates that men were much more apt than women to commit suicide because of poverty or fi-nancial reversals. Although female suicides were proportionally poorer than their male counterparts—while a little over a third of male suicides were clearly poor, fully half the females were—of the fifty-eight suicides motivated by financial problems (forty-eight after 1750), only ten were women. Though often poor, most female suicides generally were not killing themselves directly because of their poverty. True, the servant Marie Pernette Etier, twenty-five, drowned herself in 1747 after her master accused her of stealing from him.[27] Another servant, Françoise Dupont, twenty-two, was pregnant for the second time when she drowned herself in the Rhône River in January 1779.[28] While these young women were of very modest means and risked facing more abject poverty, financial reversals weighed most heavily on those who had at one time enjoyed the prospects of making a comfortable living.

Since they had only limited economic opportunities both before and after 1750, female wage-earners were less likely to experience as dramatic a drop in income as their male counterparts. The experiences of watchmakers were especially noteworthy. Watchmaking was eighteenth-century Geneva's most lucrative artisanal industry, employing over a fourth of Geneva's male work force. In 1785, however, watchmaking suffered a severe crisis that lasted into the nineteenth century.[29] Thereafter, male watchmakers committed suicide in disproportionately large numbers. While watchmaking employed 28.4 percent of Geneva's male work force in both 1788 and 1798,[30] after 1780 those employed in the various stages of watchmaking comprised 34.2 percent of the male suicides whose occupation is known. In other words, suicides among watchmakers were 20.4 percent more common than their importance in the work force would have dictated. For some watchmakers, a difficult situation was made worse by technological change, which rendered obsolete certain skills. Before shooting himself in 1787, the watchmaker Pierre Dombre wrote a number of letters explaining his action. He complained, among other things, that the switches he made for watches had become obsolete, replaced by "rollers" which he did not know how to make. Unemployed and bemoaning his recent poverty, Dombre said that he had neither the courage nor the will to learn a new trade.[31] He and other watchmakers had acquired knowledge and skills through lengthy apprenticeships and years of work. Having enjoyed the best standard of living of all Genevan artisans, they suffered from frustrated expectations and had trouble coping with the reduced opportunities in the trade in which they had invested so much of themselves.

Genevan women did not share these sentiments. In Geneva, as elsewhere in early modern Europe, women generally did not identify themselves with a particular occupation. Female work identity tended to be weak in part because they usually received little formal training. Unlike male artisans, Genevan women generally did not learn their skills through formal apprenticeships and were not members of guilds. Women in Geneva never enjoyed the prospects of being master artisans or performing the most highly paid jobs. They were also invariably paid less than men even when performing the same work, rarely earning more than half the wages of their male counterparts.[32] In early modern Europe, the labor, be it paid or unpaid, of both married and unmarried women most often served to bolster the family economy. While the family life cycle had little impact on men's work, women's work depended to a considerable extent on their marital status and on the number and ages of their children. Consequently, women had to be flexible in regard to work, changing their work habits to adapt to different stages in their lives, to the needs of their families, and to changes in market conditions. For these reasons, early modern women identified themselves much more with their families or neighborhoods than with a particular line of work.[33]

Since women's professional expectations were lower, they were less likely to be disappointed and reacted quite differently from male artisans to economic reversals. Even though women comprised up to 30 percent of those employed in Genevan watchmaking, generally restricted to the less prestigious and more poorly paid tasks,[34] none of the twenty-one women who took their lives from 1785 on worked in watchmaking. Simply put, men enjoyed far more opportunities for economic success than women, but they accordingly were much more likely to suffer loss of status and economic reward and had many more reasons to feel like failures.

These findings bring to mind a number of sociological studies on twentieth-century suicide which show an important connection between work failure and high suicide rates among males. Changes in the labor market had a direct bearing on the suicide rates for males but far less impact on the frequency with which women killed themselves. As in early modern Europe, women in twentieth-century Western societies were often restricted to low-status, low-wage jobs which did not foster strong job identification. As a result, work failure or job loss generally did not produce the same feelings of failure as they did for men.[35]

Among married couples in early modern Geneva, the husband was invariably expected to be the principal breadwinner. Consequently, men were more likely than women to feel they had failed to provide for their families. True, various studies have shown that early modern women, as those who actually put food on the table, often initiated grain riots.[36] From the seventeenth century on, however, Genevans never ran the risk of starvation. The Republic of Geneva established *La Chambre des Blés* in 1628, which effectively stockpiled grains and intervened in times of crisis to assure that Geneva's population could be fed.[37] Of course a family could be adequately fed yet still suffer from abject poverty. In such cases it was the father who most suffered guilt feelings. Four men committed suicide in the turbulent years of 1789–1794 specifically because they felt they had failed as providers. A former baker, Jean Marc Champury, 35, committed suicide in September 1793, explaining in a note that he could no longer endure seeing his wife and four children suffer.[38] In general, men who were married and had dependent children were especially prone to take their lives because of poverty—though the majority of all suicides was unmarried, only a third of the men who took their lives directly because of poverty were bachelors. Since married women's labor was intended to supplement their husbands' income, they felt less guilty if their family lived in poverty.

As the last two decades of the eighteenth century witnessed political as well as economic crisis, one might expect to find many suicides that were politically motivated, just as France witnessed a large number of suicides among political leaders in the Revolutionary period.[39] The Republic of Geneva had been ruled by an oligarchy, the bourgeoisie, admission to which had become increasingly restrictive and expensive. The foreign-born *habitants* and Genevan-born *natifs* were legal residents who did not enjoy citizenship. Members of these groups agitated for change in the 1780s and 1790s and succeeded in overthrowing the Old Regime in December 1792, extending citizenship to all males who previously had been simply residents. The peak year for suicide throughout the early modern period was, not coincidentally, 1793, the first year of the democratic regime, when seventeen people, all men, took their lives. Was this surge in suicide a result of members of the former bourgeoisie despairing over losing their privileged status? For the most part, no. Of these seventeen, only six had enjoyed citizenship before the Revolution. As they made up about a fifth of the population but a third of the suicides for this year, the ex-members of the bourgeoisie evidently were somewhat more prone to suicide during those twelve months than members of other former political rubrics. But most suicides for that year were precisely those who in theory benefited most from the Revolution: the former *natifs* and *habitants*.

How then do we explain that more suicides were committed in the first twelve months of the new regime than in any other year in early modern Geneva? If we trust the descriptions of motives in the criminal investigations, only a handful of suicides appeared to be even partially motivated by politics. The suicide of 1793 that was most clearly politically inspired was entirely independent of Genevan political events: a Frenchman shot himself because he was upset about events back home; in a suicide note, he said that he was "going to join Cato" and complained bitterly about the Jacobin dictatorship and the Reign of Terror.[40] Indeed only one suicide of the 1790s involved a member of the bourgeoisie who was explicitly motivated to take his life by the advent of democracy in Geneva. George Charles Boin, 44, shot himself in October 1792, leaving a suicide note in which he complained, "Having been heartbroken several times upon learning of the cruel atrocities committed since the reign of modern philosophy and seeing this terrible spectacle drawing near to our dear country, I had neither the strength nor the courage to tolerate being a passive eyewitness to such cruelties."[41]

Although the increase in self-inflicted deaths in the late 1700s affected all classes of people, socioeconomic and political factors help explain why suicide became increasingly a male phenomenon at this time. The events preceding and immediately following the Revolution of December 1792 caused much disruption in Geneva. Combined with an economic crisis that continued unabated, the Revolution nurtured a certain angst that cut across political and class lines. Even if for the most part people were not killing themselves specifically because of the fall of the Old Regime or the advent of democracy, they were disturbed by the tumultuous times in which they lived and concerned about their finances and the futures of their children. Men alone were political actors in the Republic of Geneva, and the economic turmoil affected most adversely artisans who had heretofore enjoyed a certain affluence. During this period of political and economic instability, the well-being of most women depended in large part on the fortunes or misfortunes of their husbands and fathers. While the political and economic downturn certainly affected the lives of Genevan women directly, they were psychologically better able to cope with it than their male counterparts.

Regardless of the status of their husbands and fathers, women themselves had no political voice either before or after 1792. At no point were the political rights of women an issue in these conflicts; Geneva produced no Mary Wollstonecraft, and its female inhabitants never threatened or even seriously questioned the male bastions of political and economic privileges. As was often the case in early modern Europe, even when women were actively involved in popular protests—as they certainly were in the Genevan unrest—they generally were not agitating for the rights of women.[42] The absence of feminist revolutionary activists surely explains why Genevan male insurgents saw little need to embrace the aggressive antifeminism in contemporary France, where Jacobins shut down women's clubs and silenced female revolutionaries in October 1793.[43] Simply put, no evidence indicates that women rebelled against the political and economic limitations placed on their sex in Geneva. As a result, while they undoubtedly shared the hopes and fears of male family members, political setbacks weighed less on Genevan women than on their husbands and fathers. In this age of patriarchy, men had more to win and more to lose politically and economically. All told, the political and especially the economic developments of the late 1700s contributed in an important way to the huge increase in self-inflicted deaths and the widening gender gap among suicides.

Though important, the political and economic crises alone cannot explain the explosion in suicides of the late eighteenth century. Genevans had experienced a severe economic downturn a century earlier, as the area around Geneva and western Europe in general suffered serious famines in the 1690s.[44] At that time, the cost of wheat skyrocketed in Geneva, increasing by about 150 percent in a matter of months in 1693. Aggravating the situation was the presence, ever since the Revocation of the Edict of Nantes in 1685, of large numbers of refugees from

France. To make matters worse, the most dynamic part of Geneva's economy in the latter seventeenth century—the manufacture of gilded braids and trimmings—went through a very difficult period beginning in 1690. From that date the huge German market was effectively closed to Genevan gilded articles, a reprisal for Geneva's allegedly favoring Louis XIV in his war against the Holy Roman Empire.[45] In spite of the economic dire straits, only one Genevan committed suicide during this crisis: a woman from an affluent, prestigious family, who drowned herself in a state of delirium in January 1699. Clearly her suicide was not provoked by food shortages or poverty.[46]

Ultimately, the appearance of growing numbers of suicides for financial reasons after 1750 reflected cultural change, having more to do with changing mores than with economic downturns or poverty per se. Poverty is likely to be a motive for suicide only in highly developed capitalistic societies. In an underdeveloped society where poverty is ubiquitous, few would likely be pushed to end their lives as a result of their material status. In a capitalistic society, however, the loss of money can bring with it a loss of political power, prestige, and self-esteem.[47] By 1750 Geneva had certainly attained a much higher level of commercial development and greater overall wealth than ever before. In addition to watchmaking, late-eighteenth-century Geneva was home to some of the most successful bankers of Europe; it served as a distribution center for goods from all over the world; and it was one of the most important centers for the production of printed cloth. Moreover, the eighteenth-century economic boom brought with it the concentration of great sums of wealth in the hands of certain Genevans who were not averse to indulging in conspicuous consumption that would have violated the sumptuary laws of earlier periods.[48] As the gap between the rich and the poor increased and as Genevan society became more materialistic, individuals were less willing to tolerate poverty. Higher material expectations were more difficult to fulfill, and the increasing difficulty in realizing aspirations provoked dissatisfaction and helped fuel suicidal tendencies.

Perhaps cultural developments also effected changes in attitudes toward suicide in the eighteenth century. From the time of Augustine, whose unequivocal condemnation of suicide had a profound impact on Western attitudes toward voluntary death, thinkers who defended the right to take one's life were few and far between prior to the eighteenth century. Calvin gave little thought to "self-murder," writing at length about it only twice—in two sermons Calvin categorically condemned self-murder primarily because it was a rebellion against God, a refusal to submit to God's will. He further asserted that it was evil because it was unnatural and resulted from diabolical possession. These views aptly reflected contemporary attitudes toward suicide shared by the elite and common folk, clergy and laity, Protestants and Catholics. He wrote so little on suicide largely because it was a nonissue—in effect everyone agreed that it was wrong. True, inspired by Stoicism, Montaigne and Pierre Charron made moderate defenses of suicide in the late sixteenth and early seventeenth centuries, and John Donne made a more radical defense of suicide which was published posthumously in 1647.[49] These, however, were isolated voices.

Only in the eighteenth century did anything resembling a debate on suicide occur. Many philosophes, such as Voltaire and Montesquieu, defended the right to take one's life under certain circumstances, provided one acted rationally. The most emphatic defense of suicide came from the Scottish philosopher David Hume, who claimed the rational person had the right to end his or her life and insisted that suicide was not a crime.[50] The philosophes had a great admiration for some of antiquity's "heroic" suicides, such as Cato, the defender of the Roman Republic who took his life rather than submit to the rule of Julius Caesar, and literary and theatrical works of the eighteenth century portrayed many suicides in a sympathetic light.[51] Moreover, Enlightened writers unanimously condemned the traditional penalties against suicide, decrying the desecration of corpses and the confiscation of goods of those who took their lives as inhumane and utterly useless.[52]

Could it be that through their writings, the philosophes were, wittingly or unwittingly, helping unleash suicidal tendencies that Christian moralists had effectively restrained for over a millennium? Some contemporaries certainly thought so. Critics in France bemoaned a dramatic increase in suicides in that country beginning in the 1760s, which they blamed on "Anglomania" and on the secular values of the philosophes. In spite of such rhetoric, however, the philosophes cannot be viewed as advocates of suicide. A host of eighteenth-century thinkers never shared this enthusiasm for suicide. Echoing Aristotle, several viewed suicide as a rejection of one's responsibilities toward society. Though deploring the traditional penalties levied against suicide, Delisle de Sales and Diderot, the likely author of the *Encyclopédie*'s article on suicide which was quite critical of voluntary death, emphasized these responsibilities and maintained that killing oneself is an egocentric act without regard to the harm inflicted on others. Similarly, eighteenth-century Geneva's most famous son, Jean-Jacques Rousseau, was at best ambivalent in regard to suicide. Though admiring Cato and conceding that suicide by the terminally ill may be excusable, Rousseau offered in *La Nouvelle Héloïse* (1761) a strong argument against the right to end one's life voluntarily. Basically he believed that life is worth living and that obligations to others must not be shirked. The most important eighteenth-century critic was the German idealist Immanuel Kant, who condemned suicide under all circumstances, deeming self-inflicted deaths as a violation of nature that was intrinsically immoral to others and especially to oneself.[53]

Even if the philosophes did not promote suicide, the Enlightenment might have contributed to a decline in religious beliefs and practices. Sociologists have long recognized the protection against suicide that strong religious beliefs provide. Religion can offer both social integration and regulation of behavior, serving as a source of both authority and solace.[54]

One deficiency with many sociological studies on the impact of religion on suicide is that they pay scant attention to the content of religious beliefs. Durkheim generally believed that religion deterred suicide more as a means of integrating individuals through shared beliefs than as a source of life-sustaining ideas. He claimed, for example, that Catholics committed suicide less often than Protestants not because of doctrinal differences but because Catholics formed a much more tightly integrated religious community.[55] Religion, like marriage and parenthood, can reduce suicide through subordination of the individual to a collective body. The content of religious faith, however, can be very important with respect to suicide. A belief in an afterlife can effectively serve as a prophylactic against suicide. Like the biblical Job, the believer may suffer hardships in this life yet persevere out of the belief that these afflictions are part of a divine plan and that eternal happiness awaits those who endure adversity. Moreover, as Christianity has often glorified poverty, religion can provide a moral status to rival mundane prestige: a person who lives in misery can take solace in being morally rich.[56]

During the course of the early modern period, Genevans' religious convictions and, concomitantly, their attitudes toward suicide changed dramatically. Residents of Calvin's Geneva were very much concerned with the devil. Although belief in Satan predated the Reformation by centuries, the sixteenth century witnessed the growing "demonization" of the world. Never before had the devil seemed so powerful and menacing, capable of assuming an ever increasing variety of forms. Many theologians from the Reformation era, both Protestant and Catholic, thought that "melancholy" and other mental infirmities resulted directly from diabolical possession. Insanity could also be a cause rather than a consequence of demon possession since the devil supposedly thrived in the bodies of melancholic people.[57]

The view that suicide was linked to demonic temptation was widespread and is aptly seen in Genevan judicial proceedings from the sixteenth and early seventeenth centuries. At that time, religious leaders, judicial authorities, and common folk all shared the belief that suicide was caused by diabolical possession or temptation. As noted in the Introduction to this volume, the simple farmer Jean Jourdain associated voluntary death with the devil when he stabbed himself in a forest in 1555. Before dying of his wounds, Jourdain admitted to authorities that, when he was in the woods, he had asked the devil to come kill him. Although he heard no voice in response and the devil did not assist him in cutting short his life, Jourdain's testimony reveals that even suicidal people believed "self-murder" was under the purview of the devil.[58]

The rather wealthy Elisabeth Paschal, who had been mentally deranged for several weeks before committing suicide in November 1625, believed she was possessed. Often incoherent, Paschal repeatedly said she felt possessed by demons. A witness reported that several days before her death Paschal declared that "the evil spirit wanted to make her kill herself and she prayed to God to protect her from it." One evening, after reading from the Bible, Paschal managed to jump out an upper-story window to her death. A fascinating document in this criminal proceeding is a report made by Dr. Dauphin, a physician who made numerous house calls over a period of months. In treating her "melancholy," Dauphin resembled more a pastor than a physician, praying with her and asking her to think of God. On one occasion, Dauphin led her in reciting the Lord's Prayer, and Paschal had trouble getting past the words "lead us not into temptation." When asked why, she replied that the devil was trying to prevent her from praying. Dauphin concluded that God allowed some people to behave in such a bizarre way that the ills of their souls could not be cured. These cases might be initiated by avarice or some other sin, which produced a corporal illness as "the melancholy humor took root and through its vapor . . . took over the brain."[59] Paschal herself was convinced that the devil possessed her; Dauphin at least agreed that sin was the root cause of her mental illness and seemed to imply that it was divinely rather than diabolically inspired. Although the devil is not mentioned in every investigation of suicides in Reformation Geneva, evidence nonetheless shows that authorities and common folk shared the conviction that suicide was of diabolical origin; prayer therefore was the best medicine.

The belief that the devil caused suicide, however, disappeared along with the fear of witchcraft. In 1686 two men believed that God, not demons, had afflicted them with maladies which eventually pushed them to kill themselves. The gardener François Cartier, forty-eight, took his life after suffering from a fever that left him frequently deranged and paranoid. His pastor reported having consoled Cartier many times during his illness and declared that Cartier was a genuine, God-fearing Christian who always resigned himself to the will of God. During lucid moments, Cartier even thanked God for the affliction, always assured of his eternal salvation.[60] Similarly, François Dunand of the rural village of Avully drowned himself in September 1686 after suffering from a serious fever. According to his wife, Dunand had stoically said that he had to accept his illness, as it was God's will. Regardless of whether he actually said these words, her testimony indicates that the proper attitude of the sick was to resign oneself to the will of God, who was responsible for all illnesses.[61]

More important than such subtle changes is the fact that religion thoroughly permeated Genevan society throughout the sixteenth and seventeenth centuries. Armed with the power to excommunicate, the Consistory, created by Calvin himself, effectively ensured that Genevans regularly attended church services and refrained from swearing, dancing, taking part in "popish" rituals, and committing other actions offensive to Reformed morality.[62] Living in a world in which God and demons seemed omnipresent, Genevans supplemented their diligent church attendance with private devotions and scriptural readings in the home. Religious devotions at home and in church were part of the daily routine of Jacques Rigoumier, for example, a wealthy jewelry merchant who took his life in March 1679 after suffering from an unspecified physical illness. On a Friday, Rigoumier, forty-five, went to the morning church service and later asked his servant to let him know when it was time to go to church for afternoon prayers. In her testimony, the servant expressed no surprise at this, thus indicating that it was not unusual for Rigoumier to attend church twice on a weekday. Early that afternoon, he read aloud from the Bible for half an hour in his apartment, a habit that he performed daily. When the servant notified him at 3:30 that it was time for the afternoon prayer service, however, Rigoumier went into his room and fatally shot himself.[63]

What is most striking, however, is that so few Genevans chose death in the sixteenth and seventeenth centuries. True, diligent private devotions, church attendance, and Scripture readings ultimately did not prevent Rigoumier, Paschal, and a handful of others from taking their lives. If commonly followed by Genevans in general, however, such practices would have, one would think, a strong deterring effect on suicide. More important, while the widespread belief in diabolical power led to a witchcraft craze in Reformation Europe, the contemporary view that the devil was responsible for suicide served as one of the most important deterrents to taking one's life. The alternative belief that suffering was divinely inflicted was also a very effective restraint on suicidal proclivities. From Augustine to Calvin and beyond, theologians warned Christians that, like Job, they must bear hardships patiently and never hasten their own end. Though it did not prevent either Cartier or Dunand from taking their lives, this Calvinist emphasis on the judgmental nature of God was enough to discourage most Genevans from voluntarily ending their lives. In short, through the seventeenth century, Calvinist piety served as an important deterrent to suicide, as the fear of both God and the devil fostered an abhorrence of suicide.[64]

A decidedly more secular atmosphere prevailed, however, after 1750. To be sure, eighteenth-century Geneva was still a Reformed republic, and the vast majority of its residents were still self-avowed Protestants. Be that as it may, Calvinism did not pervade the everyday lives of Genevans anywhere near the extent that it had during the Reformation: the Consistory had long lost its ability to require all residents to attend church, and excommunication was no longer an effective means of social control. While many of the most influential thinkers of the sixteenth century were theologians, theology was pushed to the fringe of European thought in the 1700s. Although Geneva had been the city of Calvin in

the Reformation era, it was the city of Rousseau and Voltaire in the Enlightenment. Early modern Geneva witnessed the transformation from a religious culture to a religious faith. By the eighteenth century, religion had become one
aspect of Genevan culture rather than the very basis of its culture, as had been
the case in Calvin's time.[65]

The Reformed faith itself assumed a much more "liberal" character, as Geneva's most prominent pastors and theologians had more in common with pro-
ponents of natural law and the philosophes than with the thought of Calvin.
Jean-Alphonse Turrettini (1637–1737) and Jacob Vernet (1698–1789), professors
of theology at the Genevan Academy, both gave great importance to reason in
defining their religious views. Though rejecting the atheism and deism of various Enlightenment thinkers, Turrettini and Vernet embraced a form of enlightened orthodoxy or natural theology, accepting only those aspects of the Christian
faith that were in accord with reason. Having spent time in Paris, the pastor Vernet was on familiar, if not always friendly, terms with Voltaire, Rousseau, and
Montesquieu. Though he complained about the unbelief of his contemporaries
(for which he held the philosophes partly responsible), Vernet was rather evasive
on the divinity of Jesus and thus ultimately contributed to the unintentional
movement toward deism that had begun among Genevan pastors with Turrettini. By the late 1700s, theologians at the Genevan Academy went so far as to
deny the Trinity and Incarnation, a stand that would have warranted being
burned at the stake in Calvin's time.[66]

Most important with respect to suicide, while Calvin had viewed the devil as
responsible for self-murder, eighteenth-century intellectuals in effect killed Satan. Among the various tenets of Christianity, the belief in the devil, whose existence could not be verified through sense experience, was surely among the
most difficult to reconcile with the new scientific mentality that came to pre-
dominate among eighteenth-century intellectuals. Philosophes saw little need to
attack the notion of Satan since few Christian intellectuals defended the existence of the devil, and many philosophes dismissed hell as merely a thing that
priests had created.[67] Although Calvin delivered few sermons without referring
to Satan, the devil in effect disappeared from the sermons of eighteenth-century
Genevan pastors.[68] Moreover, Vernet and others suggested that an eternal hell
was irreconcilable with the benevolence of God.[69] Also absent in their theology
was the fear of God so prevalent in Calvinist thought, as Vernet and other pastors stressed the benevolent as opposed to the judgmental side of God. As he and
others questioned the traditional belief in an eternal hell, the fear of damnation
obviously declined. Most important, the piety promoted by Geneva's church
leaders of the late 1700s served the religious values of rank-and-file Genevans
much better than did traditional Calvinism.[70]

This changing religious atmosphere was accompanied by changes in attitudes toward suicide among Genevans. By the late eighteenth century, authorities, clergy, and common folk all shared new attitudes toward suicide that were thoroughly secularized and medicalized. In the late 1700s, Genevans of all social levels attributed suicide to mental illness rather than diabolism. Natural explanations for suicide were not altogether new. But, as the Paschal case indicates, into the seventeenth century, witnesses often associated insanity with demon possession. By the eighteenth century, as belief in diabolical power waned, only the natural explanations for suicide remained, as mental illness was stripped of demonic undertones.[71] By the mid-eighteenth century, Geneva had clearly experienced an important "desacralization" of society, whereby people began downplaying the importance of the supernatural, seeking rational or scientific explanations in human affairs and natural phenomena.[72] No longer did anyone attribute suicide to the devil in the 1700s. As the devil was consigned to the dustbins of Genevan history and God became increasingly transcendent and removed from mortals, voluntary death seemed less terrible, even though religious leaders and magistrates still deplored it. The content of religious beliefs and practices, especially with regard to divine judgment and damnation, was fundamentally important in determining the degree to which religion diverted suicidal proclivities. Quite simply, restricting the domain of the supernatural contributed fundamentally to the dramatic increase in suicides in the late 1700s.

Could increasingly secular attitudes also help explain the gender gap with regard to suicide? Perhaps Protestant Geneva experienced a feminization of religion similar to that found in nineteenth-century Catholic France, the seeds of which were sown in the eighteenth century.[73] Could it be, as some scholars have suggested for other periods, that the gender gap in suicide was directly related to the gender gap in education; denied equal access to education, were women less disturbed by "the unsettling influence of independence of thought, the weight of abstract problems of life and death"?[74] According to Durkheim, suicide is higher among the better educated because intellectual development contributes to "the weakening of traditional beliefs" and thus to "the state of moral individualism."[75]

Evidence does indicate that Genevan men enjoyed a higher literacy rate and were better read than women.[76] While Rousseau was merely the most prominent of native Genevan male authors, from the conversion to Protestantism until the nineteenth century, there were no works published by a female author who was both born and raised in Geneva. Unlike their contemporaries in France, Genevan women did not organize any important salons for eloquent conversation and poetry readings.[77] As for reading habits among suicides, from 1779 to 1793, three male apprentices in their late teens, but no females, were inspired to take their lives after reading Goethe's *The Sorrows of Young Werther*.[78] Records further reveal that of those who took their lives, a few men, but no women, ex-

Figure 11. *The Suicide of Werther,* anonymous engraving, undated, Library of Congress, Prints and Photographs Division [reproduction number, LC–USZ62–77670].

pressed religious sentiments that bordered on the deism of many philosophes. A case in point is the suicide of Jean-Jacques Aimé Mellaret, a twenty-two-year-old watchmaker, who shot himself in his room in July 1769. He was an avid reader, as evidenced by the numerous books found on his desk, which included Enlightenment works by writers such as Voltaire. Of greatest interest, however, is Mellaret's own handwritten treatise, "Reflections on Suicide" which is fascinating and, though a bit rambling, even eloquent. A strong religious theme runs throughout this treatise, in which Mellaret defended the taking of one's life. In this work, Mellaret revealed an affinity for Enlightened thought in his celebration of nature. With religious passion, he sang the praises of nature and, like many philosophes, of God as creator of an ordered, beautiful universe. Mellaret was inspired by Enlightenment thought which was strongly tempered by Christianity. With some misgivings about the afterlife, Mellaret concentrated much more on the benevolent than the judgmental side of God, convinced that God's love was greater than his wrath.[79] In short, although Mellaret's values can hardly be described as entirely secular, his religious convictions were far removed from those of Calvin. Similarly, the previously mentioned Pierre Dombre, the watchmaker who was the victim of technological change, wrote a prayer just before shooting himself in June 1787. There was nothing decidedly Christian about this prayer—which was addressed to "God or Heavenly Being," terms that sound vaguely similar to the Cult of the Supreme Being, celebrated a few years later during the French Revolution—and the fear of God was virtually absent.[80] Mellaret and Dombre at least clearly believed in an afterlife, whereas another man who took his life obviously had his doubts. Before shooting himself in 1793, Charles Dalloz, the thirty-five-year-old revolutionary referred to in the Introduction to this volume, wrote to a friend, "If there is anything after death, I will try to inform you about it."[81] Quite simply, the religious convictions of Mellaret, Dombre, or Dalloz would not have offered much of a deterrent to suicide.

For the most part, however, Genevans who committed suicide in the late 1700s were not drawing inspiration directly from Enlightened apologists for suicide, nor were they little philosophes in their own right. In Geneva, as in France, suicide notes that were "enlightened" in tone were in the minority.[82] While a handful of Genevan residents were apparently inspired by the examples of Werther and Cato, the waning of religious deterrents to suicide was a far more significant factor than any positive attraction to voluntary death in the post-1750 explosion of self-inflicted deaths.[83] Similarly, changing religious mores almost surely played a role in the dramatic growth in Geneva of other forms of "aberrant" behavior, as seen in the huge increases after 1750 in the numbers of illegitimate births, abandoned infants, and divorces.[84] Moreover, although no women left suicide notes expressing "Enlightened" religious sentiments, a feminization of religion was at most a minor factor behind the suicide gender gap. The desacralization of Genevan society in the eighteenth century affected virtually everyone, male and female. When intellectuals, judicial authorities, and common folk alike lost their fear of divine wrath and dissociated killing oneself from diabolical temptation, the abhorrence of suicide waned. The most common motives for suicide cited in the late eighteenth century were mental and physical illnesses. While previous generations of Genevans had stoically borne similar afflictions, the decline in the fear of God and the devil made people more vulnerable to suicidal proclivities. Men were more likely to succumb to suicidal tendencies not so much because they were less religious than women; rather, the decline of religious deterrents to suicide simply made them more vulnerable to the wider range of motives they faced. Thus while three-fourths of female suicides were motivated by mental or physical infirmities, less than half the male suicides were motivated by poor health.[85]

In short, the political and economic crises of the late eighteenth century may have been more immediately responsible for both the explosion in suicides and the growing disparity between the numbers of male and female suicides. But the cultural change involving a more secular mentality ultimately played a most decisive role in forming modern attitudes toward and patterns of suicide.

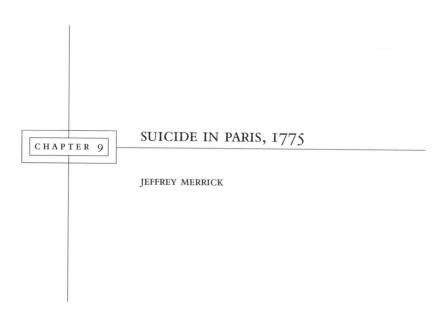

| CHAPTER 9 | SUICIDE IN PARIS, 1775 |

JEFFREY MERRICK

In the last few decades before the Revolution, French subjects disagreed about the causes and legitimacy of suicide, but they agreed that men and women were shooting and drowning themselves in record numbers all around them. The playwright and journalist Louis Sébastien Mercier, who blamed the government for not reducing the burden of taxes and the price of bread, claimed that suicide was more common in Paris than in any other city in the world, that most of its victims lived in attics or furnished rooms, and that as many as a hundred and fifty of those impoverished individuals took their lives every year.[1] The printer and bookseller Siméon Prosper Hardy, who blamed the intellectual leaders of the Enlightenment for undermining traditional values and popularizing English vices, lamented that "examples of suicide multiply daily in our capital" and reported that the lieutenant-general of police had counted a hundred cases in just four months.[2] Since the publication of Albert Bayet's monumental history of debates about the morality of suicide over the centuries, more than a few scholars have quoted Mercier and Hardy, but no one has investigated the epidemic of self-destruction that they deplored.[3] The intellectual history of suicide during the eighteenth century has been written and rewritten, usually as an episode in the ideological confrontations between advocates of Enlightenment and defenders of orthodoxy, but its social history has been largely neglected.[4] This chapter demonstrates that the social history of the subject can be written by using archival sources and provides some sense of what can be done with those sources by analyzing the police reports from one year and juxtaposing them with contemporary texts.

French subjects who killed themselves were supposed to be punished by having their bodies dragged through the streets on a hurdle, hung by the feet in the gallows, and excluded from burial in consecrated ground and by having their property confiscated by the crown. If the magistrates had enforced the laws systematically, it would be possible to locate large numbers of suicides in the records of the Châtelet, the royal court with jurisdiction over the capital, and the Parlement of Paris, the royal appeals court with jurisdiction over a third of the kingdom.[5] Fortunately for suicides then but unfortunately for historians now, the magistrates enforced the laws sporadically and selectively.[6] According to the incomplete but nonetheless useful inventory of cases appealed from the Châtelet and other courts, the Parlement reviewed at least sixteen cases of suicide in the 1770s.[7] They sentenced two soldiers who shot themselves together on Christmas Day 1773 to be hanged but only in effigy.[8] They imposed no posthumous punishments in 1775 and none after 1777. By this time the judges were no longer inclined to subject the bodies of the dead to the public abuse that may have deterred some Parisians from following their example but probably reminded others that there was a way out of lives that seemed worse than death. Instead of enforcing the letter of the law, they routinely embraced the legal fiction that men and women who cut their throats or jumped out windows were at least temporarily out of their minds and therefore not legally responsible for their own deaths.[9]

The judicial records for 1775 do not include any prosecutions for this crime, but *nouvelles,* contemporary collections of news and gossip, do include some accounts of attempted and completed suicide in that year. The *Mémoires secrets,* the most voluminous and informative of these *nouvelles,* mentioned half a dozen cases, only two of which took place in Paris.[10] In one case, a jealous courtesan who poisoned herself in June remarkably survived the attempt and flippantly assured her friends that death was nothing.[11] The *nouvellistes* recounted her story in more detail but with less sympathy than that of the other Parisian suicide, a prosperous and reputable merchant from Bordeaux troubled by kidney stones and domestic problems who shot himself in August just before he was supposed to leave the capital.[12] Hardy, whose landlord was a district police commissioner and whose uncle by marriage was a magistrate in the Châtelet, mentioned more than two hundred suicides in his unpublished journal, but only a few of them took place in 1775. He mentioned a bankrupt widow who stabbed herself in the rue Saint-Etienne-des-Grès in September and a disgraced intendant (royal official in charge of the administration of a province) who shot himself in the rue Saint-Thomas-du-Louvre in December.[13]

Church and state discouraged discussion of suicide, but people talked about it anyway, with relatives, neighbors, friends, colleagues, and customers, and some of that talk ended up in the pages of the *Mémoires secrets* and Hardy's journal, which unfortunately document only three completed suicides (since the courtesan survived) within the city limits in 1775. The best sources of information about these and additional cases are the reports of the forty-eight district police commissioners, whose numerous responsibilities included investigation of sudden and suspicious deaths.[14] A royal declaration of 1712 required commissioners not only to send for a doctor to examine the body but also to scrutinize the physical evidence and collect testimony from available witnesses.[15] The papers of the commissioners in the Archives Nationales are organized by district and by date, but they are not sorted by subject or indexed in any way. Suicides are interfiled with innumerable thefts and many other offenses, month by month, and day by day. Since Hardy specified the streets where the widow and the intendant lived, researchers can find the reports about their deaths by using the relevant archival inventory to determine the numbers of the districts and names of the commissioners in those cases. By browsing through the papers of commissioners Jacques Simon Dupuy (assigned to the Saint-Benoît district on the Left Bank) and Pierre Chenon (assigned to the Louvre district on the Right Bank) for 1775, researchers will find the relevant documents, dated 22 September and 31 December, respectively. Since the *Mémoires secrets* provided no such details about the merchant from Bordeaux, there is no simple way to track him down or to locate other suicides who were not mentioned in contemporary sources.

The only way to write a comprehensive social history of suicide in eighteenth-century Paris, or at least as comprehensive as the sources allow, is to look through all the papers of all the commissioners. Any team of researchers that could complete that daunting task, at the prescribed rate of just five bundles of documents per day, would not necessarily have the whole truth, and nothing but the truth in their hands. We do not know, in many cases, if the individual died deliberately or accidentally, and we do know, in some cases, that the commissioner went along with relatives in describing the death as something other than suicide.[16] In the case of a stationer who was found dead in his room after his neighbors had not seen him for several days, the commissioner Formel concluded the death was not self-inflicted because he did not find any marks on the body or any "instrument" indicating that the deceased "had made an attempt on his life."[17] But commissioner Leger did not know what to conclude about a surgeon who had been sick for eight months. He left home early one morning without saying a word to his wife, went to visit a friend who lived on the fourth floor in another building, and fell (or jumped?) out a window.[18]

The commissioners whose districts lined the Seine wrote dozens and dozens of reports about corpses reclaimed from the river, but more often than not they had no way of knowing if the dead men and women had intentionally drowned themselves or if they had simply fallen in while loading boats or washing clothes.[19] Some of these individuals were eventually identified by people who came looking for them, but many were listed anonymously in the registers of the morgue.[20] Commissioner Thierion did not know the name, address, or occupation of the man pulled out of the Seine along the Port de la Conférence on the afternoon of 6 May, so he did what he could by describing the victim in detail: about forty years old, wearing a wool coat and vest and a muslin shirt, black breeches and white stockings, and shoes with silver buckles on them. This man had a small key, coins worth six livres and twelve sols, a tortoise snuffbox with a woman's portrait on it, and a worn blue and white linen handkerchief in his pocket. He also had somewhat mangled features and blood coming out of his mouth, but why?[21] Was he injured, by himself or by someone else, before he fell or as he fell into the water? Only one drowning was reported by a witness, a watchman who stated that a man "hurled himself" off the Pont Royal on Sunday, 11 June about nine in the evening. The watchman sounded the alarm, and the man was retrieved downstream at the Poitevin baths, but he was already dead.[22]

One could read about the bodies, clothing, and possessions of men and women whose lives ended in the Seine, but many of them drowned accidentally and most of them must be excluded from this study of suicide for that reason.[23] This exclusion undoubtedly and artificially reduces the number of poor and female victims listed in table 9.1. The following pages are based on twenty cases collected from the papers of the commissioners involving Parisians who unquestionably killed themselves in 1775. The nineteen men ranged in age from sixteen to seventy-seven and in status from laborer, servant, and clerk to merchant and intendant. Some of them were married or widowed, but more of them were single. They shot, stabbed, hanged, or drowned themselves, cut their throats, or jumped out windows. The one woman, a forty-five-year-old widow with three children, cut her throat. All of these individuals, except for the man who threw himself into the Seine, took their lives where they lived, in many cases by themselves, at all times of day and night, on six of the seven days of the week, in eight of the twelve months of the year.[24] Some of the reports do not include information about all of these variables, but researchers who managed to read all the papers of all the commissioners for the whole eighteenth century could obviously reconstruct the sociology, geography, and chronology of suicide in Paris in considerable detail. They could identify changes and continuities over time and make comparisons with other cities and centuries. In collaboration with other researchers, they could reassess conventional wisdom about the impact of demographic trends, economic fluctuations, and political events on patterns of suicide.

It does not make much sense to quantify the limited evidence from 1775 without having additional evidence from preceding and following years in hand for purposes of prosopographical and longitudinal analysis.[25] It does make sense to ask what else one might do with and learn from the police reports, which not only document personal tragedies but also illustrate social networks and collective attitudes.[26] More often than not, the reports contain answers to the relatively straightforward "who," "how," "when," and "where" questions and, furthermore, provide information about the more complicated "why" question. Men and women who killed themselves were connected to and observed by relatives, neighbors, and friends who found their bodies, remembered their words, and explained their deaths by combining specific knowledge about individual circumstances with generic assumptions about human motives.

All of the victims isolated themselves in order to commit suicide, but none of them avoided discovery for long. In many cases they made some sort of noise that prompted others to investigate or send for the commissioner. After Crispin LeChantre carried a chamber pot up to his room in the attic, his mother called his name and asked "if he was taking a dump." He responded "yes," but he was actually cutting his throat, slashing his abdomen, and bleeding into the chamber pot. When he collapsed, he knocked it over, and that noise brought her running up the stairs.[27] Three weeks later Antoine Denis shot himself just as the night watch passed in front of his shop in the rue Sainte-Anastase. His five-and-a-half-year-old daughter, awakened by the noise, told the watch that he had bumped his head and fallen asleep.[28] The child did not understand that her father was dead, but adults who discovered bodies, whether moments or days after the fact, always realized what had happened and usually reacted in the same way. They were horrified and frightened. One neighbor refused to follow the others into the room where Etienne Giraudier had hanged himself and told them that he did not have "the strength to see such a sight."[29] Several male witnesses in other cases expressed the same sentiments.

Shocked but not silenced, individuals acquainted with the dead blamed a few suicides on misconduct and many more on physical or mental disorders. Twenty-two-year-old Tesson de Boisval from Coutances squandered the money that his family sent him on theater tickets and shot himself when the butcher demanded immediate payment of his accumulated bills. He admitted his mistakes in a package, letter, and note addressed to his brother and uncle and to the district commissioner, respectively.[30] Sixteen-year-old Dominique Ledos gambled, drank, fought, and "libertinized," so his hardworking father sometimes punished him for his own good. The boy tried not only to run away but also to drown himself and subsequently hanged himself in the backroom of the family shop.[31] Witnesses did not denounce Tesson de Boisval and Ledos in so many words but did suggest that their deaths were the result of actions that they were personally responsible for.[32] In this regard these two wastrels, the next to youngest and the youngest of the twenty suicides in 1775, were exceptions rather than the rule.

Crispin LeChantre's mother acknowledged that her son had killed himself but declared that he did so only under the influence of delirium caused by the fever that had afflicted him for the last four days. Françoise Pliarz's cousin did not know why Pliarz had left her three children in one room, locked herself in another, and cut her throat, but she was sure that the widow "could have committed this act only because she had a violent fever." The daughters, aged sixteen and fourteen, and the son, aged eleven, added that their troubled and agitated mother had threatened for the last two days to jump out the window.[33] Ribail de Foutareau, a lieutenant in the service of the Compagnie des Indes, suffered from "sadness," "distress," "vapors," "bewilderment," "derangement," "madness," and "frenzy," in the vague vocabulary of the time, after unsuccessful surgery for kidney stones.[34]

Others succumbed to suicidal urges not because of ailments that weakened their bodies and minds but because of problems that troubled or even obsessed them. The widowed stocking maker François Antoine Fererot drank out of "despair" over the misconduct of his twenty-year-old daughter.[35] The "melancholy" domestic servant Bernard Mazère drank because he was returning to his place of birth in the Caribbean or, as he put it, "going to hell."[36] Etienne Giraudier "raved" about individuals who were trying to destroy his reputation. Jean Jacques Cellier, who acted normally, and Charlemagne Guillaume and Louis André Fournier, who both acted strangely, all "imagined" that people were following them with sinister intentions.[37] The master wig maker Antoine Denis not only said and did "outlandish" things (he threatened to burn the house down and refused to eat) in his "violent rages" but also beat his wife, apprentices, and neighbors.[38]

Witnesses commonly assumed or at least asserted that men and women who committed suicide were not themselves at the time, if not for days, weeks, or months before. In one case they did not believe a man who lived long enough to claim that an intruder had stabbed and robbed him, since the window in his bedroom was shut and his money and jewels were still there on the dresser.[39] In other cases they noticed but downplayed signs or words through which victims took responsibility for their acts. Before expiring, LeChantre informed his mother through gestures that he had wounded himself, and Fererot told a neighbor in no uncertain terms that he was dying by his own hand, but the mother and the neighbor attributed these deaths to physical or mental disorders. Suicides discovered after their deaths could no longer speak for themselves, so the police sometimes looked for notes. They did not find one in Fournier's room, but they did find one in Cellier's case. The clerk identified his death as a suicide, not a murder, and explained his delusions in lucid language: "If I am in despair it is because for some time I have seen spies behind me. The fear of being detained in prison makes me do this, and I will act quite innocently. I have never registered anything except in the interest of the Farmers General and their agents or wronged anyone in any way. May God have my soul."[40]

Cellier appealed for divine mercy, and Fererot declared that he had not grasped "the horror of the crime that he was committing" until it was too late. Not a single witness, however, mentioned the religious principles or statutory prohibitions that were supposed to prevent French subjects from killing themselves. Parisians knew what they were supposed to think of individuals who shot or drowned themselves, but they typically described suicides as private tragedies without reference to sin or crime. They rarely blamed the dead and routinely exculpated them, as the magistrates did, by attributing their deaths to sickness or madness. Like the butcher who went downstairs after presenting Tesson de Boisval with his bills and heard the gunshot without putting two and two together, they did not expect people they knew to take their lives.[41] But like the longtime friend who declared that Cellier could not be suspected of misconduct and must have been out of his mind, they knew how to make sense of or at least what to say about these deaths.[42]

Parisians constructed suicide narratives out of information and speculation about the health and wealth of the dead. When they talked to the police, they generally absolved their late relatives, neighbors, and friends of responsibility for their own deaths, in part, no doubt, to avoid any possibility of posthumous prosecution. Perhaps they talked differently among themselves, as they exchanged news and gossip in stairwells and courtyards, streets and shops, markets, and cafes. Based on rumors as well as facts, sometimes corrupted and sometimes corrected, unofficial versions of the cases sometimes ended up in sources other than the police reports. The *Mémoires secrets* mentioned that the merchant from Bordeaux, that is to say the ship's lieutenant Ribail de Foutareau, had domestic problems, but Guillaume Joseph Choler specifically told the commissioner that his uncle had no such troubles. Hardy mentioned that the widow with three daughters had loaned her own money, along with funds that did not belong to her, to someone who went bankrupt, but Marie Jeanne Mazurier did not tell the commissioner anything about the financial problems of her cousin, who actually had two daughters and a son. Mistakes on the part of Parisians who heard and told the stories or omissions on the part of the witnesses intended to prevent people, especially the police, from thinking that their relatives had good reason to kill themselves without being out of their minds?

In the case of the only suicide that turned into something of a cause célèbre, it is possible to compare official and unofficial narratives in detail. According to his valet Boutigny, Etienne Louis Journet, the fifty-nine-year-old intendant of Auch, seemed agitated and distracted when he reached his residence in the rue

Figure 12. *Apprehension of Robespierre, July 27, 1794,* English engraving inspired by Michael Sloane, undated, Dawson Collection, Morrab Library, Penzance, United Kingdom. About to be arrested, Robespierre attempts unsuccessfully to commit suicide. Reproduced with the permission of the Morrab Library.

Saint-Thomas-du-Louvre late at night, late in December 1775.[43] After Boutigny shaved him on the 29th, Journet dismissed him, without completing his toilette, and spent two hours in conversation with his friend Joseph Parlongue, an official involved in the administration of the royal domain. The intendant was distraught because controller-general Turgot had summoned him to the capital. After urging Journet to stop his "shameful raving" and "be a man," Parlongue went to speak with Turgot on his behalf, but Journet slammed his hand down on a table and exclaimed that even Parlongue had abandoned him. When the latter returned, Boutigny found the door to his master's room locked from the inside and received no response when he knocked. Parlongue sent for commissioner Pierre Chenon, who had the door opened and found Journet seated on the commode, still in his nightshirt, with his throat cut and a razor in his right hand. The valet and the friend did not volunteer much information, and the commissioner did not ask many questions. The Keeper of the Seals directed the police to hush up the circumstances of the intendant's death.

Despite "all the precautions taken to prevent the scandal" that Journet's "tragic end" would "naturally" cause, people were soon talking about the case "in all societies."[44] Two days after the fact, the bookseller Hardy recorded the following version of this suicide constructed from such conversations. Having received complaints from the field, the controller-general had summoned the intendant to account for his mismanagement of a large sum of money that he was supposed to use to compensate farmers for losses resulting from the cattle plague. When Journet showed up in Paris, Turgot berated him, reminded him that the king did not want his agents to mistreat his subjects, and warned him that he would be punished severely. Journet could not justify himself and "lost his head immediately." When he got home, he found a razor, locked the door, removed his outfit, took his seat, and cut his throat. Unable to get into his master's room, his valet went directly to the lieutenant-general of police, who delegated Chenon to investigate.[45] Chenon expressed no suspicions about Boutigny in his report, but the valet was detained for two months anyway, which seemed "a bit cruel" to Hardy.[46] Turgot's enemies spread the rumor that the controller-general was responsible for the death of Journet, whom they described as a thoroughly respectable character, and they hoped that it would bring about the minister's downfall. Others, however, knew that the intendant had neglected his duties because he was preoccupied with the study of belles lettres and that he had allowed his subordinates to commit injustices in his name.

Two weeks after the fact, the self-styled "English Spy," actually the prolific *nouvelliste* Matthieu François Pidansat de Mairobert, reported that Parisians had been confused about the case, in no small part because Journet's relatives, in order to clear his name, had spread the rumor that he had been killed by his valet.[47] The relatives argued that if he had cut his own throat, he would have dropped the razor, which therefore must have been planted in his hand to mislead the police. They supposedly paid Boutigny well to go along with them, but people could not understand why he would have put himself at risk in this way and recognized the subterfuge for what it was. Having rejected this version of the story, the Spy blamed the intendant's death on his "excessive sensibility." Journet was distressed by Turgot's rebukes on paper and in person about his mishandling of the cattle plague reimbursements. He was also humiliated by the fact that his colleague Clugny, intendant of Bordeaux, had been directed to sort things out in Auch during his absence. People understood Journet's problem but not his solution. They talked about his *folie,* which could mean simple foolishness or genuine madness, because he had a large income and could have lived very well without royal favor. This commentary, of course, revealed as much about them, or perhaps about the Spy who recorded their sentiments, as it did about Journet, since it implied that money mattered more than honor.

Like other Parisians interested in the case, Hardy and Mairobert did not have access to Turgot's letters or Chenon's papers. Their accounts are limited, because they did not know all the facts and, indeed, did not present the same version of the facts, but also extremely informative because they reported evidence and discussed speculations not included in official sources. Hardy misunderstood the specificity and Mairobert exaggerated the severity of the controller-general's remarks about compensation for livestock killed to prevent the spread of the cattle plague.[48] Both stated that Journet died on 30 December, which suggests that the authorities managed to keep the matter quiet for a day, and neither knew anything about Parlongue's role in the events before and after his demise. Parlongue did not mention a meeting between Journet and Turgot, and the well-connected abbé de Véri specifically denied that any such meeting had taken place.[49] Contemporaries assumed that a confrontation had preceded and prompted the suicide, but they did not exculpate the deceased on those grounds. In the end they rejected the charges against Turgot as well as Boutigny and emphasized the intendant's weakness of character. They implied that if he was guilty, he deserved to be reprimanded, and that if he was not guilty, he should have been able to vindicate himself. In Paris, if not in the provinces as well, he behaved irresponsibly and irrationally. By losing his senses and taking his life, he reminded the English Spy that humans, on the one hand, could have recourse to suicide but, on the other hand, should make every effort to avoid this last resort.[50]

Voltaire, who learned the latest news about the court and the capital from his many correspondents, appropriated Journet's death for his own purposes. He suspected that the intendant could be counted as a philosophe, since he reportedly "read lots of English books."[51] As much as he admired society and culture on the other side of the Channel, Voltaire claimed that there were more works "in support of suicide" in French than in English and implied that the dissemination of these works had something to do with the incidence of suicide in distant Paris, as well as nearby Geneva. Using typically sarcastic language, he declared that "we have clearly shown our faith through deeds." The "faith" in question was the faith in and cause of reason preached by the leaders of the Enlightenment, all of whom challenged the authority of the Bible and the clergy, and some of whom justified suicide outright. They argued, as Voltaire did here, that humans had more liberty than Christianity allowed and that "it is permitted to leave one's house when one is badly housed there." The "deeds" in question included the deaths of the two soldiers who shot themselves together on Christmas Day 1773 and, of course, Journet's more recent suicide. In this case, no one mentioned philosophical motivations, any more than religious reservations, but Voltaire enrolled Journet in his own "faith." The deceased did not speak for himself, but others did not hesitate to speak for him.[52]

Parisians had many things to talk about in the course of 1775, including the recall of the provincial parlements (Journet was involved in the reinstallation of the Parlement of Pau), the meeting of the assembly of the clergy (the bishops issued warnings against suicide and other manifestations of irreligion), the changes in the ministry, the reforms of Turgot, the coronation (and alleged impotence) of Louis XVI, the favorites (and alleged extravagance) of Marie-Antoinette, the success of *The Barber of Seville,* the proliferation of marital separation cases, the bread riots in and around the capital, the suppression of the Pugachev rebellion, and the outbreak of the American Revolution.[53] They did not always believe what the authorities told them (for example about grain supplies), and they did not always tell the authorities what they wanted to know or even hear. Sometimes they remained silent when they were expected to say something, for example to mourn the late Louis XV, and sometimes they expressed themselves when they were expected to say nothing, for example about court intrigues and royal policies. Invoked by parlements, bishops, ministers, and pamphleteers, public opinion was out of control by the time Journet cut his throat.[54] As suggested by the unofficial accounts provided by the royalist Hardy and the subversive Mairobert, contemporaries politicized his death by reading it in context and contrasting the worthy/selfish intendant with the wicked/selfless minister.[55] They did not editorialize about the other suicides in 1775, at least not when they talked to the police, by blaming these deaths on prices or Enlightenment. By repudiating the language of sin and crime, by deciding what to reveal and what to conceal, and by attributing most of these deaths to sickness or madness (in the same way that the magistrates did), they nevertheless claimed or at least exercised the right to judge these cases, like many other matters, for themselves.

TABLE 9.1.
Suicides documented in the papers of the district police commissioners, 1775

Y*	Date	Name	Age	Status	Identity	Method
13685	24 Mar.	Etienne Giraudier	48	s	manual laborer	hanged
12185	8 Apr.	Jean Jacques Cellier		s	Protestant clerk	cut throat
13790	19 Apr.	Dominique Ledos	16	s	shopkeeper's son	hanged
11400	26 Apr.	Michel–François Bauchereau	55	m	retired merchant	cut throat
14102	3 Jun.	Claude Boissonet		m	water carrier	jumped
13790	8 Jun.	Tesson de Boisval	22	s		shot
14560	11 Jun.	unidentified man				drowned
13127	25 Jun.	Crispin LeChantre	27	s	discharged soldier	cut throat
15977	19 Jul.	Antoine Denis		m	master wig maker	shot
11016	22 Aug.	Ribail de Foutareau	45	m	ship's lieutenant	shot
15076	30 Aug.	Bernard Mazère		s	black servant	hanged
12791	22 Sep.	Françoise Pliarz	45	w		cut throat
11494	26 Sep.	Noël Pelletier		s		jumped
12679	2 Oct.	Jean Baptiste Fleury	77	w	financier	shot
14102	6 Oct.	Charlemagne Guillaume	30	s	stocking worker	cut throat
12186	26 Oct.	Nathan Lifman	45	m	Jewish merchant	hanged
15665	10 Dec.	Jean Baptiste Petit	75	m	bourgeois	shot
14824	15 Dec.	Louis André Fournier	38	s		stabbed
14102	28 Dec.	François Antoine Fererot		w	stocking maker	cut throat
11402	29 Dec.	Etienne Journet	60	m	royal intendant	cut throat

*Document numbers in the Archives Nationales in Paris.

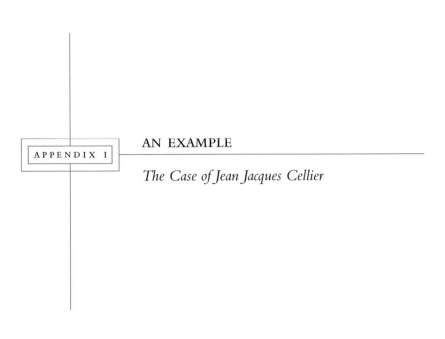

AN EXAMPLE

The Case of Jean Jacques Cellier

Report

In the year 1775, on Saturday, 8 April, at 5:45 A.M., having been sent for, we, Louis Michel Roch de La Porte, counselor of the king and commissioner, investigator, and examiner of the Châtelet of Paris, went to the rue du Grenier-Saint-Lazare, to the building with the district post office in it, where, having gone into the courtyard, we found several persons gathered and occupied in looking at the window of a room on the fifth floor, on the sill of which one saw the head and shoulders of a man whose nightshirt is all covered with blood and from whose head lots of blood flowed onto the pavement, as it seemed to us, which individual we were told is named Cellier, clerk in the office of the tax on gold and silver goods, living in said room for fifteen to seventeen years, alone, that he had been seen last night coming back at 11 o'clock and that there is reason to believe that he died from a stroke, that since this man lived alone he could not get any help.[56] For this reason we sent for Monsieur Charles Basse, master locksmith in Paris, living there in the rue du Grenier-Saint-Lazare, in the parish of Saint-Nicolas-des-Champs, with whom, having gone up to the fifth floor, to the door of said Cellier's room, which was locked, we had it opened by sieur Basse in the presence of Louis François Salis, upholsterer and porter of the building we are in, and Va Vit Godot, master founder, also living in the building we are in, and several other neighbors. Which opening accomplished after having made the bolt, which was closed on the inside, fall, we entered the room, being in which we noticed that the bed is covered with blood, that on the fireplace close to the bed is an open razor covered with blood, with the names Paris, Henroi stamped on it with a [illegible word]. Then, having approached the cadaver, we had it lifted up and saw that it had its throat cut in the front and had it put back on his bed. Then, having searched said room, the pockets and clothes of the deceased, in the course of which we found, on a guilloche lathe behind the door, a large sheet of ordinary paper with writing only on the front side of it, beginning with these words, "List of what I own," and after said list, which finishes a third of the way down the front, is another written text containing these words, "Let no one be bothered. If I am in despair it is because for some time I have seen spies behind me. The fear of being detained in prison makes me do this, and I will act quite innocently. I have never registered anything except in the interest of the Farmers General and their agents or wronged anyone in any way. May God have my soul. I have a note for 1200 livres and 15 sols that belongs to Monsieur the chevalier Playette. I believe I owe the painter 12 francs. I owe the locksmith payment for my locks," which we took possession of, namely the text and the razor, to turn them over to the clerk of the criminal court, after which we signed and initialed said text, ne variator, and signed with us.[57]

[signed]Basse, Salisse, [and] Godot

This done, we left said cadaver in the possession of Jean Jacques Jisser, master clock maker in Paris, living there in the rue Saint-Louis, near the Palais de Justice, in the parish of Saint-Barthélemy, distant cousin of the deceased, who informed us that the deceased was named Jean Jacques Cellier, fifty-five years old, native of La Neuveville in Switzerland, in the principality of Porrentruy, who was of the Protestant religion, who takes responsibility for the body in order to have it buried. That after it has been seen and examined by the doctors and surgeons of the Châtelet and after it has been so directed by order of Monsieur the lieutenant-general of police, based on the decision of Monsieur the royal prosecutor, and in light of the act involved, we state that it is going to be investigated by us at the request of Monsieur the royal prosecutor in the Châtelet, of all of which we have drafted this report for that reason. Jisser signed with us.

[signed] Jisser [and] De La Porte

Having seen the report, I do not, on behalf of the king, prevent the cadaver of said Jean Jacques Cellier from being buried quietly, without any scene or show, in the cemetery for foreigners. Agents of the watch and the police to be directed to see to it and lend assistance if needed and they are asked for it. Done this 8 April 1775.

[signed] Moreau [royal prosecutor in the Châtelet]

To be done as it is directed, this 8 April 1775.

[signed] Lenoir [lieutenant-general of police]

Investigation

Official investigation conducted by us, Louis Michel Roch de La Porte, counselor of the king, commissioner, investigator, etc.

At the request of Monsieur the royal prosecutor in the Châtelet.

In execution of our order to determine the motives that might have led Jean Jacques Cellier, clerk in the office of the tax on gold and silver goods, to take his life as it is established by the report that we drafted about the matter today separately from the present document.

In the course of which official investigation we heard the witnesses found in said house.

On Saturday, 8 April 1775, at 7 A.M.

1. Louis François Salis, 47 years old, upholsterer in Paris, living there in the rue du Grenier-Saint-Lazare at the corner of the rue Saint-Martin, in the house where we are, in the parish of Saint-Nicolas-des-Champs, who, after taking the oath to tell the truth, stated that he is not a relative, in-law, servant, or domestic of the parties involved.

Testifies about the matter in question, after the report was read to him, that he had known said Cellier for a year, that he was calm and very regular in his habits, treating everyone politely; that he had not seen him yesterday; that this morning at 5:30, being in the courtyard and seeing blood on the ground, he looked up and saw said Cellier in his nightshirt, leaning on the window sill, with half of his body outside and his nightshirt covered with blood on the back, which seemed extraordinary to him, such that he alerted us and, having witnessed the opening of the door of said Cellier's room ordered by us, he entered with us and despaired to see that he had his throat cut; that he saw the razor on the fireplace close to the bed, with which it seemed that he cut the same, and believes that he did it in his bed, since it was covered with blood, heard nothing last night and does not know at what time he might have struck this blow, which is all that he says he knows. After his deposition was read to him, said that it contains the truth, reaffirmed it, and signed.

[signed] Salisse [and] De La Porte

2. Va Vit Godot, more than 29 years old, master founder in Paris, living there in the house where we are, in the parish of Saint-Nicolas-des-Champs, who after taking the oath to tell the truth, stated that he is not a relative, in-law, servant, or domestic of the parties involved.

Testifies that he knew said Cellier for seven years; that he was upright and liked by all his neighbors; that in the morning, being in the courtyard with said Salis, after having seen blood on the ground at the base of the wall, he looked up and saw a man leaning on the window sill, with his head bent over and his nightshirt covered with blood on the shoulders and the back; that having come with said Salis to alert us, he returned with us to the room; that having found the bed covered with blood and nearby, on the hearth of the fireplace, an open razor also covered with blood, he suspected that he had taken his life; that then he helped to put him on the bed and saw that he had his throat cut, which is all that he says he knows. After his deposition was read to him, said that it contains the truth, reaffirmed it, and signed.

[signed] Godot [and] De La Porte

3. Jean Jacques Jisser, 48 years old, master clock maker in Paris, living there in the rue Saint-Louis near the Palais de Justice, in the parish of Saint-Barthélemy, who after taking the oath to tell the truth, stated that he is not a relative, in-law, servant, or domestic of the parties involved, except that he is a distant cousin of said Cellier.

Testifies about the matter in question etc., that he knew the deceased since his childhood; that he is a native of La Neuveville in Switzerland in the principality of Porrentruy and was a Protestant; that he was married and had been a widower for about fifteen years; that he had only one daughter, who married a clock maker in that place, La Neuveville, named Thieche; that this man had very regular habits, was liked by his superiors and by all who knew him; that five years ago said Cellier had a fit of madness that lasted a month; that at the time he imagined all the while that he saw spies who watched for a chance to arrest him; that this fit passed; that for about a month and a half said Cellier had begun to have the same fears and believed that he saw spies all the time; that this, however, did not prevent him from fulfilling the responsibilities of his job; that the deponent even saw him yesterday at his office; that he seemed uneasy and bewildered; that he did what he could to reassure him; that since his conduct was not subject to any suspicion, he would not have believed that he thought of taking his life; that this morning he was surprised to learn about this accident and can only attribute it to mental disorder. The deponent adds that said Cellier's father died eighteen to twenty years ago and that for the last four or five years of his life he was out of his mind; that his mother later died weak-minded, which is all that he says he knows. After his deposition was read to him, said that it contains the truth, reaffirmed it, and signed.

[signed] Jisser [and] De La Porte

Having seen the report and the investigation, along with the text attached to it, I order, on behalf of the king, that the investigation be continued and, however, that the corpse of said Jean Jacques Cellier be seen and examined by the doctors and surgeons of the Châtelet in order to determine the cause of his death and communicated to us in their report.[58] Done this 8 April 1775.

[signed] Moreau

To be done as it is directed, this 8 April 1775.

[signed] Lenoir

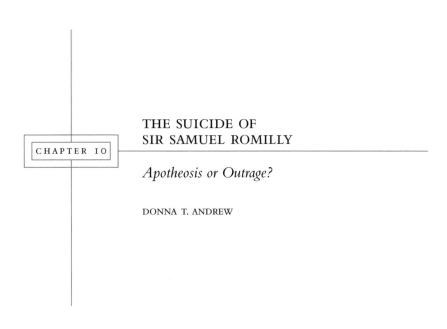

THE SUICIDE OF
SIR SAMUEL ROMILLY

CHAPTER 10

Apotheosis or Outrage?

DONNA T. ANDREW

When Sir Samuel Romilly, member of Parliament, eminent civil lawyer, crusader for the abolition of the slave trade and the reduction in the severity of criminal law, killed himself on November 2, 1818, London's newspapers were filled with the story. In the following weeks, the story of Romilly's demise continued to be discussed as the press not only published reports of the inquest, details of the funeral, the contents of his will, and the ramifications of his death for the political situation, but also poems, editorials, and letters to the editor eulogizing his life and bemoaning his death. Seldom has the demise of a nonroyal received so much public attention. This chapter examines the press reports and comments on this event, using this particularly intensely felt and widely reported episode of the self-inflicted death of a man much in the public eye as an entry point into early-nineteenth-century attitudes toward suicide.

When someone died in unusual or unknown circumstances, English law required that a coroner's inquest be called, a jury sworn in, and a decision reached on the cause of death. A variety of possible verdicts could be found for someone who had died by their own hand. "Accident" or "visitation of God" were two possible judgments, but most commonly the verdicts were "*felo de se*" (that is, self-murder, premeditated and done in a rational state of mind) or "lunacy." If the verdict was self-murder, the deceased might have his estate forfeited to the crown, and could not receive proper Christian burial; if the verdict was lunacy, no such culpability was attached to the act. Through the eighteenth century the number of *felo de se* verdicts steadily declined, while, at the same time, a wave of interest grew in the causes of suicide, the best ways of preventing it, and the most appropriate punishments or actions on its commission. Whereas one body of thought argued that all suicides were the result of illness, and should thus be treated medically rather than criminally, another body of thought reacted to suicide as a crime, viewing the act and its consequences with horror, fear, and revulsion. William Combe's rather trite poem expressed the commonly held early-nineteenth-century's visceral and intellectual antipathy to self-murder.

> Philosophy, in all its Pride,
> Cannot defend the Suicide,
> By any Law, by any rule
> In Reason's or Religion's school:
> Life's the peculiar gift of Heav'n,
> And He alone by whom 'tis given,
> Can have alone the power to give
> The stroke by which we cease to live.[1]

Since Samuel Romilly both killed himself, and was, as we shall soon see, enormously loved and respected, in the accounts of his death we can observe early-nineteenth-century writers attempting to come to terms both with the man and with his heinous end.

Romilly was one of the preeminent lawyers and parliamentarians of his day. In both spheres he attempted to make legal practices more rational, more consistent, and more humane. He fought for a reduction in the frequency of hanging, transportation, or confinement in the hulks (ships used as prisons) as appropriate criminal penalties. Four years before his death he campaigned for and won a mitigation of the law of treason and attainder. By 1817 he was "the life and soul of the opposition" and argued against the suspension of the Habeas Corpus Act and the suppression of public discussion. An ardent campaigner for the emancipation of Catholics and African slaves, he was active in many philanthropic movements of the day. After the deaths of Charles James Fox and Samuel Whitbread, Romilly was perhaps the best known Whig of his day. Described as "one whom we must consider, for a time, as the most celebrated man in this country" it is no wonder, then, that he was so grievously missed.[2]

It is instructive to consider press reports of the mourning occasioned by Romilly's death. It was said that "never perhaps was a more sincere tribute of respect and veneration paid to an individual, than what was exhibited on Tuesday morning in the two Courts of Equity." The Lord Chancellor, glancing at the spot where Romilly normally had stood, "could no longer restrain his feelings; the tears rushed down his cheeks; he immediately rose and retired to his room, to give vent to his feelings."[3] But grief spread far wider than the courts; the loss of

Figure 13. Henry Wallis, *The Death of Chatterton,* 1856. Reproduced with the permission of the Tate Gallery, London / Art Resource, New York.

Romilly, "that incomparable person . . . filled the metropolis with sorrow."[4] It seemed a special public nerve had been touched, for contemporaries noted the strength and depth of the expressed grief: "Since the day when the public was made acquainted with the fall of the immortal Nelson, we do not recollect one, in which the mourning was so deep and universal as on the death of Sir Samuel Romilly; and never was there an occasion when there was a more general expression of profound sorrow in all ranks of the people."[5] It was, judging from peoples' reactions, as if a terrible national calamity had occurred: "We have never witnessed a sensation at once so strong and so general as what at this time occupies all minds."[6] But to judge his death merely as a national disaster did not seem enough for commentators. Thus one writer, noting that "his death is indeed a great national calamity," went on to add that the loss was "not confined to his country, for the range of his mighty and extraordinary mind encompassed every class of his fellow beings, and, as if conscious of the high commission of that power, who had thus distinguishedly gifted him, every energy of that mind was directed to their good."[7] Rather than being presented only as an exemplary Englishman and as an ardent advocate of improvement, his death was described as having "given a shock, wholly without example, to every heart which cherishes a hope for the advancement of its species."[8] By these accounts Romilly appeared as a hero for all humanity.

The qualities most lauded posthumously were threefold. Romilly was mourned for three sorts of excellencies: as an uncorrupted law maker and politician, as a self-made man of business and endeavor, and as an exemplary family man, a father, husband and son. Described as a patriot and sage, lauded for "the purity of his intentions" and characterized by his "love of constitutional liberty," in his public capacity Romilly seemed to exemplify a particularly valuable and perhaps rare set of qualities.[9] His humility was matched, it was said, only by his zeal for his fellow creatures and his general benevolence.[10] "His political views were generous, manly, and extensive" and he was "uncorrupted by wealth—undazzled by rank—unblemished by ambition."[11] These attributes of the statesman were matched by his devotion to his profession, and his success at it. The press repeatedly insisted that though Romilly's father, a jeweler, had given him a good education, "all the rest had been achieved by himself." He was a model of the rewards of hard work and industry, having "acquired those habits which usually promote health and success in life." Rising early, he caught "those moments for improvement, which others too often waste in indolence." Almost all the papers carried the story of how, as a young man wishing to marry, he explained to his fiancée that it would be a good while before they could be wed. Supporting his aging parents, Romilly would not enter into married life before he had made two fortunes by his own endeavors, the first dedicated to the support of his kin, the second to establish his new family.[12] Known as a "most indefatigable labourer," he was widely praised for his "knowledge, learning and eloquence."[13] In a phrase redolent of his philosophic mentor Jeremy Bentham, the *Constitution* summed up his life as "useful."[14]

While rather over-heated panegyrists hailed him as "the Citizen of the World" and "the Father of his Country,"[15] it was his personal virtues, his self-acquired talents, which received most praise. Only a year before, in 1817, Princess Charlotte had died, but the press noted that while the Princess and her stillborn child "were beings out of the sphere of ordinary occupation: Sir Samuel Romilly was one of ourselves."[16] Unlike "the Great," Romilly was seen as an ordinary man, albeit one of extraordinary achievement. The *Monthly Magazine* presented his life as epitomizing the new self-made leaders of the country; in the new nineteenth century, it boasted, "no longer looking up to nobility for true greatness, men were beheld starting daily from the democratic floor, and snatching away the prize of knowledge, learning and eloquence" from the privileged orders.[17] Much was made of his middling station, especially when describing the curiosity the public had in his life and his death. "The loss was sensibly felt in every quarter; for though he was not in that high station, with which the generality are apt to connect so much consequence, yet his talents, his worth, and the honourable distinctions . . . gave every one an interest in his character." The *Imperial Weekly Gazette* even went so far as to say that "though born in a private state, the luster and dignity of virtue, has placed him above all the Monarchs of the world."[18]

But if any aspect of his life or career was praised, if any role was considered illustrative of and central to all his other virtues, it was his conduct as the head of his family, "as a son, a father, a husband, and a master." On the one hand it is not surprising that this side of his life received so much attention; for, it was said, he had killed himself because of his grief at the death of his much-loved wife. On the other hand, this sentimental exaltation of the domestic life of a married man was surely something relatively recent. When thirty years before, a Mr. Green hanged himself in his chamber following the death of his wife, the inquest jury sat for seventeen hours before they arrived at the verdict of lunacy. Commenting on the verdict, the *Times* rather facetiously noted that "to be inconsolable for one's wife, and to follow her to the grave—is *madness*." But by the time Romilly committed the same act for the same reason the tone was graver, more respectful and much more sympathetic. The *Lady's Magazine,* for example, noting that "in the bosom of his family . . . he was the tender husband—the fond father," presented his familial devotion and his public service as inextricably combined. "This weakness and this wisdom—this combination of all that is delicate and all that is great, shew human nature in a point of view, which commands at one and the same time our utmost love and highest veneration."[19] The *Lady's Magazine* was neither alone nor unusual in its praise of Romilly's domestic virtues; several other papers also commented on this aspect of his conduct.[20] Contemporaries, however, went far beyond the merely complimentary in their descriptions of Romilly's home life. Despite the manner of his death, the weight of his domestic despair illustrated not only the superiority of his country and age, but the hidden springs of his public life. The *British Review,* for example, presented Romilly as

> the example of a virtuous English gentleman in his family, and in private society. This is by some considered to be but a slight commendation, as having reference to duties of easy performance; and some regard the high credit in which they stand as the mark of the rarity of their occurrence. . . . It is honourable in the age in which we live, that it is principally from the private lives of the great that the people take the measure of their real greatness. It is in the recesses of the characters of eminent men that we sometimes find those shady refreshing spots, on which the eyes, tired with brilliancy, delight to repose.[21]

For many of Romilly's contemporaries, such as his friend, George Crabbe, the public and the private man, the political and the domestic talents, were of a piece, "the best of guides to my assuming pen, / The best of fathers, husbands, judges, men." The anonymous poet who described Romilly as "Father of his Country" preceded that attribution by describing him as "Blessed with a heart, as gentle and refin'd / As e'er found solace in domestic joys!" Claiming that Romilly's reputation was "inferior to none, in the annals of modern times," another newspaper writer declared that "beginning with his own family, the circle of his attachment increased until it included friends, relatives, his country, and finally, the whole human species."[22] Yet another mixed the domestic and public, addressing Romilly's orphaned children:

> Ye orphan Pledges of their mutual love,
> Heaven grant you in your Father's path to move!
> . . . And oh! than rather not be like your Sire,
> Live as he has lived, and then like him expire.[23]

This view came perilously close to condoning or even approving the closing act of Romilly's life, and may have strengthened the backlash to this sort of extenuation, to which we will shortly turn.

Perhaps Romilly's rash act prompted less speculation about its larger causes (most seemed to feel that the recent death of his wife was reason enough) than praise for his character, his public and private conduct, and his critical political importance,[24] but we do have a number of interesting comments which hint at contemporary understandings of these other causes. Of course, many press reports gave multiple explanations and interpretations for his self-destructive act.

An examination of these does not present us with a coherent and comprehensive account of Romilly's suicide but illustrates contemporaries' efforts to try, with considerable unease and some mystification, to explain and understand, if not to justify, the event.

First, of course, were those sorts of explanations that arose most easily and naturally from the inquest itself. "Sir Samuel Romilly when he committed the act was in a state of mental delirium. He was suffering under a brain fever. . . . He was unconscious of crime at the time, and GOD and the world will, we trust, judge him accordingly. . . . The whole tenor of Sir Samuel's unsullied life . . . contradicts the idea, that there could be a premeditated motive for self-destruction. And, indeed, the evidence before the Coroner proves that it arose from an instantaneous paroxysm of the brain."[25] The *British Neptune* agreed, commenting that Romilly's death

> was merely the result of disease and derangement. The evidence is convincing of his clear and powerful mind, imbued as it was with honourable and religious principle, having sunk under the pressure of fatigue, affliction, and disease. Suicide in such a case is merely a symptom of physical disorder, and no more to be connected with the moral condition of the sufferer than any of the bodily ills that flesh is heir to. It has nothing of the imposing energy, or guilt, or imbecility, or mistaken virtue, which strike the attention of the heroes of antiquity, or the victims of passion, profligacy, or criminality in modern times, who have fallen by their own hands. We contemplate it only as one of the results of intense bodily suffering, and turn gladly from the disgusting exhibition.[26]

The *Constitution* presented the act as almost foreordained: "There was too much upon his mind, there was too much upon his heart; the one became deranged, the other broke."[27]

Shortly after the event, the *Courier* launched an attack on this sort of mitigation of Romilly's action, arguing instead that many had borne what Romilly had suffered and had not had recourse to suicide, that Romilly's act betrayed if not an irreligious frame of mind then perhaps an insufficiency of character and resolve. Comparing the stoic responses of Princess Charlotte's husband and of Edmund Burke to the deaths of their loved ones (in the first case, a wife and child, in the second, an only son), the *Courier* remarked: "Surely these and similar examples of religious fortitude under the severe visitations of this life, are those which should obtain our highest sympathy, and greatest admiration. The weakness which bends, which falls, before the storm, may call forth our pity, but no more." The responses to the *Courier's* comments were immediate. Not only were they held to be invidious but also incorrect, for, as several papers asked, "must similar results arise in the minds of various men from causes apparently similar? Human reason cannot be measured like objects of sense, nor can the experience of one individual's endurance be considered as evidence of what another can safely encounter. The cases, however, are very far from being similar."[28] In attempting to answer the calumnies of the *Courier,* the press came to propose a variety of extenuating circumstances by which to explain what in this particular case caused Romilly's act.

One common explanation for Romilly's deed was the years of toil which he had endured, not only in building his career, but in fighting for and defending the causes to which he was committed. The *Country Herald and Weekly Advertiser* argued that "it seems beyond a doubt, that the mental derangement to which Sir Samuel Romilly fell a victim, was brought on in part by the unremitted professional toil which had first weakened his frame." His many activities "left no time for bodily exercise, mental relaxation, or domestic comfort. . . . He became a devoted servant to the Public, he made more than fair use of his talents; and this probably tended to subdue that vigour which had well known how to advise and to exercise equanimity and resignation in the hour of affliction," commented the *Gentleman's Magazine.* The *Monthly Magazine* concurred, remarking that it was "easy to trace the causes of the frenzy which destroyed him. Its foundations had been laid in years of inconceiveable and distracting labour." Unlike those who led "less irksome or artificial lives" Romilly, having "passed his whole life in the careful and unhealthy routine of the law, with a perpetual wear and tear on his spirits, and cooped up from air and exercise in the Courts" was the inevitable victim of the first emotional storm he experienced.[29]

The most prevalent explanation for Romilly's act, however, was his extreme tenderness of feeling, which, it was held, was also the source of his many virtues. His speech against the slave trade, for example, was described as exhibiting "the most melting pathos, the most overwhelming eloquence." Similarly it was this very "tenderness of nature which led Sir Samuel Romilly to embrace with love the whole of his fellow creatures, and to exert himself to serve them, [that] was most fervent, as it ought to be, at home" and which led to his death. Romilly's final act was described as springing "from an excess of feeling, or rather from a sentiment, which is the most binding one in our social system" and thus rather too much of a good thing than a crime or an evil.[30] Writers burst into verse to express this sentiment:

> Nor judge too harshly of that closing act
> O'er which a nation droops in grief profound.
> Excess of feeling caus'd it—of feeling
> Closely allied to virtue! Affection's links

> So long had been entwin'd around his heart,
> They form'd a part of it! Death snapped the chain—
> The shock unseated reason. Muse!—no more.[31]

"To [Romilly], unfortunately, his virtues have proved holy traitors," commented the *Globe*. "With a heart less susceptible and feelings less acute, Sir Samuel Romilly would be now living." The *New Times* summed it up most succinctly; Romilly it said, "fell a victim to the acuteness of his sensibility."[32]

Before we leave this strand of explanation, however, we must consider some minor though intriguing understandings of the connection between Romilly's outer and inner life, between his enormous dedication to the intricacies of his profession and the psychological and intellectual resources with which he faced domestic trials. Both the *Examiner* and the *Monthly Magazine* explained Romilly's suicide by noting his lack of imagination. Commenting on his death, the latter noted that "The springs by which his spiritual nature should have been nourished and invigorated, were dried up within him. . . . He was essentially a practical man, destitute, for the most part, of fancy and imagination. . . . Hence he was little prepared to draw consolation from things unseen; to rest on sentiment or unearthly hopes; to cherish sweet fancies and tender thoughts which soften the grief that incites them, or to indulge in that gentle pensiveness which throws a rich, yet sober enchantment over the grave." The *Examiner* expanded on the value of the imaginative faculty; "if imagination on the one hand may be supposed to create pains as well as pleasures to itself according as health or morbidity predominates, yet upon the whole, according to the natural impulse of humanity, it leans more to the pleasurable than the painful, and takes even a pride in summoning its numerous servitors to its assistance." Whether invoking imagination as the wellspring of spirituality, or seeing it as the source of pleasure, both magazines agreed that its absence had a deleterious effect on Romilly's psyche. Living a life of duty, a life bereft of even the consolations of fancy and imagination, Romilly sought above all to appear unruffled and calm. It was this very laudable stoicism that the *News* felt must have given him the coup de grace:

> The endeavour to keep his grief in a subdued state, appeared to claim all his attention. . . . This tension of feeling at length produced its natural consequence. It broke down the frail barrier which separates man from the brute which perisheth, and in the momentary bereavement of his faculties, the act of suicide was committed. Whether the indulgence of grief, and the burst of feeling consequent on it, may not in some cases tend to preserve the mind; though it may exhaust the body, is a question which we feel incompetent to decide.

Lacking the consolations of imagination, Romilly fell prey to the dark gloom of his bereavement.[33]

We have seen how the press and the public seemed overwhelmed and puzzled by Romilly's death, unable to offer a satisfactory explanation for his act or to find words adequate to express their pain. The *British Review* remarked that "every one who heard was struck dumb with the intelligence; or had only the power, for the moment, to utter some ejaculation of astonishment." The *Morning Advertiser,* discussing the effects of the double deaths of the Romillys on their children said, "the heavy domestic afflictions occasioned by these lamentable events may be conceived but they are such as language has not the power to describe." But newspapers are filled with words, and despite the shock, the Romilly suicide was a story which fascinated and troubled the reading public; simply put, bad news makes good sales. Everyone, it seemed, wanted to read and discuss this horrifying death. Thus the *Philanthropic Gazette,* describing "the gloom [spread] over the country" by Romilly's demise, commented on what was most newsworthy about it—"the manner of it being still more painful than the event itself."[34]

When we look closely at the phrases used to describe this death, a rather surprising consistency emerges. The images employed by the press imply that Romilly was removed or in some other way effaced; his agency, even a demented or deranged willfulness, was denied, and the act was presented as an accident or the mysterious decree of some divine plan. We have already noted the description of Romilly as victim; other accounts talked of his "sudden and fearful disappearance," of his being "called away" or having "fallen, like an eagle from his rock, smitten down in a moment by the lightening of heaven." The *Monthly Repository* continued this dramatic tone: "Death again struck his triumphant dart and levelled with the dust one of the greatest men that his nation has produced." Many took a more sober, less colorful line, holding fate responsible. Thus the *Morning Chronicle* summarized the widely held belief that "Sir Samuel Romilly . . . has sunk under the severe visitation of Providence."[35] It was but a short step from this sort of palliation, of blaming an impersonal fatality rather than Romilly himself, to the image of Romilly as warrior, fallen in battle. We have already seen a hint of this in the earlier comparison of the grief over Romilly's death with that of Nelson's; the *News* employed the metaphor directly and overtly. Though prefacing its remarks with the mandatory disclaimer, that is, that it "lament[ed] the manner of [Romilly's death]," the *News* went on to comment that "Yet not more natural is it for a warrior to die on the field of battle, than it was for this most amiable man to fall a sacrifice to the excess of his affections and tenderness." This is as close to an apotheosis for his private virtues that a public man has ever come.[36]

There were those however, who, like the *Courier,* discerned in Romilly's ac-

tion an insufficiency of religious attachment, a proof of the necessity for absolute
faith and reliance on God in all of life's adversities. The *Independent Whig* saw this
lack of faith and overreliance on reason not only as a flaw in Romilly's constitution, but as a symptom of the age: "This instance of the dreadful infirmity of
human nature, and the insufficiency of the mind of man, however exalted and
cultivated, to sustain himself, in the hour of heavy calamity, is by no means a soli-
tary occurrence, even in modern times." Some accounts, of course, advised the
public to be charitable in their opinions about Romilly's faith: "It ill becomes us
to pronounce a sentence which God hath not pronounced; or rashly and cruelly
to make [the suicide] a proof that his virtue wanted the support of religious, of
Christian principle." The radical *Black Dwarf* asserted that "the private virtues of
Sir Samuel, and his public worth, will not be lessened in the opinion of any worthy man by the *manner* of his death."[37] And one poet even went so far as to portray his death as Heaven's gift:

> Nor think Religion wanted all her power,
> To soothe his spirit in that torturing hour;
> But rather say, that Heaven, in pity, gave
> A friendly refuge in the sheltering grave.[38]

But despite the exculpatory tone of the press in general, those papers which took
a harder, more censorious attitude toward Romilly's death, did so, not surprisingly, on religious grounds.[39] Most of these condemnations focused on the act
as betraying a lack of proper Christian submission, an insufficiency of Christian
faith. Condemning not only the act itself, but attacking the verdict of the inquest
jury as well, *Bell's Weekly Messenger* remarked that, "it is the express command of
our religion . . . to exert all our human powers of body and mind [to fight against
adversity] . . . and if we find those powers insufficient, to call for that divine
aid. . . . Human resolution is [usually] found sufficient to restrain other sallies of
inordinate passion. And if they break out in despite of such restraint . . . the human legislator does not the less punish them, because they were the acts of a passion, blind, furious and uncontrollable, in the instant of the communication."
Romilly's act was thus presented by some accounts as idolatrous, as more moved
by human than Divine love. "It does seem, therefore, a little extraordinary how
. . . any sensible man of sixty can suffer even the sweetest and holiest ties of this
passing world so to wind round his heart as to dispute the property of that heart
with Him who has declared his jealousy in that respect." Denounced as an act of
cowardice, a betrayal of friends and family, Romilly's suicide seemed to some the
undeniable proof of his pride and his irreligion. "We are left only to lament that
his resignation to the dispensations of Providence was not sufficiently humble,
nor his reliance on the support of Him who is our strength and our safety, and

who loves while he chastens, sufficiently great to enable him to bear up against so severe a trial," proclaimed the *St. James's Chronicle.*[40]

Other periodicals presented Romilly's act as that of a man whose principles, if not corrupted, at least were unhinged, and even perhaps fatally tainted by the miasma of deism. Most papers were only willing to hint at this, as when the *Philanthropic Gazette,* commenting on Romilly and Whitbread's suicide, argued that "whether we impute their derangement to intense attachment on the one hand, or to disgust of the world's ingratitude on the other, it is sufficiently evident that some principle must be wanting, that is necessary to support the mind under trials and bereavements." Whitbread, like Romilly, an ardent Whig reformer, had killed himself three years before, overwhelmed, it was said, by the difficulties he had encountered in his attempt to rescue the Drury-lane Theatre from debt, though the *Gazette* implied that what really impelled both men to their fatal ends was their rationalist irreligion.[41] The *Morning Post* was franker, rhetorically asking its readers, "who does not acknowledge and lament the awful inroads made on our moral character as a nation by the diabolical *Modern Philosophy,* which aims at extinguishing every principle from the human heart on which our present and future hopes are founded." The clearest and harshest criticism, however, was not made of Romilly's act overtly; this would have been considered in rather bad taste. But when Thomas Belsham, a Unitarian minister, delivered and published a funeral oration for Romilly, the condemnation was intense and severe. Both the *Anti-Jacobin Review* and the *British Review* denounced Belsham's palliation of the sin, the crime of suicide. In ringing tones, the *British Review* justified its attack: "We should have felt ourselves interdicted from touching a topic so full of domestic anguish; but truth must not be sacrificed to a drivelling delicacy of sentiment. There is but one religion for all the world; for a Sir Samuel Romilly and the meanest man in the realm." Both journals explicitly denounced Belsham's view (which, as previously discussed, appeared in the press as well) that Romilly had been "taken" or "summoned away," arguing that such an explanation not only was sophistical, but revealed the "cloven foot of deism." It required only a small step to make the connection between such exculpatory views of Romilly's death and the radical ideology of continental philosophers, a step which the *Anti-Jacobin Review* fearlessly made. Such excuses, it claimed, "amount to a complete justification of suicide and a vindication of the *patet exitus* [the door is open (between life and death)] taught by [Adam] Weishaupt and the Illuminées of Germany."[42] In linking Romilly's death with the writings of Weishaupt, the antiroyalist German freemason who founded the mysterious Order of the Illuminati, the *Anti-Jacobin Review* argued that an intimate connection existed between such acts and radical religious and political activity.

For such critics, Romilly's action appeared less than glorious, his end not resembling the soldier on the field of battle, but a death which "dash[ed] every better feeling with horror and agony. Human nature seems humiliated by this catastrophe." Especially worrying was the possibility that Romilly's death might cause others to imitate it, and, when in fact such a suicide occurred within days, some of the papers did attribute this second death to a terrible sort of mimicry.[43] There was a widespread feeling that such acts were becoming more common. "Such events, now alas," commented the *Morning Post,* were "so frequently recurring." The *Independent Whig* agreed, "let us hope that fatal act will less frequently take place among us, especially with men of probity, virtue and worth; that such men will make a gallant stand against the evils they may have to encounter, and thereby overcome the weaknesses incident to mortality." Thus some newspapers, though unwilling to forgo publishing accounts of well known suicides, insisted that they owed it to their readers and to the nation to present such culpable deeds without sugar-coating or exoneration. "We intend nothing against the memory of so good a man as the late Sir Samuel Romilly . . . but there is nothing more *contagious* than examples which appeal strongly to the public passions. . . . Any theatric exhibition, or dramatic and ostentatious dressing-up of such actions to popular effect, are amongst the most culpable efforts of public writers, inasmuch as it is attacking mankind through their best feelings and misleading them into vice by their admiration of eminent virtue."[44]

In discussions of the death of Sir Samuel Romilly we can see three contemporary themes emerging. The first is the lack of agreement about whether Romilly's self-destruction was caused by sickness or sin. Part of a much larger discussion of the causes of suicide and the best means by which those fatal acts could be lessened, the publicity surrounding Romilly's death added a poignancy to the debate hitherto unknown. How shocking some found the public revelations, the newspaper intrusions into the private affairs and grief of the Romilly family! And yet others saw his death as an awful warning. "How painfully instructive the awful lesson which it reads, upon the instability of this world's greatness, upon the insecurity of man's proudest hopes." Some thought that the case proved the need to do away completely with coroners' juries. "I must own," commented a columnist to the *British Monitor* in a piece about Romilly's demise, "that I have ever considered the institution of a Coroner's jury incompatible with the character and feelings of a civilized nation." Others thought that the problem with coroner's juries was their excessive kindness, their failure to find correct verdicts and through a mistaken kindness, to promote charity at the expense of justice. Such "a false sense of clemency," if extended, would render the law a dead letter. If this should occur, "Suicide will remain, as it has so long been, the reproach of our nation; and the impunity of the past will ever prove a lamentable encouragement to the future."[45] While the notion that the English had an especial penchant for suicide was a cliché by this time, some commentators argued that the stringent and unmitigated operation of a stern coroner's jury could diminish if not eradicate the reality from which this platitude arose.[46]

Accompanying these discussions about inquest juries and their operations came a disquieting recognition of the social biases of such bodies and of the public itself. One observer, for example, noted that the public's interest in this story had more to do with Romilly's prestige than with the nature of his death. "Not a week passes," commented X.Y., in a letter to the *Sunday Advertiser*, "without our having a report of three or four instances of the kind; but numerous as these are, they excite very little attention. It is only when a man of celebrated talents, is impelled, by whatever cause, to rid himself of life, that we take alarm, and meditate on the crime." Even more damaging was the point made by another anonymous correspondent who remarked "that not once in a thousand did a Coroner's Jury bring in a verdict of *Felo-de-se* against a rich man, but principally against poor criminals alone." Charging that the law was tenderer to the rich and famous than to the poor and condemned, that inquest verdicts depended on the class rather than the guilt of the accused, was a very serious, and unusually frank accusation.[47]

But, as we have already noted, Romilly was generally not described as a man of rank or riches, but rather was presented as an ideal man of the middle class: self-made, publicly active though emotionally grounded in the familial, hard working, and dedicated to social improvement. After his death, a great deal was made of the fortune he had acquired through his own laudable efforts: "It is stated, that Sir Samuel Romilly died worth no less a sum than [£]180,000 landed and funded property. He is supposed to have annually netted from sixteen to seventeen thousand pounds, by his professional exertions. Sir Samuel's law library is said to have been the most choice and valuable of any possessed by the profession."[48] How could such a man, with so much character, so widely admired, and so successful, have come to kill himself? Was there perhaps some inevitable price to pay for pulling oneself up by one's bootstraps? The *European Magazine* certainly raised this possibility. Romilly's "industry and perseverance were not only proverbial" they noted, "but had almost grown to a fault."[49] Romilly's death raised, but did not answer any of these questions. When aristocrats, dandies, or criminals killed themselves, their acts confirmed rather than challenged common wisdom: vice, self-indulgence, or law breaking not surprisingly led to despair and death. But the enigma of Romilly's suicide seemed more troubling, for in his case it seemed his virtues which caused his demise, his sentiments which led to his fatal act. Though his death could be read as the inevitable outcome of philosophic radicalism, of Enlightenment self-confidence, the anxiety raised by the event suggests contemporaries saw in it the specter not only of an individual but of a class of men flawed by the very attributes that made them admirable.[50]

| ACKNOWLEDGMENTS |

As with all collaborative ventures, this volume required the contributions of many individuals. My biggest debt of course is to the other ten scholars who have written chapters for this volume. I laud them all for their fine, diligent work and am quite grateful to David Lederer for his suggestions about possible contributors and to Arne Jansson, who, though accepting the invitation to contribute on short notice, still made important recommendations for this volume. My greatest debt is to Jeff Merrick who, from the early planning stages to the publication of this collection, has been most generous in sharing his time and invaluable ideas.

We deeply appreciate Vera Lind's efforts in organizing a conference for all contributors in December 2001 at the German Historical Institute (GHI) in Washington, D.C. The conference, at which we discussed in detail all the chapters, generated much constructive criticism, giving this project an enormous boost. We are profoundly indebted to director Christof Mauch and the entire staff of the GHI for their generosity and kind hospitality in hosting the conference and for providing a very generous subvention for this publication. Special thanks to David Lazar for his constant support and guidance toward the publication of this collection.

Widely esteemed for his expertise in the history of suicide, Michael Mac-Donald generously shared some helpful insights over the past decade and a half. I also thank Erik Midelfort, Margaret and Patrice Higonnet, and Paolo Bernardini for their encouragement and suggestions and to Ron Brown for some useful tips concerning illustrations.

I sincerely appreciate the professional manner in which John Ackerman and the superb staff at Cornell University Press have handled all phases of the publication of this volume. Special thanks to Sheri Englund whose diligent efforts, along with those of her assistant, Julie Brown, have been vitally important in completing this work. For their fine work, kudos also go to Karen Laun and Susan MacKay, the production editor and copyeditor, respectively.

Here at the University of Mississippi, I am grateful to my chair, Bob Haws, for his support of and genuine interest in this collection, and to my colleagues, Les Field and Joe Ward, for their valuable advice. Finally, I thank Isabella Watt for enduring countless conversations about the morbid subject of suicide and for kindly assisting me with her computer know-how.

An earlier version of Craig Koslofsky's chapter appeared in *Continuity and Change* 16 (2001): 45–71. For their chapters, Vera Lind, Arne Jansson, and Jeffrey Watt drew material from their respective books: *Selbstmord in der Frühen Neuzeit: Diskurs, Lebenswelt, kultureller Wandel am Beispiel der Herzogtümer Schleswig und Holstein,* Veröffentlichungen des Max-Planck-Instituts für Geschichte, vol. 146 (Göttingen: Vandenhoeck und Ruprecht, 1999); *From Swords to Sorrow: Homicide and Suicide in Early Modern Stockholm* (Stockholm: Almqvist & Wiksell, 1998); and *Choosing Death: Suicide and Calvinism in Early Modern Geneva* (Kirksville: Truman State University Press, 2001). We warmly thank the various publishers for their permission to reuse material here.

Introduction

1. Archives d'Etat de Genève, Procès Criminel 552; Registres du Petit Conseil 50: 23v, 25v, 27–28.

2. Archives d'Etat de Genève, Procès Criminel 17079.

3. See Yolande Grisé, *Le suicide dans la Rome antique* (Montreal, 1982); Anton J. L. Hooff, *From Autothanasia to Suicide: Self-killing in Classical Antiquity* (London, 1990).

4. Augustine, *City of God,* 1. 16–27. Augustine did acknowledge that God could actually order someone to take his life. The church father argued that Samson's death, though self-inflicted, was justified because he was fulfilling an order from God; ibid., 1. 20.

5. For the medieval period, see Alexander Murray's excellent *Suicide in the Middle Ages,* 2 vols. (Oxford, 1998–2000).

6. Henry Romilly Fedden, *Suicide: A Social and Historical Study* (New York, 1972), 309; Howard I. Kushner, *American Suicide: A Psychocultural Exploration* (New Brunswick, 1991), 6–7; Georges Minois, *History of Suicide: Voluntary Death in Western Culture,* trans. Lydia G. Cochrane (Baltimore, 1999), 320.

7. Fedden, *Suicide,* 322–23; Kushner, *American Suicide,* 3–6.

8. Such researchers have tended to modify the connection between suicide and mental illness: rather than insisting that all suicides are psychologically disturbed, they tend to look for varying degrees of risk for suicide among different diagnostic groups; David Lester, *Why People Kill Themselves: A Summary of Research Findings on Suicidal Behavior* (Springfield, 1972), 193.

9. Enrico Morselli, *Il Suicidio: Saggio di statistica morale comparata* (Milan, 1879). See also Steven Stack, "Suicide and Religion: A Comparative Analysis," *Sociological Focus* 14 (1981): 207–20.

10. Emile Durkheim, *Suicide: A Case Study in Sociology,* trans. John A. Spaulding and George Simpson, ed. George Simpson (New York, 1951).

11. See, for example, Albert Bayet, *Le Suicide et la morale* (Paris, 1922; reprint, New York,

1975); Minois, *History of Suicide;* Murray, *Suicide in Middle Ages,* vol. 2, *The Curse on Self-Murder;* S. E. Sprott: *The English Debate on Suicide from Donne to Hume* (La Salle, 1961).

12. An excellent example is Olive Anderson, *Suicide in Victorian and Edwardian England* (Oxford, 1987). Another fine quantitative study is Victor Bailey, *"This Rash Act": Suicide across the Life Cycle in the Victorian City* (Stanford, 1998).

13. Jack Douglas, *The Social Meanings of Suicide* (Princeton, 1967), 275.

14. Michael MacDonald and Terence Murphy, *Sleepless Souls: Suicide in Early Modern England* (Oxford, 1990), 351.

Chapter 1. The Judicial Treatment of Suicide in Amsterdam

I would like to thank a number of people for their various contributions to this essay. M. F. Gijswijt-Hofstra, H. F. K. van Nierop, S. Faber, J. van Herwaarden, and E. Lissenberg all provided me with valuable comments on my master's thesis, which has formed the basis of the present document. I am also most grateful to Jeffrey R. Watt for his stimulating and supportive advice during the writing of this chapter. Finally, I want to thank my father, Jan Peter Bosman, for his help in translating it.

1. Amsterdam City Archives (hereafter GAA), Judicial Archives (hereafter RA) 635: Dec. 1792.

2. In recent years there has been considerable research on the judicial treatment of suicides in early modern Europe, thanks to the growing use of court records as important historical sources. See, for example, Vera Lind, *Selbstmord in der Frühen Neuzeit: Diskurs, Lebenswelt und kultureller Wandel am Beispiel der Herzogtümer Schleswig und Holstein,* Veröffentlichungen des Max-Planck-Instituts für Geschichte, vol. 146 (Göttingen, 1999); Michael MacDonald and Terence R. Murphy, *Sleepless Souls: Suicide in Early Modern England* (Oxford, 1990); Markus Schär, *Seelennöte der Untertanen: Selbstmord, Melancholie und Religion im Alten Zürich, 1500–1800* (Zurich, 1985); Jeffrey R. Watt, *Choosing Death: Suicide and Calvinism in Early Modern Geneva* (Kirksville, 2001). But until now this trend has not affected scholarship on the Dutch Republic. Prior to this research project, the most recent article on the legal practices governing Dutch suicides dated from 1871, and no publication on the legal treatment of suicides in early modern Amsterdam has occurred since 1838; M. C. van Hall, "Verhandeling over het zinnebeeldige in de oud-Nederlandse regten," in idem, *Regtsgeleerde verhandelingen en losse geschriften* (Amsterdam, 1838), 117–244; J. H. de Stoppelaar, "Het geregt van desperatie," *De oude tijd* 3 (1871): 121–23, 135–38, 219–23, 262–66, 328–30, 360–62. Both studies labor under the nineteenth-century malady of wishing to cast the eighteenth century in an unfavorable light. Consequently, this article is exploratory in nature, and research had to start from scratch. See also Machiel Bosman, "De laatst bestrafte zelfmoordenaars in Amsterdam, eind achttiende eeuw," *De achttiende eeuw* 33 (2001): 125–33.

3. Soldiers had to fear from the law as well. Their suicides were equated with desertion and punished by confiscation of the deceased's property. If, however, the suicide had its origin in *taedium vitae* or in other absolving circumstances, the estate remained intact; Andreas Wacke, "Der Selbstmord im römischen Recht und in der Rechtsentwicklung," *Zeitschrift der Savigny Stiftung für Rechtsgeschichte-Romanische Abteilung* 64 (1980): 52–54, 65–76.

4. Wacke, "Selbstmord im römischen Recht," 55–61.

5. Augustine, *De Civitate Dei,* 1. 19; Jürgen Dieselhorst, "Die Bestrafung der Selbstmörder in Territorium der Reichsstadt Nürnberg," in *Mitteilungen des Vereins für Geschichte der Stadt Nürnberg* 44 (1953): 68. Augustine's position was largely motivated by the Donatists, an early Christian movement that Augustine deemed heretical, whose followers at times courted martyrdom in a manner that bordered on suicide; Wacke, "Selbstmord im römischen Recht," 33.

6. Gratian, *Decretum,* C. 23, q. 5, c. 12, in *Corpus iuris canonici,* ed. Emil Friedberg (Leipzig, 1879–81), 1: 935. See also Albert Bayet, *Le Suicide et la morale* (Paris, 1922; reprint, New York,

1975), 387–88;Alexander Murray, *Suicide in the Middle Ages*, vol. 2, *The Curse on Self-Murder* (Oxford, 2000), 183; Lieve Vandekerckhove, *Van straffen gesproken. De bestraffing van zelfdoding in het oude Europa* (Tielt, 1985), 21. Religious ceremonies were similarly denied to the funerals of another category of the damned: the excommunicated. Such burials came to be given the unflattering designation of asses' burials, a term taken from Jeremiah 22:19: "He shall be buried like a dead ass, dragged along and flung out beyond the gates of Jerusalem"; Dieselhorst, "Bestrafung," 70–71.

7. MacDonald and Murphy, *Sleepless Souls*, 18–19; Murray, *Suicide in Middle Ages*, vol. 2, *Curse on Self-Murder*, 28–53.

8. Vandekerkhove, *Van straffen gesproken*, 67.

9. Filips Wielant, *Verzameld werk I. Corte instructie in materie criminele*, ed. Jos Monballyu (Brussels, 1985), 86.

10. Murray, *Suicide in Middle Ages*, vol. 2, *Curse on Self-Murder*, 63–77.

11. See, for example, Tobias Boel, Jr., *Amstelredams privilegie en poorter-regt; raakende de verbeurte van lyf, en goed, ter saake van misdaad; verklaard, en in syn volle kragt voorgesteld* (Amsterdam, 1713), 127; Genootschap van Rechtsgeleerden, *Rechtsgeleerde observatien dienende tot opheldering van verscheide duistere, en tot nog toe onbewezene passagien uyt "De inleyding tot de Hollandsche rechtsgel." van wijlen Mr. Hugo de Groot* (The Hague, 1777), 66.

12. J. P. H. de Monté Verloren and J. E. Spruit, *Hoofdlijnen uit de ontwikkeling der rechterlijke organisatie in de Noordelijke Nederlanden tot de Bataafse omwenteling*, 5th ed. (Deventer, 1972), 181–82.

13. Joost de Damhouder, *Practycke in criminele saken*, ed. J. Dauwe and J. Monballyu (Roeselare, 1981), 143–44.

14. De Monté Verloren and Spruit, *Hoofdlijnen*, 215. Though written from 1619–21, Grotius's *Inleidinge in de Hollandsche regtsgeleertheit* was not published as a book until 1633.

15. Genootschap van Rechtsgeleerden, *Dertig rechtsgeleerde vraagen uit de Inleidinge tot de Hollandsche Rechts-geleerdheid van wijlen Mr. Hugo de Groot* (The Hague, 1776–77), 3.

16. R. W. Lee, *The Jurisprudence of Holland by Hugo Grotius* (Oxford, 1936), 2: 71.

17. Hugo de Groot, *Inleidinge tot de Hollantsche regts-geleertheyt, bevestigt met Placcaten, Hantvesten, oude Herkomen, Regten etc.*, ed. Simon van Groenewegen van der Made (Amsterdam, 1667), 52.

18. Willem van Alphen, *Papegay ofte formulier-boek van allerhande requesten, mandamenten conclusien, als anders, in de dagelijcksche practijcke dienende voor de respective Hoven van Justitie in Hollandt* (The Hague, 1683), 52.

19. In addition to works already mentioned, see Martinus Caesar, *Jus Hodiernum ofte hedensdaeghs Recht* (Amsterdam, 1656); Simon van Leeuwen, *Het Rooms-Hollands-regt* (Leiden, 1664); Petrus Peckius, *Verhandelinge van hand-opleggen ende besetten*, ed. Simon van Leeuwen (Amsterdam, 1712); Eduard van Zurck, *Codex Batavus, waer in het algemeen Kerk- publyk en burgerlijk recht van Hollant, Zeelant en het ressort der generaliteit kortelyk is begrepen* (Delft, 1727).

20. Peckius, *Verhandelinge van hand-opleggen*, ed. Van Leeuwen, 182. See also Caesar, *Jus Hodiernum*, 352; Van Leeuwen, *Rooms-Hollands-regt*, 415; *Consultatien, advysen en advertissementen, gegeven ende geschreven by verscheyden treffelijcke rechts-geleerden in Holland* (Rotterdam, 1645), 6: 140.

21. Genootschap van Rechtsgeleerden, *Rechtsgeleerde observatien*, 64.

22. The best introduction to the Amsterdam legal archives is provided by Sjoerd Faber, *Strafrechtspleging en criminaliteit te Amsterdam, 1680–1811. De nieuwe menslievendheid* (Arnhem, 1983).

23. Jean A. G. Jüngen, "God betert. De Amsterdamse lijkschouwingsrapporten in de jaren 1560, 1570, 1580, 1590" (Master's thesis, Vrije Universiteit Amsterdam, 1982); idem, "Doodslagers en hun pakkans in het 16e-eeuwse Amsterdam," in *Scherp toezicht. Van "Boeventucht" tot "Samenleving en Criminaliteit"*, ed. C. Fijnaut and P. Spierenburg (Arnhem, 1990). Jüngen counts

twenty-three suicides, but I have not included one man who succumbed to self-inflicted injuries during a fight.

24. GAA, RA 567: 31.

25. This verdict can be found in *Sententien en gewezen zaken, van den Hoogen en Provincialen Raad in Holland, Zeeland en West-Vriesland* (Rotterdam, 1662), 1: 336–39.

26. Ibid., 337.

27. Jan Wagenaar, *Amsterdam in zyne opkomst, aanwas, geschiedenissen etc.* (Amsterdam, 1760–67), 2: 108.

28. W. van Iterson, *Geschiedenis der confiscatie in Nederland. Een rechtshistorische studie aan de hand van noord-Nederlandse, een aantal zuid-Nederlandse en andere bronnen* (Utrecht, 1957), 417.

29. *Sententien en gewezen zaken,* 1: 339–43.

30. Van Iterson found the same principle of automatic confiscation of a suicide's estate in Holland in the late Middle Ages; *Confiscatie in Nederland,* 177–78.

31. GAA, RA 567: 69v, 117, 231, 285; RA 568: 111v.

32. GAA, RA 567: 89v, 106, 119v, 150, 192v, 325; RA 568: 107v; RA 569: 16.

33. GAA, RA 567: 192v.

34. Ibid., 355v.

35. Ibid., 101, 161v; GAA, RA 568: 116v. Of those with criminal records who killed themselves only one seems to have escaped punishment; RA 567: 167.

36. GAA, RA 567: 37, 156.

37. Ibid., 213.

38. Sjoerd Faber, "Crime and Punishment in Amsterdam," in *Rome and Amsterdam: Two Growing Cities in Seventeenth-Century Europe,* ed. P. van Kessel and E. Schulte (Amsterdam, 1997), 289.

39. Pieter Spierenburg, "Lange termijn trends in doodslag. Theoretische overdenkingen en Nederlands bewijsmateriaal, 15de–20ste eeuw," *Amsterdams sociologisch tijdschrift* 20–21 (1993): 88.

40. Pieter Spierenburg, *The Spectacle of Suffering. Executions and the Evolution of Repression: From a Preindustrial Metropolis to the European Experience* (Cambridge, 1984), 56.

41. Machiel Bosman, "'Vol-recht heeft niemand over sijn leven.' De strafrechtspleging inzake zelfmoord te Amsterdam, zestiende tot eind achttiende eeuw" (Master's thesis, Universiteit van Amsterdam, 1998), 35–36.

42. GAA, Collection of Manuscripts (hereafter CH), Collectie Bontemantel 32: 429.

43. I have not been able to find out where they were recorded, having looked in the *schepenen minuut register,* the *schoutsrol,* the *arrestrol,* and the *Groot Memoriaal.*

44. These latter two suicides are discussed respectively in Jacobus Koning, *Geschiedkundige aanteekeningen betrekkelijk de lijfstraffelijke regtsoefening te Amsterdam, voornamelijk in de zestiende eeuw* (Amsterdam, 1828), 97; and Spierenburg, *Spectacle of Suffering,* 56.

45. GAA, CH, Collectie Bontemantel 31: 149. Although the quotation deals with hanging, no doubt Bontemantel was referring to all methods of suicide since he mentioned in the margin a suicide who shot himself. Another marginal note says, "Is no longer practiced in the case of persons drowned." As is well known, it is extremely difficult to determine whether death by drowning is accidental or intentional. This is probably why it had become customary not to try drowned persons.

46. GAA, RA 580: 125v.

47. GAA, RA 583: 27v.

48. GAA, CH, Collectie Bontemantel 33: 5–7. Cf. Peckius, *Verhandelinge van hand-opleggen,* 182. Bontemantel showed that he was conversant with the latest legal views as this quotation was taken verbatim from Simon van Leeuwen's annotations of 1659 on a work by Petrus Peckius (1529–1589). In the margins of his notes on suicide, Bontemantel also referred to the works of the lawyers Rooseboom, De Damhouder, Poppius, and Van Groenewegen.

49. GAA, CH, Collectie Bontemantel 32: 429.

50. Hans Bontemantel, *De regeeringe van Amsterdam, soo in 't civiel als crimineel en militaire (1663–1672),* ed. G. W. Kernkamp (The Hague, 1897), lxxxiv.

51. Bosman, "Vol-recht heeft niemand over sijn leven," 49–51.

52. Watt, *Choosing Death,* 90.

53. For a discussion of suicides who had not committed a crime before killing themselves, see Machiel Bosman, "Uit 'onvergenoegdheid' van de brug af. Zelfmoord in de 18de eeuw," *Ons Amsterdam* 54 (2002): 252–55.

54. GAA, CH, Aantekeningen van mr. M. Weveringh 55: 63.

55. I thank Sjoerd Faber for making available to me his findings on wardens' bills for the period 1732 to 1788. I consulted the bills for the subsequent years through 1795. Altogether thirteen suicides can be found in the wardens' bills: GAA, RA 631: March 1741, Dec. 1744; RA 632: Oct. 1752, July 1760; RA 633: Feb. 1764, Jan. 1765, May 1766, Sept. 1771, March 1773; RA 634: May 1779, April 1786, June 1786; RA 635: Dec. 1792. A fourteenth suicide can be found in the diary of Jacob Bicker Raye from Amsterdam (1703–77). This concerned a case from 1763, a year for which no wardens' bills can be found. GAA Library, manuscript of Jacob Bicker Raye's diary 54: 276.

56. GAA, RA 430: 90.

57. The bodies of people shot dead during revolts were also hanged upside down.

58. GAA, RA 413: 256.

59. For example, GAA, RA 446: 381.

60. H. C. Jelgersma, *Galgebergen en galgevelden in West- en Midden Nederland* (Zutphen, 1978), 22–23.

61. Montesquieu, *Persian Letters,* trans. C. J. Betts (Harmondsworth, Eng., 1973), 152.

62. I have found nothing to indicate that Amsterdam's judicial treatment of suicide was atypical in the eighteenth-century Dutch Republic. In studying Middleburg in the province of Zeeland, De Stoppelaar makes no mention of punishments imposed on suicides without criminal pasts after 1685; "Het geregt van desperatie," 265. In the province of Friesland, the famous physician, Petrus Camper (1722–89), wrote the following in 1774: "By now punishments such as the hurdle, the gibbet, and the confiscation of estates have passed completely out of use, except for those who either inside or outside of jail kill themselves in order to escape punishment: even in present-day Friesland such people will be dragged on a hurdle to the gallows-field, there to be hanged or to be put on the rack"; *Gedagten van Petrus Camper over de misdaad van kindermoord; over de gemakkelijke wijze om vondelinghuizen in te voeren; over de oorzaken van kindermoord; en over de zelfmoord* (Leeuwarden, 1774), 34.

Chapter 2. Suicide and the Vicar General in London

1. London Metropolitan Archive (henceforth, LMA), DL/C/338, Vicar General Book, 1601–05, 16–5, 4v–5v. Spelling and punctuation here and in all quoted manuscript material has been modernized.

2. Thomas Roger Forbes, *Chronicle from Aldgate: Life and Death in Shakespeare's London* (New Haven, 1971), 168.

3. The literature on suicide in early modern Europe is vast. In addition to the works cited in this study, one might mention the recent articles by Jeffrey R. Watt: "The Family, Love, and Suicide in Early Modern Geneva," *Journal of Family History* 21 (1996): 63–86; "Calvin on Suicide," *Church History* 66 (1997): 463–76; and "Suicide in Reformation Geneva," *Archiv für Reformationsgeschichte* 89 (1998): 227–45; Luke Wilson, "Hamlet, Hales v. Petit, and the Hysteresis of Action," *English Literary History,* 60 (1993): 17–55; Michael MacDonald, "The Strange Death of the Earl of Essex, 1683," *History Today* 41 (1991): 13–18; and more generally Georges Minois,

History of Suicide: Voluntary Death in Western Culture, trans. Lydia G. Cochrane (Baltimore, 1999) and Alexander Murray, *Suicide in the Middle Ages,* 2 vols. (Oxford, 1998–2000).

4. Michael MacDonald, "The Secularization of Suicide in England 1660–1800," *Past and Present* 111 (1986): 50–97; Michael MacDonald and Terence R. Murphy, *Sleepless Souls: Suicide in Early Modern England* (Oxford, 1990), 24–28, 346–53; Michael Zell, "Suicide in Pre-industrial England," *Social History* 11 (1986): 306–7; S. J. Stevenson, "The Rise of Suicide Verdicts in South-east England, 1530–1590," *Continuity and Change* 2 (1987): 41–51; Forbes, *Chronicle from Aldgate,* 166–67.

5. John Weever, *Ancient funerall Monuments within the united Monarchie of Great Britaine* (London, 1631), 22.

6. Charles Moore, *A Full Inquiry into the Subject of Suicide* (London, 1790), vol. 1, 308n. Alexander Murray notes that in the later Middle Ages "a bishop might occasionally have to judge a disputed question concerning burial"; *Suicide in Middle Ages,* vol. 1, *The Violent against Themselves,* 138.

7. See LMA, Vicar General Book, 1561–74, DL/C/332; Vicar General Book, 1574–83, DL/C/333; Vicar General Book, 1583–90, DL/C/334; Vicar General Book, 1590–95, DL/C/335; Vicar General Book, 1595–97, DL/C/336; Vicar General Book, 1597–99, DL/C/337; Vicar General Book, 1601–05, DL/C/338.

8. Evidently the coroner's jury in each case had returned a verdict of *felo de se,* since had this not been the case no special license would be required. For example, when the coroner's jury met at St. Botolph's Aldgate on 10 July 1624 to investigate the death of John Blackman, it was determined that "he died of a wound which he gave himself in his sickness, being as it were distraught and light headed, and after the coroner's inquest had viewed him, order was appointed to have him laid in Christian burial," to which account the parish clerk added the comment that "it seemed he was ill looked unto in his sickness." Forbes, *Chronicle from Aldgate,* 31.

9. Thomas Beard, *The Theatre of Gods Judgments,* 3d edition (London, 1631), 306–7. The second edition, published in 1612, contained this chapter for the first time.

10. Rowland Wymer, *Suicide and Despair in the Jacobean Drama* (Brighton, 1986), 15.

11. For King, Abbot, and Cartwright, see S. E. Sprott, *The English Debate on Suicide from Donne to Hume* (LaSalle, 1961), 3–5, 33.

12. John Sym, *Lifes Preservative against self-Killing. Or, An Useful Treatise Concerning Life and Self-murder* (London, 1637), 262–63, 267–73, 278.

13. Ibid., sig. A2v.

14. Ibid., 212–24, 184.

15. John Prince in his *Self-Murder Asserted to be a very heinous Crime* (London, 1709), 54, urged his readers specifically to return to works of a century earlier "for the healing of wounded consciences," "such as are *Mary Magdalen's Tears wip'd off,* Mr. Robert Bolton's *Directions for the Cure of afflicted Consciences,* Mr. Perkins's *Cases of Conscience;* the Works of Mr. Greenham; and some others of like kind, if you can light upon them."

16. Sym, *Lifes Preservative,* sigs. A1r, A1v.

17. For evidence suggesting that no great increase in the number of London suicides occurred in the year or so before Prince published his treatise, see the appendix in Sprott, *English Debate on Suicide,* 159. My figures for suicides and total deaths for 1636 come from the table compiled from the Bills of Mortality by John Graunt, *Natural and Political Observations . . . made upon the Bills of Mortality* (London, 1662), the Table of Casualties, found between pages 74 and 75.

18. Graunt notes that between 1603 and 1624 the Bills show 829 drownings and 222 suicides. There is no way to improve on Graunt's compilations for the early Stuart period, because the records of coroners' reports for London do not exist for this period in the King's Bench series exploited by MacDonald and Murphy. A coroners' roll for London between May and November 1590 was found in the Corporation Records Office by Thomas Forbes: seven of the

thirty-five deaths investigated were purported to be suicides, "a man and two women by hanging, two men by stabbing, and two women by jumping and by poisoning." Thomas R. Forbes,
"London Coroner's Inquests for 1590," *Journal of the History of Medicine and Allied Sciences* 28
(1973): 385 – 86.

19. MacDonald, "Secularization of Suicide," 78.

20. The entry is dated 17 October 1639: LMA, Vicar General Book, 1637 – 62, DL/C/344,
61r.

21. LMA, Vicar General Book, 1627 – 37, DL/C/343, 56r-v.

22. MacDonald and Murphy, *Sleepless Souls*, 248, table 7.1. Michael Zell's study of Kentish
suicides in Elizabeth's reign shows a ratio of 1.9: 1, a ratio of men to women suicides much
closer to the London figures produced here than to those, based on much larger totals, used by
MacDonald and Murphy; "Suicide in Pre-industrial England," 311, table 2. S. J. Stevenson, again
using a different data base, estimated male suicides running at 1.5 to 2.5 times that of females;
"Social and Economic Contributions to the Pattern of 'Suicide' in South-east England, 1530 –
1590," *Continuity and Change* 2 (1987): 240 – 41. Stevenson notes that in 1951 the figure for male
suicides in England and Wales was 1.9 times that of females.

23. "Suicide in Pre-industrial England," 311, table 2.

24. John Graunt found that the Bills of Mortality, 1603 – 24, gave totals of 229,250 as having died in London, of which 829 were listed as having drowned. Graunt, *Natural and Political
Observations*, 15 – 17; Forbes, "London Coroner's Inquests," 385.

25. LMA, Vicar General Book, 1616 – 23, DL/C/341, 55r-v. In early modern England, the
new year officially began 25 March. Consequently while we would consider the above license
to have been granted in January 1618, for contemporaries the suicide and burial took place in
January 1617. Only in 1752 did England officially adopt the Gregorian calendar which provided, among other things, that the new year begins the first of January.

26. LMA, Vicar General Book, 1623 – 27, DL/C/342, 225v.

27. LMA, Vicar General Book, 1627 – 37, DL/C/343, 101r-v.

28. Ibid., 134r-v, 142r-v, 147r, 203r-v.

29. License to bury was granted 26 April 1615: LMA, Vicar General Book, 1611 – 16, DL/
C/340, 148v.

30. License to bury was granted 11 May 1615: ibid., 151r.

31. Vicar General Book, 1623 – 27, LMA, DL/C/342, 55r.

32. License to bury was granted 7 October 1616: LMA, Vicar General Book, 1616 – 23, DL/
C/341, 11r.

33. Ibid., 179r.

34. Ibid., 41v.

35. William Ames, *Conscience with the Power and Cases Thereof* (n.p., 1639), book 1, sig. F2r.

36. Kenneth L. Parker and Eric J. Carlson, *"Practical Divinity": The Works and Life of Revd
Richard Greenham* (Aldershot, 1998), 188.

37. The petitioners on behalf of John Stafford, B.D., who had hanged himself, nevertheless
claimed that the act was not premeditated but was committed as a result of a severe illness, so
"that they verily believe he died not without repentance for his sins." Vicar General Book,
1607 – 11, LMA, DL/C/339, 159r-v.

38. As noted, the petitioners preferred to believe that Stafford had repented. The second
case involved Henry Thorneton, who had cut his throat but had lived long enough to repent,
and the third, Anne Gibson, a servant whose master petitioned on her behalf, had also cut her
throat but had, so her master claimed, convincingly repented; Vicar General Book, 1611 – 16,
LMA, DL/C/340, 148v, 151r. For Gurling, see ibid., 160r.

39. Vicar General Book, 1616 – 23, LMA, DL/C/341, 67r.

40. Vicar General Book, 1627 – 37, LMA, DL/C/343, 166v.

41. Vicar General Book, 1616 – 23, LMA, DL/C/341, 11r.

42. Ibid., 179r.

43. Vicar General Book, 1623–27, LMA, DL/C/342, 37r.

44. Vicar General Book, 1627–37, LMA, DL/C/343, 101r, 134r.

45. Ibid., 203r-v.

46. Beard, *Theatre of Gods Judgments,* 307; Sym, *Lifes Preservative,* 246.

47. Vicar General Book, 1627–37, LMA, DL/C/343, 203r.

48. See, e.g., MacDonald and Murphy, *Sleepless Souls,* 42–75; Keith Thomas, *Religion and the Decline of Magic* (London, 1971), 469–77; Paul Seaver, *Wallington's World: A Puritan Artisan in Seventeenth-Century London* (Stanford, 1985), 64–65.

49. Vicar General Book, 1616–23, LMA, DL/C/341, 67r, 179r.

50. It is also impossible to know whether some petitions were turned down, since the vicar general books record only licenses granted.

51. The three were all from city parishes, and therefore fell within the cognizance of the Bills. In fact, aside from Henry Thorneton of Fulham, Gresham Hogan of Hackney, and Sir George Southcote of Kensington, all the suicides occurred in urban parishes.

52. In this respect it is worth noting that those who petitioned in the case of John Stafford in 1610 included two parishioners from St. Bride's in Fleet Street outside the western wall of the city and one petitioner from St. Olave's in Hart Street which is across the city along the eastern wall. How a merchant resident in St. Olave's came to know and care about a preacher at St. Bride's is unknown.

53. *The Complete Works of St. Thomas More,* ed. Edward Surtz and J. H. Hexter, vol. 4, *Utopia* (New Haven, 1965), 186–87.

54. British Library, Add. MS 27,632, 122r–125v. Although John Harington's name precedes the title of this manuscript, it is not apparently in Harington's handwriting and may be a misattribution.

55. John Donne, *Biathanotos. A Declaration of that Paradoxe, or Thesis, that Self-homicide is not so Naturally Sinne, that it may never be otherwise* (London, n.d. [1646]), 18.

56. Donne, *Biathanotos,* 31, 32. William Doddington, a London merchant who committed suicide in 1600, left a suicide note implying a belief that penance was still possible and efficacious even if done before the act. He wrote: "And O Lord forgive me this cruel fact upon mine own body, which I utterly detest, and most humbly pray him to cast it behind him, and that of his exceeding and infinite mercy he will forgive it me with all my other sins"; BL, Lansdowne MS. 99, no. 32. See also MacDonald and Murphy, *Sleepless Souls,* 66–67.

57. Donne, *Biathanotos,* 45, 46, 49, 71, 74.

58. Ibid., 79, 81, 88, 89.

59. Ibid., 91.

60. Ibid., 99.

61. For Montaigne and Sidney, see MacDonald and Murphy, *Sleepless Souls,* 90–91; Raleigh's letter is quoted in Wymer, *Suicide and Despair,* 20.

62. *The Tragical History of Doctor Faustus,* act 2, sc. 2.

63. *Doctor Faustus,* act 4, sc. 5.

64. *The Tragedy of Hamlet, Prince of Denmark,* act 3, sc. 1.

65. *Julius Caesar,* act 5, sc. 5.

66. As quoted in Wymer, *Suicide and Despair,* 114.

67. In addition to the many dramatic and poetic versions dating from the Elizabethan period, one could cite a story that echoes the Lucretia story in prose, told by Thomas Nashe's incorrigible hero, Jack Wilton, who recounts how he witnessed the rape of "the chaste matron, Heraclide," who, after pronouncing that "the only repeal we have from God's undefinite chastisement is to chastise ourselves in this world . . . ; nought but death be my penance," stabbed herself to death. *The Unfortunate Traveller* (1594), ed. John Berryman (New York, 1960), 110, 115–17.

68. As quoted in Wymer, *Suicide and Despair,* 138.

69. Ibid., 156.

70. Vicars general had material motives to increase their business, and it is worth noting that the early Elizabethan volume, 1563–74, had fewer than 100 folios (LMA, DL/C/332), whereas that of 1583–90 contained 350 folios (LMA, DL/C/334).

71. St. Botolph Bishopsgate, Parish Register, 1558–1628, Guildhall Library [henceforth GL] MS. 4515/1, no foliation; St. Swithin London Stone, Parish Register, 1614–75, GL MS. 4311, no foliation. On at least one occasion the injunction to bury the suicide against the churchyard wall was simply ignored: "Anne, daughter of Ralph Grinder, buried in the cloister the 14th July [1626]." St. Stephen Coleman Street, Parish Register, 1558–1636, GL MS. 4449/1, no foliation.

72. "A Memorial of God's Judgments," British Library, Sloane MS. 1457, 6r–7v.

73. See Joseph P. Ward, *Metropolitan Communities: Trade Guilds, Identity, and Change in Early Modern London* (Stanford, 1997), chapters 1 and 4.

74. See, for example, Dagmar Freist, *Government by Opinion: Politics, Religion and the Dynamics of Communication in Stuart London 1637–1645* (London, 1997); the rapid mobilization of vast crowds of Londoners in the early 1640s would not have been possible in the absence of a public demand for information and the capacity to communicate it across the city: see, for example, Keith Lindley, *Popular Politics and Religion in Civil War London* (Aldershot, 1997). For a description of Samuel Pepys's rich and complex social network in the 1660s, see Ian W. Archer, "Social Networks in Restoration London: The Evidence of Samuel Pepys's Diary," in *Communities in Early Modern England: Networks, Place, Rhetoric,* ed. Alexandra Shepard and Phil Withington (Manchester, 2000), 76–94.

75. *The Staple of News,* act 1, sc. 2, and act 3, sc. 2.

76. MacDonald, "Secularization of Suicide," 61, table 2.

77. GL, MS. 204, 8. As Michael MacDonald noted, "melancholy became a badge of fashion during the late sixteenth and seventeenth centuries, and the fascination with this classical malady fostered the belief that suicidal behavior was a sign of mental illness, rather than a religious crime"; *Mystical Bedlam: Madness, Anxiety, and Healing in Seventeenth-Century England* (Cambridge, 1981), 135.

Chapter 3. Controlling the Body of the Suicide in Saxony

1. For their generous assistance in the development of this chapter, the author wishes to thank the other contributors to this volume, and the members of the early modern Europe reading group and the German Colloquium at the University of Illinois.

2. Michael MacDonald and Terence Murphy, *Sleepless Souls: Suicide in Early Modern England* (New York, 1990), 342, see also 6, 109–216; and Donna Andrew and Michael MacDonald, "Debate: The Secularization of Suicide in England, 1660–1800," *Past and Present* 119 (1988): 158–70.

3. Martina Wagner-Egelhaaf, "Melancholischer Diskurs und literaler Selbstmord: Der Fall Adam Bernd," in *Trauer, Verzweiflung und Anfechtung: Selbstmord und Selbstmordversuche in mittelalterlichen und frühneuzeitlichen Gesellschaften,* ed. Gabriela Signori (Tübingen, 1994), 282–310; Adam Bernd, *Eigene Lebens-Beschreibung* (complete 1738 edition), ed. Volker Hoffmann (Munich, 1973), 128–30, 177–84, 376–78.

4. Markus Schär refers to "die Abwertung übernatürlicher Mächte" in his *Seelennöte der Untertanen: Selbstmord, Melancholie und Religion im alten Zürich, 1500–1800* (Zürich, 1985), 6, 201–19. See also the overview of eighteenth-century debates in Vera Lind, *Selbstmord in der Frühen Neuzeit: Diskurs, Lebenswelt und kultureller Wandel am Beispiel der Herzogtümer Schleswig und Holstein,* Veröffentlichungen des Max-Planck-Instituts für Geschichte, vol. 146 (Göttingen, 1999), 45–151.

5. See for example Georges Minois, *History of Suicide: Voluntary Death in Western Culture,* trans. Lydia G. Cochrane (Baltimore, 1999), which does not discuss the body in relation to suicide.

6. See Michael Frank, "Die fehlende Geduld Hiobs: Suizid und Gesellschaft in der Graftschaft Lippe (1600–1800)," in *Trauer, Verzweifelung und Anfechtung,* ed. Signori, 152–88; and in the same volume, David Lederer, "Aufruhr auf dem Friedhof: Pfarrer, Gemeinde und Selbstmord im frühneuzeitlichen Bayern," 189–209. Frank discusses the social consequences of contact with the body of a suicide (169–75); Lederer (199–208) examines the dishonor associated with the body of the suicide and the threats it posed to the community.

7. Most recently, see Jeffrey R. Watt, *Choosing Death: Suicide and Calvinism in Early Modern Geneva* (Kirksville, 2001), 67–125. See also Jürgen Dieselhorst, "Die Bestrafung der Selbstmörder im Territorium der Reichsstadt Nürnberg," *Mitteilung des Vereins für Geschichte der Stadt Nürnberg* 44 (1955): 189–222; Fritz-Helmut Karraß, "Die rechtliche Behandlung der Selbstmörder in der Zentverfassung des Hochstifts Würzburg (1454 bis 1806)" (Ph.D. dissertation, Universität Würzburg, 1971); Schär, *Seelennöte der Untertanen.*

8. See David Lederer, "Reforming the Spirit: Society, Madness and Suicide in Central Europe, 1517–1809" (Ph.D. dissertation, New York University, 1995), 360–437, esp. 387–403; and Lind, *Selbstmord,* 340–57. This was also the case in early modern Sweden, where civil courts determined the form of burial of suicides; Arne Jansson, *From Swords to Sorrow: Homicide and Suicide in Early Modern Stockholm* (Stockholm, 1998), 12, 25–31.

9. Lederer, "Reforming the Spirit," 389–403. In his richly detailed study, Lederer does not discuss any cases of church-state conflict over the general authority to determine the form of burial of a suicide, as in the Leipzig dispute.

10. Lind, *Selbstmord,* 351–57.

11. See Tanya Kevorkian, "Piety Confronts Politics: Philipp Jacob Spener in Dresden, 1686–1691," *German History* 16 (1998): 145–64.

12. See the recent article on "Kirchenregiment, landesherrliche" in *Theologische Realenzyklopaedie,* ed. Gerhard Krause and Gerhard Müller in association with Horst Robert Balz (Berlin, 1976–), 19: 62–64, and the literature cited there.

13. The most detailed study is Wieland Held, *Der Adel und August der Starke: Konflikt und Konfliktaustrag zwischen 1694 und 1707 in Kursachsen* (Cologne, 1999), which describes the *Landtag,* the *Ständekonvent* (which selected the members of the *Landtag*), and a subcommission of the *Landtag,* the *Ausschußtag.* See also Karl Czok, *August der Starke: Sein Verhältnis zum Absolutismus und zum sächsischen Adel* (Berlin, 1991); and the articles by Blaschke, Czok, and Hoyer in the special volume of *Saxonia* 1 (1995) on Augustus and his age (7–13, 41–47, 48–54).

14. Augustus's Catholicism was entirely political, as was his approach to confessional questions in Leipzig politics. Catholic and Protestant church historians alike agree that his conversion had no basis in faith or conviction—evidence of another aspect of secularization in this period. See Norman Davies, *God's Playground: A History of Poland* (New York, 1984), 2: 495–96.

15. See the *Übersicht über die Bestände des Sächsischen Landeshauptarchivs* (Dresden, 1955), 94; and Johannes Dürichen, "Geheimes Kabinett und Geheimer Rat unter die Regierung Augusts des Starken in den Jahren 1704–1720," *Neues Archiv für sächsische Geschichte* 51 (1930): 68–136, esp. 75. On the relationship between Leipzig and its *Landesherr,* see Karlheinz Blaschke, "Die kursächsische Politik und Leipzig im 18. Jahrhundert," in *Leipzig: Aufklärung und Bürgerlichkeit,* ed. Wolfgang Martens (Heidelberg, 1990), 23–38; and Gustav Wustmann, "Der Bürgermeister Romanus," in *Quellen zur Geschichte Leipzigs,* ed. Gustav Wustmann (Leipzig, 1889–95), 2: 263–352.

16. See Martin Greschat, *Zwischen Tradition und neuem Anfang: Valentin Ernst Löscher und der Ausgang der lutherischen Orthodoxie* (Witten, 1971).

17. See "Selbstmörder" in *Handwörterbuch des deutschen Aberglaubens,* ed. Hanns Bächtold-Stäubli (reprint Berlin, 1987), 7: 1627–33. On the medicinal use of human body parts in this

period, see Kathy Stuart, *Defiled Trades and Social Outcasts: Honor and Ritual Pollution in Early Modern Germany* (Cambridge, 1999), 149–88.

18. See Craig Koslofsky, *The Reformation of the Dead: Death and Ritual in Early Modern Germany, 1450–1700* (New York, 1999), 101–4. On the denial of Christian burial in Catholic Bavaria, see Lederer, "Reforming the Spirit," 368–73.

19. On the denial of Christian burial to members of "dishonorable professions," see Johann Glenzdorf and Fritz Treichel, *Henker, Schinder und arme Sünder* (Bad Münder am Deister, 1970), 1: 31–36; and Gisela Wilbertz, *Scharfrichter und Abdecker im Hochstift Osnabrück: Untersuchungen zur Sozialgeschichte zweier "unehrlicher" Berufe im nordwestdeutschen Raum von 16. bis zum 19. Jahrhundert* (Osnabrück, 1979), 299–300. On criminals see Richard van Dülmen, *Theater des Schreckens: Gerichtspraxis und Strafrituale in der frühen Neuzeit* (Munich, 1985); and Richard Evans, *Rituals of Retribution: Capital Punishment in Germany, 1600–1987* (New York, 1986).

20. See H. C. Erik Midelfort, "Selbstmord im Urteil von Reformation und Gegenreformation," in *Die katholische Konfessionalisierung,* ed. Wolfgang Reinhard and Heinz Schilling (Gütersloh, 1995), 296–310, 301, citing *D. Martin Luthers Werke. Kritische Gesamtausgabe. Tischreden* (WATr) (Weimar, 1912–21), Nr. 222. See also WATr, Nr. 6089.

21. Benedict Carpzov, *Jurisprudentia ecclesiastica seu consistorialis* (Leipzig, 1649), "auff dem Kirchhof an einem absonderlichen ort abends oder morgens frühe ohne läuten / singen und dergleichen ceremonien ohne allen längeren verzug begraben werden möge"; Def. 377, 580.

22. Mary Lindemann, "Armen- und Eselsgräbnis in der europäischen Frühneuzeit," in *Studien zur Thematik des Todes im 16. Jahrhundert,* ed. Paul Richard Blum, Wolfenbütteler Forschungen, vol. 22 (Wolfenbüttel, 1983), 125–40, esp. 130.

23. See the cases cited by Benedict Carpzov in his *Jurisprudentia ecclesiastica seu consistorialis,* Def. 578–82, and the 159 Nuremberg cases (1484–1778) in appendix 2 of Dieselhorst, "Selbstmörder im Territorium Nürnberg," 189–222. Criminals awaiting trial or sentence who committed suicide to escape execution were usually given the same burial as if they had been executed—typically under the gallows.

24. See Hinrich Rüping, "Carpzov und Thomasius," *Zeitschrift für die gesamte Strafrechtswissenschaft* 109 (1997): 381–90. On burial see Wilhelm Thümmel, *Die Versagung der Kirchlichen Bestattungsfeier: Ihre geschichtliche Entwicklung und gegenwärtige Bedeutung* (Leipzig, 1902), 117.

25. In practice this distinction was flexible: it could be used, for example, to shield the wellborn from dishonorable burial. See Carpzov, *Jurisprudentia ecclesiastica seu consistorialis,* Def. 581–82; on funeral sermons for suicides, see Rudolf Mohr, *Protestantische Theologie und Frömmigkeit im Angesicht des Todes während des Barockzeitalters* (Marburg, 1964), 402–4.

26. "Cognitio ergo causae praecedat, necesse est, quae ad Magistratum ecclesiasticum seu Consistorium proprie spectat, a quo modus sepulturae in casu occurente praescribendus licet"; Carpzov, *Jurisprudentia ecclesiastica seu consistorialis,* Def. 581.

27. Ibid., Def. 582; Johann Christian Lünig, *Codex Augusteus, oder Neuvermahrtes corpus juris saxonici* (Leipzig, 1724), 1: 861.

28. Carpzov, *Jurisprudentia ecclesiastica seu consistorialis,* Def. 577–80.

29. Ibid., Def. 578; "ex melancholii, furore, aliave animi impotentia."

30. Ibid., Def. 605.

31. See Hans-Jürgen Engfer, "Christian Thomasius: Erste Proklamation und erste Krise der Aufklärung in Deutschland," in *Christian Thomasius 1655–1728,* ed. Werner Schneiders (Hamburg, 1989), 21–36.

32. See Ian Hunter, "Christian Thomasius and the Desacraliztion of Philosophy," *Journal of the History of Ideas* 61 (2000): 595–617; and Horst Dreitzel, "Christliche Aufklärung durch fürstlichen Absolutismus: Thomasius und die Destruktion des frühneuzeitlichen Konfessionsstaates," in *Christian Thomasius (1655–1728), neue Forschungen im Kontext der Früaufklärung,* ed. Friedrich Vollhardt (Tübingen, 1997), 17–50.

33. These connections are examined by Peter Schröder, "Thomas Hobbes, Christian

Thomasius and the Seventeenth Century Debate on the Church and State," *History of European Ideas* 23 (1997): 59–79. See also Stephan Buchholz, "Christian Thomasius: Zwischen Orthodoxie und Pietismus—Religionskonflikte und ihre literarische Verarbeitung," in *Christian Thomasius,* ed. Werner Schneiders, 250–52. Cf. Stephan Buchholz, *Recht, Religion und Ehe: Orientierungswandel und gelehrte Kontroversen im Übergang vom 17. zum 18. Jahrhundert* (Frankfurt am Main, 1988), 109–33.

34. Greschat, *Zwischen Tradition,* 158–60.

35. The German translation, *Vom Recht evangelischer Fürsten in Mitteldingen oder Kirchenzeremonien,* was published in Thomasius's *Auserlesene und in Deutsch noch nie gedruckte Schriften* (Halle, 1705), reprinted in *Christian Thomasius: Ausgewählte Werke,* ed. Werner Schneiders (Hildesheim, 1994), vol. 23.

36. See Rolf Lieberwirth, *Christian Thomasius: Sein wissenschaftliches Lebenswerk* (Weimar, 1955), 53–54.

37. Buchholz, "Christian Thomasius," 251.

38. Thomasius, *Vom Recht evangelischer Fürsten in Mitteldingen oder Kirchenzeremonien,* 79–80. See Schröder, "Thomas Hobbes, Christian Thomasius," 62–65.

39. Christian Thomasius (praes.) and Nikolaus Peter Giedda (resp.), *De jure principis evangelici circa solennia sepulturae* (Halle, 1702). Translated as *Vom Recht evangelischer Fürsten in Solennitäten bei Begräbnissen,* in *Auserlesene und in Deutsch noch nie gedruckte Schriften* (Halle, 1705), 376–461. Reprinted in *Christian Thomasius: Ausgewählte Werke,* ed. Schneiders, vol. 23. On questions of authorship of such dissertations, see Dreitzel, "Christliche Aufklärung," 20; Buchholtz, *Recht, Religion und Ehe,* 4–14, and Lieberwirth, *Christian Thomasius,* 3. The publication of the German translation of *De jure principis evangelici circa solennia sepulturae* under Thomasius's name in 1705 also indicates that he saw the work as his own.

40. Thomasius, *Vom Recht evangelischer Fürsten,* 382–83.

41. Ibid., 379, 436.

42. Ibid., 404: "die Verwaltung der Leichenbegängnisse nicht zum Recht in innerlichen / sonder in äusserlichen Dingen gehöre."

43. Ibid., 401: "with good cause, to either increase or decrease the ceremonies typical at honorable funerals." This simplification of the Lutheran funeral was one aspect of the rise of honorable nocturnal funeral during the last third of the seventeenth century. See Koslofsky, *Reformation of Dead,* 133–52.

44. Thomasius, *Vom Recht evangelischer Fürsten,* 389.

45. Ibid., 388–89.

46. Ibid., 399.

47. Ibid., 396.

48. Thomasius's position on postmortem punishment of suicides is closely linked with his opposition to judicial torture. Lederer, "Reforming the Spirit," 398, also connects leniency in cases of suicide with the changing attitudes toward the body suggested by Michel Foucault, *Discipline and Punish: The Birth of the Prison,* trans. Alan Sheridan (New York, 1979), 3–30.

49. Thomasius, *Vom Recht evangelischer Fürsten,* 460.

50. See Werner Emmerich, *Der ländliche Besitz des Leipziger Rates: Entwicklung, Bewirtschaftung und Verwaltung bis zum 18. Jahrhundert* (Leipzig, 1936), 81–134.

51. Stadtarchiv Leipzig (hereafter SdAL), Tit. XLIV E 4 (Feud.), "Begräbnis deren welche sich selbst entleiben betr., 1702–1771," 2–3v; and the records in the Sächsisches Hauptstaatsarchiv Dresden (hereafter SHAD), Loc. 4571, Geheimes Konsilium, "Die zwischen den Rath zu Leipzig und dem Consistorio daselbst wegen Begrabung derer sich selbst ermordeten Personen entstandene differentien Ao. 1703." No documents exist concerning the dispute in the records of the Privy Cabinet.

52. Lederer, "Reforming the Spirit," 363–73; Midelfort, "Selbstmord," 299–302.

53. "Die vermuthlichen Ursachen der Autochirie," SdAL, Tit. XLIV E 4 (Feud.), 2v.–3v.

54. Ibid., 2—3v.

55. Ibid., 1. As seen in subsequent discussions, the churchmen may have been responding to the publication of Thomasius's *Solennia Sepulturae,* which put the council's practice in the threatening context of Thomasius's territorialism.

56. Ibid., 3v.

57. Ibid., 4.

58. The King-Elector put Romanus at the head of the Leipzig city council to ensure the flow of revenue from the city. See Wustmann, "Bürgermeister Romanus," 264—72. There are no extant records of the deliberations of the Leipzig city council on this issue.

59. SdAL, Tit. XLIV E 4 (Feud.), 5—6r.

60. Ibid., 5v.

61. Ibid., 5—6r. As the dispute continued, the Leipzig Consistory insisted that it had no difficulty investigating suicides in any part of its jurisdiction (SHAD, Loc. 4571, 17—20, May 30, 1703).

62. SdAL, Tit. XLIV E 4 (Feud.), 7—8v.

63. Ibid., 8.

64. Ibid.

65. Ibid., 9—10v. This is an accurate reference to Carpzov, *Jurisprudentia ecclesiastica seu consistorialis,* Def. 607—9.

66. See Johann Jakob Vogel, *Leipzigisches Geschichts-Buch oder Annales, das ist: Jahr- und Tagebücher der . . . Stadt Leipzig . . . von anno 661 . . . bis in das 1714 Jahr* (Leipzig, 1714), 953.

67. SdAL, Tit. XLIV E 4 (Feud.), 11.

68. Ibid.

69. Ibid., 15v.

70. Ibid., 13—14; cf. SHAD, Loc. 4571, Geheimes Konsilium, "Die zwischen den Rath zu Leipzig und dem Consistorio daselbst," 12, 21.

71. The draft of the council's reply is in SdAL, Tit. XLIV E 4 (Feud.), 21—23v.

72. Ibid., 22v.

73. Ibid.; 1690 was the date of the earliest case confirmed in Vogel's chronicle.

74. Vogel, *Leipzigisches Geschichts-Buch,* 884.

75. Ibid.

76. Ibid., 863.

77. SdAL, Tit. XLIV E 4 (Feud.), 22v.—23r.

78. Ibid., 22v. On this secular understanding of self-destruction, see MacDonald and Murphy, *Sleepless Souls,* 107—216; John McManners, *Death and the Enlightenment: Changing Attitudes to Death among Christians and Unbelievers in Eighteenth-Century France* (Oxford, 1981), 409—37; and Ursula Baumann, "Überlegungen zur Geschichte des Suizids (letztes Drittel 18. Jahrhundert bis erste Hälfte 20. Jahrhundert)," in *Trauer, Verzweifelung und Anfechtung,* ed. Gabriela Signori, 319—29. On the uneven course of secularization see Hartmut Lehmann, *Das Zeitalter des Absolutismus: Gottesgnadentum und Kriegsnot* (Stuttgart, 1980), 176—78.

79. On the continued protest of the Leipzig council see SHAD, Loc. 4571, Geheimes Konsilium, "Die zwischen den Rath zu Leipzig und dem Consistorio daselbst," 33—34, 37, 40v. Unfortunately, the surviving records of the Leipzig Consistory, held in the Sächsisches Hauptstaatsarchiv Dresden (Aktenzeichen II. 3. 1. 09. 1.), contain nothing regarding the Leipzig burial dispute.

80. *Codex Augusteus* 1: 1009—12.

81. As Siegfried Hoyer has observed, research on domestic politics during the reign of Augustus is still in its early stages; "Wie absolut war August?" *Saxonia* 1 (1995): 49—51.

82. On foreign councilors see Karl Czok, "Zur absolutistischen Politik Augusts des Starken in Sachsen," *Sächsische Heimatblätter* 4 (1983): 145—53.

83. See Blaschke, "Die kursächsische Politik," 23—38; Albrecht Kirchoff, *Die Anfänge kirch-*

licher Toleranz in Sachsen: August der Starke und die Reformirten (Leipzig, 1872); Wustmann, "Bürgermeister Romanus," 272–74.

84. See the review of Thomasius's 1706 tract on the bann in the journal edited by Löscher, *Unschuldige Nachrichten von Alten und Neuen Theologischen Sachen* 7 (1706): 402–20. See Greschat, *Zwischen Tradition,* 157–59, for critical references to Thomasius in the publications of Lutheran church officials.

85. As with bigamy, for example, suicide raised legal questions that highlighted the intellectual conflicts between the episcopalism of traditional Lutherans and the territorialism of Thomasius. See Buchholz, *Recht, Religion und Ehe;* and Isabel V. Hull, *Sexuality, State, and Civil Society in Germany, 1700–1815* (Ithaca, 1996).

Chapter 4. The Suicidal Mind and Body

1. Augustine and Thomas Aquinas established the foundation for this train of thought. On the symbolic importance of their arguments, see Gerald Hartung, "Über den Selbstmord: Eine Grenzbestimmung des anthropologischen Diskurses im 18. Jahrhundert," in *Der ganze Mensch: Anthropologie und Literatur im 18. Jahrhundert,* ed. Hans-Jürgen Schings (Stuttgart, 1994), 34.

2. See Gerhard Krause, "Luthers Stellung zum Selbstmord: Ein Kapitel seiner Lehre und Praxis der Seelsorge," *Luther. Zeitschrift der Luther-Gesellschaft* 36 (1965), 50–71; H. C. Erik Midelfort, "Selbstmord im Urteil von Reformation und Gegenreformation," in *Die katholische Konfessionalisierung,* ed. Wolfgang Reinhard and Heinz Schilling (Münster, 1995), 296–310. On the criminalization of suicide in north German territorial law, see Vera Lind, *Selbstmord in der Frühen Neuzeit: Diskurs, Lebenswelt, kultureller Wandel am Beispiel der Herzogtümer Schleswig und Holstein,* Veröffentlichungen des Max-Planck-Instituts für Geschichte, vol. 146 (Göttingen, 1999), 340–45.

3. On the decriminalization of suicide prior to the nineteenth century, see Lind, *Selbstmord,* 340–45.

4. Karl August Geiger, "Der Selbstmord im deutschen Recht," *Archiv für katholisches Kirchenrecht* 65 (1891): 3–36; Ossip Bernstein, *Die Bestrafung des Selbstmords und ihr Ende,* Strafrechtliche Abhandlungen, vol. 78 (Breslau, 1907); Jürgen Dieselhorst, "Die Bestrafung der Selbstmörder im Territorium der Reichsstadt Nürnberg," *Mitteilungen des Vereins für Geschichte der Stadt Nürnberg* 44 (1953): 58–230; Fritz-Helmuth Karrass, "Die rechtliche Behandlung der Selbstmörder in der Zentverfassung des Hochstifts Würzburg, 1454 bis 1806. Eine rechtsgeschichtliche Untersuchung an Hand der Zentordnungen und Verordnungen des Hochstifts" (Ph.D. dissertation, Universität Würzburg, 1971); Michael J. Seidler, "Kant and the Stoics on Suicide," *Journal of the History of Ideas* 44 (1983): 429–53; Hartung, "Über den Selbstmord," 33–53; Hans-Martin Kirn, "'Ich sterbe als büßende Christin . . .': Zum Suizidverständnis im Spannungsfeld von Spätaufklärung und Pietismus," *Pietismus und Neuzeit* 24 (1998): 252–70; Midelfort, "Selbstmord im Urteil," 296–310.

5. See essays in *Trauer, Verzweiflung und Anfechtung: Selbstmord und Selbstmordversuch in mittelalterlichen und frühneuzeitlichen Gesellschaften,* ed. Gabriela Signori (Tübingen, 1994); Ursula Baumann, "Suizid als soziale Pathologie: Gesellschaftskritik und Reformdiskussion im späten 18. Jahrhundert," *Zeitschrift für Geschichtswissenschaft* 45 (1997), 485–502; Lind, *Selbstmord.*

6. The American suicidologist Edwin Shneidman, founder of numerous pathbreaking suicide prevention centers, employs for this the term "psychological autopsy." Among his works, see "Suicide Lethality and the Psychological Autopsy," *International Psychiatric Clinics* 6 (1969): 225–50; "The Psychological Autopsy," *Suicide and Life-Threatening Behaviour* 11 (1981): 325–40. The psychological autopsy is recognized as playing an important role in court and insurance cases, where the cause of death is in question; see Douglas Jacobs and Marci Ellen Klein, "The

Expanding Role of Psychological Autopsies," in *Suicidology: Essays in Honor of Edwin S. Shneidman,* ed. Antoon A. Leenaars (Northvale, 1993), 226–28. On the possibility of predicting suicide with this method, see Shneidman's "Perturbation and Lethality as Precursors of Suicide in a Gifted Group," *Life-Threatening Behaviour* 1 (1971): 23–45; and "Prevention, Intervention, and Postvention of Suicide," *Annals of Internal Medicine* 75 (1971): 453–58.

7. On the history of emotions, see Peter N. Stearns and Carol Z. Stearns, "Emotionology: Clarifying the History of Emotions and Emotional Standards," *American Historical Review* 90 (1984): 813–36. On the history of the senses, see Robert Jütte, *Geschichte der Sinne: Von der Antike bis zum Cyberspace* (Munich, 2000). The history of the body is now a well-researched field. See, for example, Roy Porter, "History of the Body," in *New Perspectives on Historical Writing,* ed. Peter Burke (Cambridge, 1992), 206–32; Jakob Tanner, "Körpererfahrung, Schmerz und die Konstruktion des Kulturellen," *Historische Anthropologie* 3 (1994): 489–502; Richard van Dülmen, ed., *Körper-Geschichten,* Studien zur historischen Kulturforschung, vol. 5 (Frankfurt am Main, 1996).

8. In European history the most prominent proponent of psychohistory is probably Peter Gay. See his multi-volume work on the emotions of the bourgeoisie in late eighteenth- and nineteenth-century Europe, as well as his methodological analysis of psychohistory: *The Bourgeois Experience: Victoria to Freud,* 5 vols. (New York, 1984–98); and *Freud for Historians* (Oxford, 1985). See also Lyndal Roper's psychoanalytical interpretation of an early modern witchcraft accusation: *Oedipus and the Devil: Witchcraft, Sexuality, and Religion in Early Modern Europe* (London, 1994), 226–48. For a general overview see Jacques Szaluta, *Psychohistory: Theory and Practice* (New York, 1999).

9. See Elaine Scarry, *Der Körper im Schmerz: Die Chiffren der Verletzlichkeit und die Erfindung der Kultur* (Frankfurt am Main, 1992); David B. Morris, *Geschichte des Schmerzes* (Frankfurt am Main, 1996).

10. See Mary Douglas, *Ritual, Tabu und Körpersymbolik: Sozialanthropologische Studien in Industriegesellschaft und Stammeskultur* (Frankfurt am Main, 1981); Barbara Duden, *Geschichte unter der Haut* (Stuttgart, 1987), summarized in Tanner, "Körpererfahrung," 490.

11. The vast majority of these cases involved dependents in the lower orders who presumably had little or no writing ability and left no written testaments such as goodbye letters.

12. That the depositions given by third parties, i.e., people who recall what has been confided by suicides weeks or months earlier, contain a problem of objectivity has been dismissed in most modern studies by referring to the "optimized" way of the interview. See J. W. Shaffer, S. Perlin, and C. W. Schmidt, Jr., and M. Himmelfarb, "Assessment in Absentia: New Directions in the Psychological Autopsy," *Johns Hopkins Medical Journal* 130 (1972): 308–16. In another work Perlin and Schmidt write, "Following brief, neutral directions by the interviewer, the informant rates the subject in terms of the behavioural items in the scales. In order to minimize the extent to which the informant's involvement would tend to bias his reporting, all items have been worded so as to focus on specific behaviour and thereby reduce the necessity for inference or judgment"; "Psychiatry," in *A Handbook for the Study of Suicide,* ed. Seymour Perlin (New York, 1975), 159.

13. See Arne Jansson's chapter in this volume.

14. Landesarchiv Schleswig-Holstein, Schleswig, Germany (hereafter LAS), Abt. 11 Nr. 685, Attest des Pastors Moller, Flensburg, 12 October 1682. For more on this mentality, see Robert W. Scribner, "The Reformation, Popular Magic, and the 'Disenchantment' of the World," *Journal of Interdisciplinary History* 23 (1993): 475–94; Paul S. Seaver, *Wallington's World: A Puritan Artisan in Seventeenth-Century London* (London, 1985), 115–18. In such cases Catholics could call on Saint Anastasia, who was noted for being helpful in the struggle against obsession and mental disorders; Karl-S. Kramer, "Ein Mirakelbuch der heiligen Anastasia in Benediktbeuren," *Bayerisches Jahrbuch für Volkskunde* (1991): 111–38, especially 123.

15. LAS Abt. 11 Nr. 685, Attest des Arztes Scheffer, Flensburg, 12 October 1682.

16. Esther Fischer-Homberger, *Medizin vor Gericht: Zur Sozialgeschichte der Gerichtsmedizin* (Darmstadt, 1988), 128.

17. See for example the theory of the doctors Johan Wier (1515–88) and Felix Platter (1536–1614); ibid., 133.

18. Stadtarchiv Rendsburg, Germany, X. 7. Kriminalia, Nr. 237, Examen testium pro defensione Margreten Mullers, Testis Meister Gottfried, Rendsburg, 10 December 1664.

19. Stadtarchiv Rendsburg, Germany, X. 7. Kriminalia, Nr. 237, Articuli inquisitionalis, Margreten Richters Anwort, Rendsburg, 21 November 1664.

20. This could be, for example, either the reaction to marital conflict or to the loss of her husband. "The woman who loses her man is perceived to lose herself; she follows him," writes Margaret Higonnet in her literary treatment of female suicide; "Representations of the Feminine in the Nineteenth Century," *Poetics Today* 6 (1985): 108. Menstrual disruptions, menopause, and lying-in are also accepted explanatory models. In the late medieval and early modern eras, postpartum depression was not an unknown phenomenon. This illness was accepted as an explanation and excuse for female aggression that could be directed either toward the mother herself or her newborn child. Gabriela Signori has vividly described this interpretive mechanism by using late medieval miracle books; "Aggression und Selbstzerstörung: 'Geistesstörungen' und Selbstmordversuche im Spannungsfeld spätmittelalterlicher Geschlechterstereotypen (15. und beginnendes 16. Jahrhundert)," in *Trauer, Verzweiflung und Anfechtung,* ed. Signori, 113–51. See also Otto Ulbricht, *Kindsmord und Aufklärung in Deutschland,* Ancién Régime, Aufklärung und Revolution, vol. 18 (Munich, 1990), 154–56.

21. LAS Abt. 13 A Nr. 657, Stadtphysikus Führsen to Königliche Kanzlei, Schleswig, 4 September 1759.

22. These kinds of headache attacks could have been migraines. It is also possible that these symptoms were simply a metaphor for her lack of spiritual and emotional well-being which she interpreted as not feeling well in her head. LAS Abt. 65.2 Nr. 336, P.M. of Stadtphysikus Baller to Oberinspektor des Zuchthauses Amtmann von Lowtzow, Neumünster, 13 January 1795.

23. See Fischer-Homberger, *Medizin vor Gericht,* 150–52.

24. On the difference between deep, semiconscious psychological causes of suicide and those caused by personal motives with concrete goals, see Lind, *Selbstmord,* 219–73.

25. LAS Abt. 127.21 AGA V. B 1 Nr. 60 Summ. Verhöre, Protokoll, Breitenburg, 23 August 1762.

26. The original German reads, "Durch diese Reden wäre er außer sich selbst gesetzet worden, und er hätte nicht gewust, wie ihm zu muthe gewesen, und in solchem Zustande wären ihm die Gedancken in den Sinn gekommen, daß er sich zu nahe thun wollte"; ibid.

27. On interpretations of this phenomenon in modern suicide research, see John T. Maltsberger, "Confusion of the Body, the Self, and Others in Suicidal States," in *Suicidology,* ed. Leenaars, 148–71.

28. Sigmund Freud, "Totem und Tabu," in *Gesammelte Werke,* ed. Anna Freud, 4th ed. (Frankfurt am Main, 1968), 9: 185, n. 1.

29. "Der Schmerz, und ein Drang unbeschreiblicher Gefühle, habe in ihr das Sehnen nach Luft veranlaßt, und in dieser Herzensangst sey sie in den Mühlenbach gesprungen; sie habe nicht gewußt, wo sie sey, sie sey wie Dwatsch gewesen." LAS Abt. 268 Nr. 1584, Summ. Verhör, Pansdorf, 20 July 1802. "Dwatsch" means to be strange, odd, or "wunderlich" in the head; *Schleswig-Holsteinisches Wörterbuch,* ed. Otto Mensing (Neumünster, 1925), 1: 973, s.v. "Dwatsch."

30. This inner pressure or feeling that one can no longer breathe was described in other suicide cases, e.g., by the twenty-eight-year-old servant Hans Draguhn of Groß Timmendorf,

who in 1799 jumped into a hole in the ice and later explained that he wanted to do something to "get air" ("Luft verschaffen"); LAS Abt. 285 Nr. 1376, Protokoll, Groß Timmendorf, 4 March 1799.

31. LAS Abt. 108 Nr. 933, Protokoll, Ahrensbök, 7 September 1788; my emphasis.

32. There is a voluminous literature on the development of Pietism in the eighteenth century. Much of it has been synthesized in *Geschichte des Pietismus,* ed. Martin Brecht and Klaus Deppermann, vol. 2, *Der Pietismus im achtzehnten Jahrhundert* (Göttingen 1995). See also Johannes Wallmann, *Der Pietismus* (Göttingen, 1990); and W. R. Ward, *The Protestant Evangelical Awakening* (Cambridge, 1992).

33. Fischer-Homberger, *Medizin vor Gericht,* 131.

34. See Hans-Jürgen Schings, *Melancholie und Aufklärung: Melancholiker und ihre Kritiker in der Erfahrungsseelenkunde und Literatur des 18. Jahrhunderts* (Stuttgart, 1977), 77–79.

35. Adam Bernd, *Eigene Lebens-Beschreibung,* ed. Volker Hoffmann (München, 1973). See also Schings, *Melancholie und Aufklärung,* 113–15.

36. Manfred Jakubowski-Tiessen has documented the spread of Pietism in this region; "Der Pietismus in Dänemark und Schleswig-Holstein," in *Geschichte des Pietismus,* ed. Martin Brecht and Klaus Deppermann, 2: 446–71.

37. LAS Abt. 11 Nr. 685, Diakon Jessen to Inspektor Reymers, Neuenkirchen, 16 February 1752.

38. On these developments in Lutheran church practice after the Reformation, see Scribner, "Reformation," 485–86. On the instrumentalization of collective anxiety of an avenging God, see Helga Schnabel-Schüle, "Kirchenzucht als Verbrechensprävention," in *Kirchenzucht und Sozialdisziplinierung im frühneuzeitlichen Europa,* ed. Heinz Schilling, supplemental issue 16 of *Zeitschrift für Historische Forschung,* 49–64.

39. LAS Abt. 11 Nr. 685, Protokoll, Bahrenfleth, 16 February 1752, Summarisches Verhör des Kätners Marx Steffens.

40. It is interesting that the farmer's son assumed that his death would remove the curse of ill weather from his family, since according to widely-held superstition suicide could also bring natural catastrophe or some other misfortune to the land or to one's family. The threat of the *Wiedergänger,* a wanderer between the worlds of the living and the dead who cannot fully enter the realm of either because he or she did not await death's summons, was considered especially relevant if the body of a suicide had not been properly removed from the community of the living. On the connections between weather (e.g., hail, storms, and the like) and suicide in folk superstition, see Gerhard Hard, *Selbstmord und Wetter—Selbstmord und Gesellschaft: Studien zur Problemwahrnehmung in der Wissenschaft und zur Geschichte der Geographie* (Wiesbaden, 1988), 26–27.

41. Women were obviously sensitive to other things. For example, in 1776 a woman tried to poison herself and her entire family because she believed her daughter's honor had been lost when someone accused her of having stolen some roots; LAS Abt. 65.2 Nr. 273.2. On this case see also, Silke Göttsch, "'Mörderin an ihrem unschuldigen Kinde aus Überdruß des Lebens.' Ein Beitrag zum Thema 'Gewalttätige Frauen im 18. Jahrhundert,'" *Bayerisches Jahrbuch für Volkskunde* (1996): 46–47.

42. LAS Abt. 112 Nr. 155, Protokoll, o.D. Before he was arrested the servant admitted to a friend that he had to commit this act to attain grace ("dat mut ick ja wohl, wenn ich to gnaden kommen will"), adding that he wanted to "suffer for this" ("dafür leiden").

43. For more details on these cases and the juridical background, see Lind, *Selbstmord,* 153–89, 339–99. For similar examples of suicidal murders in early modern Sweden, see Arne Jansson's chapter in this volume and his *From Swords to Sorrows: Homicide and Suicide in Early Modern Stockholm* (Stockholm, 1998). In both Sweden and northern Germany most of the perpetrators were women.

44. Landsarkivet for de sønderjyske landsdele, Åbenrå, Amtsarkivet Åbenrå, L.v. Schmettaus Arkiv, Nr. 297, Protokoll, Westerhoist, 24 April 1801.

45. LAS Abt. 127.21 AGA V. B 1 Nr. 60, Summarische Verhöre, Protokoll, Breitenburg, 23 August 1762.

46. LAS Abt. 285 Nr. 1364, Protokoll, Lübeck, 7 October 1793.

47. For more details and examples about the passivity experienced by suicides, see Lind, *Selbstmord*, 157–89.

48. This observation corresponds to the comment by Robert Jütte that in the regulated, early modern social discourse on illness, a person could be publicly identified as suffering from melancholy, but caution had to be exercised when associating someone with mental illness. Whereas melancholy was foremost seen as an illness, mental problems could have their source in the spiritual and other worlds; *Ärzte, Heiler und Patienten: Medizinischer Alltag in der Frühen Neuzeit* (Munich, 1991), 129–30. The same reservation was advisable in dealing with the term "suicide."

49. . Tanner, *Körpererfahrung*, 499.

50. Of interest, superstitions regarding the danger of a *Wiedergänger* were also rooted in the belief in the passive origin of the suicidal impulse, namely the conviction that one could be led to take one's life by an evil force, including the soul of a person who has already committed suicide.

51. LAS Abt. 268 Nr. 1584, Summarisches Verhör, Pansdorf, 20 July 1802.

Chapter 5. Suicidal Murders in Stockholm

Material for this chapter was taken from Arne Jansson, *From Swords to Sorrow: Homicide and Suicide in Early Modern Stockholm* (Stockholm, 1998).

1. City Archives of Stockholm, Stockholms rådhusrätts kriminalprotokoll (Minutes from criminal cases of the Stockholm Municipal Court, hereafter Krim prot), 1668, 18/5, 123.

2. Comprehensive surveys of Swedish history are found in *New Cambridge Modern History* (Cambridge, 1968), vol. 3: chapter 12; (1970), vol. 4: chapter 12; (1961), vol. 5: chapter 12; (1970), vol. 6: chapter 20; and (1957), vol. 7: chapter 15. Material concerning Stockholm is taken from Sven Lilja, "Stockholms befolkningsutveckling före 1800. Problem, metoder och förklaringar," *Historisk tidskrift* 3 (1995): 328; Arne Jansson and Johan Söderberg, "Priser och löner i Stockholm 1600–1719," in *Dagligt bröd i onda tider*, ed. Arne Jansson et al. (Gothenburg, 1991), 30–32; and Arne Jansson, *Bördor och bärkraft. Borgare och kronotjänare i Stockholm 1644–1672* (Stockholm, 1991), 19–20, 24–32.

3. Jansson, *Bördor*, 22, 179; Ernst Söderlund, *Hantverkarna II. Stormaktstiden, frihetstiden och gustavianska tiden* (Stockholm, 1949), 262–67.

4. Krim prot 1672, 6/5, 105.

5. The years 1628–1635 are omitted because of lacunae in sources. According to official statistics, the frequency of suicide was around 4 per 100,000 inhabitants in Stockholm for 1750–1773 (Johan Söderberg, *Civilisering, marknad och våld i Sverige 1750–1870: en regional analys,* [Stockholm, 1993], 25, figure 8), but sources do not allow calculating the frequency of attempted suicides.

6. See Vera Lind's chapter in this volume and H. von Weber, "Selbstmord als Mordmotiv," *Monatsschrift für Kriminalbiologie und Strafsrechtsreform* 28 (1937): 161–81.

7. The shift from homicide to suicide is reflected in the title of my book: *From Swords to Sorrow.* Similarly, Jeffrey Watt found that in Geneva suicides increased dramatically with respect to homicides from the early seventeenth to the late eighteenth century; *Choosing Death: Suicide and Calvinism in Early Modern Geneva* (Kirksville, 2001), 53–62.

8. A key theme found in classic sociological studies such as Emile Durkheim, *Suicide: A Case*

Study in Sociology, trans. John A. Spaulding and George Simpson, ed. George Simpson (New York, 1951); and Maurice Halbwachs, Les causes du suicide (Paris, 1930). Some later studies include Unni Bille-Brahe, "Suicide and Social Integration: A Pilot Study of the Integration levels in Norway and Denmark," Acta Psychiatrica Scandinavica 76 (1987): 45–62; Nick Danigelis and Whitney Pope, "Durkheim's Theory as Applied to the Family: An Empirical Test," Social Forces 57 (1979): 1081–106; Peter Sainsbury, Suicide in London: An Ecological Study (London, 1955); William B. Bankston et al., "Religion and Suicide: A Research Note on Sociology's 'One Law,'" Social Forces 62 (1983): 521–28; Richard Quinney, "Suicide, Homicide, and Economic Development," Social Forces 43 (1965): 401–6; Mark C. Stafford and Jack P. Gibbs, "A Major Problem with the Theory of Status Integration and Suicide," Social Forces 63 (1985): 643–60, and "Change in the Relation between Marital Integration and Suicide Rates," Social Forces 66 (1988): 1060–79.

9. In this respect, the court records for Stockholm are not as rich as those of northern Germany studied by Vera Lind or as Stockholm's records from later periods.

10. Krim prot 1706, 12/11, 239.

11. Durkheim, Suicide, 171–89. See also Jeffrey Watt's chapter in this volume.

12. City Archives of Stockholm, Södra förstadens kämnärsrätts kriminalprotokoll (Minutes from criminal cases of the District Court of Southern Stockholm), 1740, 21/12 (no pagination).

13. Jansson, Bördor, 22.

14. Werner Pursche, Timmermansämbetet i Stockholm före 1700 (Stockholm, 1979), 331, table 35.

15. Hans Andersson, "Folklig rättskultur i stormaktstidens Stockholm" (Licentiate dissertation, Institute of Economic History, Stockholm University, 1996), 33.

16. Jansson and Söderberg, "Priser," 20, 28, 74–81.

17. Arne Jarrick, Kärlekens makt och tårar (Stockholm, 1997), 47–56.

18. Durkheim, Suicide, 73, 100–103; Anthony Giddens, "The Statistics of Suicide," in The Sociology of Suicide: A Selection of Readings, ed. Anthony Giddens (London, 1971), 422; Ronald W. Maris, Social Forces in Urban Suicide (Homewood, 1969), 92–93.

19. Jean Baechler, Suicides, trans. Barry Cooper (New York, 1979), 284–85. See also Arlette Moullembé, Florence Tiano, Gérard Anavi, Claude Anavi, and Jean-Marc Parichon, "Conduites suicidaires, approche théorique et clinique," Bulletin de Psychologie 27 (1973–74): 872; Seymour Perlin and Chester W. Schmidt, Jr., "Psychiatry," in Handbook for Study of Suicide (New York, 1975), ed. Seymour Perlin, 153.

20. Durkheim, Suicide, 152–64.

21. Arne Jansson, "Mäster Samuel och rike herr Lars," Karolinska förbundets årsbok 2000: 230–47.

22. Jansson, Swords, 165–69, Appendix 1: A Study of Literacy in Stockholm during the Seventeenth and Beginning of the Eighteenth Centuries.

23. Durkheim, Suicide, 168.

24. Jansson, "Mäster Samuel," 230–40.

25. In 1707 the distinguished jurist, Count Nils Gyldenstolpe, chair of the commission entrusted with the revision of Swedish civil and penal law, declared that suicide was in fact a more heinous crime than the murder of another person. Moreover, Swedish law affirmed in 1734 that attempted suicide was punishable, a confirmation of earlier practice; Ann-Sofie Ohlander, Kärlek, död och frihet. Historiska uppsatser om människovärde och livsvillkor i Sverige (Stockholm, 1986), 47–51, 55.

26. Södra förstadens kämnärsrätts kriminalprotokoll, 1740, 8/12 (no pagination).

27. City Archives of Stockholm, Stockholms rådhusrätts tänkebok (Minutes from the Stockholm Municipal Court), 1651, 28/5, 225–29.

28. Krim prot 1686, 3/7, 372–76.

29. Södra förstadens kämnärsrätts kriminalprotokoll, 1740, 8/12 (no pagination).

30. Krim prot 1676, 27/5, 128–30; City Archives of Stockholm, Norra förstadens käm-

närsrätts kriminalprotokoll (Minutes from criminal cases of the District Court of Northern Stockholm), 1727, 29/ 5, 319–22.

31. City Archives of Stockholm, Stockholms rådhusrätts tänkebok, konceptversionen (Minutes from the Stockholm Municipal Court, concept version), 1651, 28/ 5, 178.

32. Krim prot 1696, 28/ 8, 1161–72.

33. Michael MacDonald, "The Secularization of Suicide in England 1660–1800," *Past and Present* 111 (1986): 90.

34. Louise Hagberg, *När döden gästar* (Stockholm, 1937), 501– 5, 554– 58.

35. Ibid., 501– 5.

36. David Lindquist, *Studier i den svenska andaktslitteraturen under stormaktstidevarvet* (Uppsala, 1939), 378–84. The author of this prayer is unknown but is assumed to have been a layman or a clergyman of low status.

37. Norra förstadens kämnärsrätts kriminalprotokoll, 1727, 16/ 3, 168–70.

38. Ibid., 178

39. Krim prot 1667, 28/ 6 (no pagination).

40. The National Archives of Sweden, Stockholm, Svea hovrätt (Svea Court of Appeal), Resolutioner, series 3, vol. 61, 252– 55; Södra förstadens kämnärsrätts kriminalprotokoll, 1767, 18/ 5, 599–603. Of interest, these two relatively late cases, along with the case described immediately following, were the only suicidal murders in which the Prince of Darkness appeared as a tempter. By contrast, Vera Lind found many references to diabolical temptation in cases from seventeenth-century northern Germany; see her chapter in this volume.

41. Krim prot 1699, 23/ 10, 1153; 25/ 10, 1167–69.

42. Södra förstadens kämnärsrätts kriminalprotokoll, 1740, 21 / 12 (no pagination).

43. Krim prot 1706, 3/ 10, 205, 506.

44. For an interesting discussion concerning cultural codes for understanding the causes of suicide, see Vera Lind's chapter in this volume.

45. Ibid.

46. Stockholms rådhusrätts tänkebok, 1651, 28/ 5, 225–29; Weber, "Selbstmord," 161.

47. Krim prot 1696, 24/ 10, 1836–38.

48. Jonas Liliequist, *Brott, synd och straff. Tidelagsbrottet i Sverige under 1600-och 1700-talet* (Umeå, 1991), 99–113. Records reveal no crime other than murder or bestiality being used as a means of indirect suicide in Sweden. In early modern Germany, however, other crimes punishable by death, such as arson and destroying holy relics, were reportedly used with the same suicidal intent; Weber, "Selbstmord," 168.

49. See Georges Minois, *History of Suicide: Voluntary Death in Western Culture,* trans. Lydia G. Cochrane (Baltimore, 1999), 153–54.

50. Stockholms rådhusrätts tänkebok, 1652, 28/ 2, 49.

51. Peter Englund, *Poltava. Berättelsen om en armés undergång* (Stockholm, 1988), 63.

52. Göran Rystad, *Karl XI. En biografi* (Lund, 2001), 61.

53. Claes Wahlöö and Göran Larsson, *Slaget vid Lund. Ett mord och icke ett fältslag* (Lund, 1998), 71.

54. *Årstrycket* (Yearbook of laws and statutes issued in Sweden), 1662, 23/ 12.

55. *Årstrycket,* 1741, 12/ 12; *Samling af Kongl. Maj:ts bref, hwilka på inkomna förfrågningar om lagens rätta förstånd . . . , utfärdade blifwit* (Directives from the Swedish government concerning the interpretation of laws), ed. Johan Jusléen (Stockholm, 1787), 379; *Samling af Love og anordninger af mere almindelig interesse* (Danish laws and statutes), 1683–1859, ed. C. S. Klein (Copenhagen, 1861), 1: 120–21.

56. Martin Bergman, *Dödsstraffet, kyrkan och staten i Sverige från 1700–tal till 1900–tal* (Lund, 1996), 108–9; *Samling af love,* 1: 191–92.

57. Jacob Flintberg, *Lagfarenhets-Bibliotek* (Stockholm, 1803), 5: 208.

58. C. Nyholm, *Dödsstraffen efter almindelige lovgivningsgrundsatser og dansk ret* (Copenhagen, 1858), 35.

Chapter 6. Ambivalence toward Suicide in Golden Age Spain

1. Michael MacDonald and Terence R. Murphy, *Sleepless Souls: Suicide in Early Modern England* (Oxford, 1990); Jeffrey R. Watt, *Choosing Death: Suicide and Calvinism in Early Modern Geneva* (Kirksville, 2001); Fernando Martínez Gil, *Muerte y sociedad en la España de los Austrias* (Madrid, 1993), 149–52.

2. Bartolomé Bennassar, *The Spanish Character: Attitudes and Mentalities from the Sixteenth to the Nineteenth Century,* trans. B. Keen (Berkeley, 1979), chap. 8, quotation from 231.

3. Haim Beinart, *Records of the Trials of the Spanish Inquisition of Ciudad Real,* 4 vols. (Jerusalem, 1985). The edited case records can be found at *Records,* 2: 539–93, 1r–34v. Translations from this source are Elizabeth Dickenson's. See *Records,* 2: 587–90: 32v–34r, for the sentence of the inquisitorial court at Toledo.

4. 31 May 1512; see trial of Juan Ramírez in *Records,* 3: 30–36, 16v–19r.

5. The sin of Judaizing was assessed against persons accused of having converted to Christianity and then relapsed into Jewish religious practices. Examples of Judaizing taken from the trial records include observing the law of Moses, keeping the Jewish Sabbath, refusing to eat pork, and circumcising males. Women were often accused of lighting candles with new wicks on Friday nights to welcome the Sabbath, wearing clean clothes on Saturdays, and teaching Jewish religious and cultural traditions to their children. Historians have long observed that inquisitors were apt to construe indiscriminately traditional cultural practices as Judaizing, regardless of accompanying doctrinal content. See, for example, Cecil Roth, *The Spanish Inquisition* (New York, 1964), 76, who introduces an inquisitorial "Edict of Faith" of 1519 with the comment that "the prominence given to unimportant customs and mere superstitions is noteworthy."

6. See Confession of Isabel de los Olivos y López, *Records,* 2: 544–49, 4r–6v.

7. The trial records of Diego Sánchez de Madrid and others have been lost, but case summaries have been reconstructed by Haim Beinart from extant records, such as those from the related trials of Isabel de los Olivos y López and Juan Ramírez. See ibid., 3: 303–8, for the case summaries. See also testimony from the trial of Isabel de los Olivos y López in ibid., 2: 557–69, 12r–19r, regarding the confessions and examinations of Alonso Sánchez under torture.

8. 3 May 1513; see ibid., 2: 575–77, 24r–25v, for the jailer's testimony on the "demencia" of Isabel de los Olivos y López. Inquisitors determined that she was "distraught" beginning about the same time that she first recanted her previous testimony. See ibid., 569–75, 20r–24r, for testimony of women in prison concerning the "demencia" of Isabel de los Olivos y López.

9. Testimonies on the suicide of Isabel de los Olivos y López are given in ibid., 577–86, 26r–31v, by Saavedra and members of his household, including servants.

10. Michael R. McVaugh, *Medicine before the Plague: Practitioners and their Patients in the Crown of Aragon, 1285–1345* (Cambridge, 1993), 233–34.

11. For her sentence, see *Records,* 2: 587–90, 32v–34v, especially 589–90, 34v. "Otrosy declaramos los hijos e descendientes de la dicha Ysabel de los Olivos, por las lineas masculina e femenina, fasta el primero grado ynclusiue, ser privados de todos beneficios e oficios, eclesyasticos e seglares e honras mundanas, e ynabiles e yncapazes para poder aver e tener otros de nuevo perpetuamente; e que no puedan traer ni traigan sobre sy ni en sus bestiduras oro ni seda ni grana ni chamelote ni corales ni aljofar ni perlas ni piedras preciosas, ni traygan armas ni caualguen a cauallo, ni sean fisycos ni boticarios ni canbiadores ni arrendadores ni abogados ni procuradores, ni tengan ni usen de los otros oficios publicos de honor prohevidos en derecho, so las penas en el contenidas."

12. For a useful analysis of the relationship of the Inquisition to racialist attacks on *conversos,* see Henry Kamen, *The Spanish Inquisition: A Historical Revision* (New Haven, 1997), 230–54.

13. See especially Baruch A. Brody, "A Historical Introduction to Jewish Casuistry on Suicide and Euthanasia," in *Suicide and Euthanasia: Historical and Contemporary Themes,* ed. Baruch

A. Brody (Dordrecht, 1989), 39–76. See also *The Jewish Encyclopedia of Moral and Ethical Issues,* ed. Nachum Amsel (Northvale, 1994), 65–66. For the Ashkenazi tradition of medieval martyrdom, including suicide, see Susan L. Einbinder, *Beautiful Death: Jewish Poetry and Martyrdom in Medieval France* (Princeton, 2002), 23–25, 51.

14. Not until the nineteenth century would the law of Spain be recast to reflect a secular absolution of self-murder. See Enrique Díaz Aranda, *Dogmática del suicidio y homicidio consentido* (Madrid, 1995), 28; idem, *Del suicidio a la eutanasia* (Mexico City, 1997), 21.

15. Joseph O'Callaghan, *A History of Medieval Spain* (Ithaca, 1975), 110–12, provides a brief summary. For more detailed analyses, see Kenneth Baxter Wolf, *Christian Martyrs in Muslim Spain* (Cambridge, 1988); Jessica Coope, *The Martyrs of Córdoba: Community and Family Conflict in an Age of Mass Conversion* (Lincoln, 1995). On the martyrs as voluntary suicides, see Clayton J. Drees, "Sainthood and Suicide: The Motives of the Martyrs of Córdoba, A.D. 850–859," *Journal of Medieval and Renaissance Studies* 20 (1990): 59–90.

16. David Nirenberg, *Communities of Violence: Persecution of Minorities in the Middle Ages* (Princeton, 1996), 62 (quotation concerning Judas) and chap. 7 (about Holy Week).

17. See *Women in the Classical World,* ed. Elaine Fantham, Helene Peet Foley, Natalie Boymel Kampen, Sarah B. Pomeroy, and H. Alan Shapiro (Oxford, 1994), 170. For a discussion of Seneca's views on this issue, see Arthur Droge and James Tabor, *A Noble Death: Suicide and Martyrdom among Christians and Jews in Antiquity* (New York, 1992), 34–37.

18. Darrel W. Amundsen, "Suicide and Early Christian Values," in *Suicide and Euthanasia,* ed. Baruch A. Brody, 108.

19. Augustine, *City of God* 1. 19. See also Droge and Tabor, *Noble Death,* 171–79, for a discussion of Augustine's theology and writings concerning suicide.

20. Augustine, *Contra Gaudentius, in Corpus Scriptorum Ecclesiasticorum Latinorum* (Vienna, 1910), 53: 201–74; Droge and Tabor, *Noble Death,* 169–73. See also Alexander Murray, *Suicide in the Middle Ages,* 2 vols. (Oxford, 1998–2000), for a general history of suicide in medieval Western Europe.

21. Karl Josef von Hefele, *History of the Councils of the Church,* trans. and ed. William Clark (Edinburgh, 1883–96; reprint, New York, 1972), 4: 385.

22. *Corpus iuris civilis,* trans. and ed. Samuel Parsons Scott, 17 vols. (Cincinnati, 1932). See especially vol. 11: 129–31 (Digest 48. 19. 38. 12) and vol. 15: 85 (The Code of Justinian 9. 50. 1–2). Something akin to this notion of suicide as a multiplier of criminality seems to have been at work in the Inquisition's punishment of Isabel de los Olivos y López, discussed previously.

23. *The Visigothic Code (Forum iudicum),* trans. and ed. Samuel Parsons Scott (Boston, 1910), 354.

24. *Isidori Hispalensis Episcopi, Etymologiarum sive Originum Libri XX,* 2 vols., ed. W. M. Lindsay (Oxford, 1911). See also Ariel Guiance, *Los discursos sobre la muerte en la Castilla Medieval* (siglos VII–XV) (Valladolid, 1998), 173, 362.

25. Hefele, *History,* 5: 245.

26. *Las Siete Partidas,* trans. and ed. Samuel Parsons Scott (Chicago, 1931), 1446–47. This useful translation has recently been reprinted in five volumes (preserving the original pagination) under the editorial supervision of Robert I. Burns; the text under discussion here appears in *Las Siete Partidas,* vol. 5, *Underworlds: The Dead, the Criminal, and the Marginalized* (Philadelphia, 2001). See also Alejandro Morin, "Suicidas, apóstatas y asesinos: la desesperación en la Séptima Partida de Alfonso el Sabio," *Hispania* 61 (2001): 179–220.

27. *Songs of Holy Mary of Alfonso X, The Wise: A Translation of the Cantigas de Santa María,* trans. Kathleen Kulp-Hill (Tempe, 2000), 36–37, 108–9, 241–42.

28. *Novísima Recopilación,* vol. 4, in *Los códigos españoles concordados y anotados* (Madrid, 1850), 10: 73 (ley XV).

29. *Nuevo Código Penal de 1995* (Barcelona, 1996), Lib. II, Art. 144, 295.

30. *Siete Partidas,* 7: 27 in *Siete Partidas,* vol. 5, *Underworlds,* ed. Burns, 1446.

31. See *Novísima Recopilación*, vol. 4, in *Códigos españoles*, 10: 73 (ley XV).

32. For a clear explanation of Augustine's views, see Droge and Tabor, *Noble Death*, chap. 7.

33. *Arte de bien morir, y breve confesionario* (Zaragoza, c. 1479–84), ed. Francisco Gago Jover (Barcelona, 1999), 97.

34. For a well-annotated critical edition incorporating a Spanish translation, see "Del homicidio," in *Obras de Francisco de Vitoria: Relecciones teológicas*, ed. Teófilo Urdanoz (Madrid, 1960), 1070–130.

35. Ibid., 1123.

36. Ibid., 1128–29.

37. Sebastián de Covarrubias Orozco, *Tesoro de la lengua castellana, o española [1611]*, 2d modern edition, ed. Felipe C. R. Maldonado and Manuel Camarero (Madrid, 1995), 414. Sara Nalle provides illuminating and tantalizing insights into elite (inquisitorial) and more popular notions of madness and its exculpatory qualities in *Mad for God: Bartolomé Sánchez, the Secret Messiah of Cardenete* (Charlottesville, 2001), esp. chap. 8. And see the synodal ruling of 1626 (Cuenca) mentioned in Martínez Gil, *Muerte y sociedad*, 152.

38. On martyrdom in the Reformation era and the controversies surrounding it, see Brad Gregory, *Salvation at Stake: Christian Martyrdom in Early Modern Europe* (Cambridge, Mass., 1999).

39. *The Life of Saint Teresa by Herself*, trans. J. M. Cohen (Harmondsworth, 1957), 24.

40. See the intriguing account by Elizabeth Rhodes, "Luisa de Carvajal's Counter-Reformation Journey to Selfhood (1566–1614)," *Renaissance Quarterly* 51 (1998): 887–911, quotation from 895.

41. See E. W. Bovill, *The Battle of Alcazar: An Account of the Defeat of Don Sebastian of Portugal at El-Ksar el-Kebir* (London, 1952), 14–15; H. V. Livermore, *A New History of Portugal* (Cambridge, 1969), 154.

42. The exact circumstances of the cardinal's death remain unclear, but some accounts convey an unmistakable suggestion of despair as its cause. This interpretation emerges most vividly in Martin A. S. Hume, *Philip II of Spain* (London, 1897; reprint, New York, 1969), 193; compare Luciano Serrano's explanation—not denying Philip's displeasure, but chalking Espinosa's death up to overwork and failing health—in *Correspondencia diplomática entre España y la Santa Sede durante el pontificado de S. Pío V*, ed. L. Serrano (Madrid, 1914), 2: lxxxiii.

43. See Francisco de Rojas Zorrilla, *Numancia cercada y Numancia destruida*, ed. Raymond MacCurdy (Madrid, 1977), editor's introduction, xiv–xvii.

44. See Bennassar, *Spanish Character*, 213.

45. Mariana, *Historia general*, book 3, chap. 10, in *Obras del padre Juan de Mariana* (Madrid, 1923), 1: 69–71.

46. Among recent treatments, see Rachel Schmidt, "The Development of Hispanitas in Spanish Sixteenth-Century Versions of the Fall of Numancia," *Renaissance and Reformation* 19 (1995): 27–45; Jack Weiner, "La Numancia de Cervantes y la alianza entre Dios e Israel," *Neophilologus* 81 (1997): 63–70; and Ceferino Caro López, "'Que se vuelva el mundo como se estaba': literatura y religión en el tema americano del siglo de oro. La polémica política," *Anuario de Estudios Americanos* 56 (1999): 441–62.

47. Miguel de Cervantes, *La destrucción de Numancia*, ed. Ricardo Domenech (Madrid, 1967), with the colloquy of España and Duero at 56–61. Julio Caro Baroja provides some interesting observations about the continuing patriotic significance of Numantia in modern Spain in his inaugural address to the Real Academia de la Historia, Madrid, *Interpretaciones de la guerra de Numancia: discurso leído el día 24 de febrero de 1968* (Madrid, 1968), esp. section 10.

48. Cervantes, *Numancia*, 130–31. Quoted here from the translation of Roy Campbell, in *Life is a Dream and other Spanish Classics*, ed. Eric Bentley (New York, 1985), 63.

49. Rojas Zorrilla, *Numancia destruida*, 133.

50. Ibid., 192–93.

51. Ibid., 193.

52. Cervantes, *Numancia*, 130.

53. See Martínez Gil, *Muerte y Sociedad*, 149, 152. The term *suicidio* does not appear in the dictionary of the Real Academia Española until 1817; *Diccionario de la lengua castellana por la Real Academia Española*, 5th ed. (Madrid, 1817), 819. (See the extraordinarily useful search function at http://buscon.rae.es/ntlle/jsp/azul.jsp)

54. Cervantes, *Numancia*, 130.

55. Rojas Zorrilla, *Numancia destruida*, 236.

56. Covarrubias Orozco, *Tesoro*, 414.

57. José Luis de las Heras Santos, *La justicia penal de los Austrias en la Corona de Castilla* (Salamanca, 1991), 219.

58. Francisco de Quevedo y Villegas, "Grandes Anales de Quince Días: historia de muchos siglos que pasaron en un mes," in *Obras en prosa*, ed. Luis Astrana Marín (Madrid, 1932), 488. *Desengaño* resists neat translation, but one of Covarrubias Orozco's definitions (*Tesoro*, 413) of the verb *desengañarse* suggests the sense: "to come to the realization that what you held for certain truth was a fraud." For contemporary notions of the good death see tracts such as the fifteenth-century *Arte de bien morir* cited in note 33, or Alejo Venegas's influential *Agonía del tránsito de la muerte con los avisos y consuelos que cerca de ella son provechosos*, first published in 1536; for the Alcalá edition of 1565, see *Escritores místicos españoles*, ed. M. Mir (Madrid, 1911), 1: 105–318. For recent scholarly treatments, see, among others, Sara Nalle, *God in La Mancha: Religious Reform and the People of Cuenca, 1500–1650* (Baltimore, 1992), esp. chap. 6; Carlos Eire, *From Madrid to Purgatory: The Art and Craft of Dying in Sixteenth-Century Spain* (Cambridge, 1995); and James Boyden, "The Worst Death Becomes a Good Death: The Passion of Don Rodrigo Calderón," in *The Place of the Dead: Death and Remembrance in Late Medieval and Early Modern Europe*, ed. B. Gordon and P. Marshall (Cambridge, 2000), 240–65.

Chapter 7. *Honfibú*

1. Comparative research on the history of suicide in Hungary was conducted within the larger framework of an ongoing study of suicide in the Holy Roman Empire, 1495–1806. Funding was provided by the Hungarian Academy of Sciences (MTÁ) and the Royal Irish Academy. Many thanks to everyone in Budapest and Debrecen for their assistance during my 1998 research visit, especially Barta János, Faragó Tamás, Klaniczay Gábor, Kristóf Ildikó, Szőnyi György, and Kulcsár Krísztina.

2. Although this is not the place to critique thoroughly the use of suicide statistics, it is worth pointing out that the reporting of suicide rates presupposes an interest in statistical record keeping on the subject. Therefore we might question whether countries with traditionally low rates (such as Ireland) simply lack either the bureaucratic infrastructure or an avid interest in reporting such statistics.

3. The nineteenth-century Durkheimian model of anomie in an industrialized Protestant society makes high rates of suicide in nineteenth- and twentieth-century Hungary about as unlikely as the Bolshevik revolution in Russia according to Marx's predictions. Also, as we shall see, there is much doubt about the rise of individualism in nineteenth-century Hungary, where the romantic and liberal movements were heavily influenced by populists and nationalists.

4. An underlying theme of nearly all his work, e.g., *The Cheese and the Worms: The Cosmos of a Sixteenth-Century Miller* (Baltimore, 1980); stories of the Livonian werewolf in *The Night Battles: Witchcraft and Agrarian Cults in the Sixteenth and Seventeenth Centuries* (London, 1983); and *Clues, Myths and the Historical Method* (Baltimore, 1989).

5. For an extended consideration of the symbolic meanings of suicide as a cultural artifact, see Irina Paperno, *Suicide as a Cultural Institution in Dostoevsky's Russia* (Ithaca, 1997), 1–17.

6. Paul Lendvai, *Hungary:The Art of Survival* (London, 1988), 101.

7. Ibid., 102.

8. Tamás Zonda, *Öngyilkos Nép-e a Magyar?* (Budapest, 1995), 250. For his general theory of suicide as a cultural phenomenon, see Tamás Zonda, *Az Öngyilkosság Kultúrtörténete (Rövid mentalitástörténet)* (Budapest, 1991).

9. Zonda, *Öngyilkos Nép-e a Magyar?* 251–52.

10. Ede Böszörményi, "Hódmezővásárh o elyi öngyilkosságok," *Történeti statisztikai tanulmányok. Központi Statisztikai Hivatal Könyvtáre, Magyar Országos Levéltar* 3 (1977): 237–304.

11. The primary focus of Böszörményi's demographic suicide studies is the discrepancy between religious groups. His most comprehensive study of the history of suicide in Hungary is *Az öngyilkosságok múltja és jelene. Történeti vázlat, különös tekintettel Magyarországra* (Budapest, 1991). See also his general work on world religions, *Az Igazságot Szeretetben: Írások az Egyház Múltjából és Jelenéből* (Debrecen, 1998).The general assumption of higher rates of suicide among Protestants than Catholics is based on the "first law" of sociology; for an historical analysis of its development, see David Lederer, "Selbstmord im frühneuzeitlichen Deutschland: Klischee und Geschichte," *Psychotherapie* 4 (1999): 196–202; H. C. Erik Midelfort, "Religious Melancholy and Suicide: On the Reformation Origins of a Sociological Stereotype," in *Madness, Melancholy, and the Limits of the Self,* ed. Andrew D. Weiner and Leonard V. Kaplan, vol. 3 of *Graven Images: Studies in Culture, Law, and the Sacred* (Madison, 1996), 41–56.

12. The generalization of consistently higher rates of successful suicides among men than women has been euphemistically dubbed the "second law," while women exceed men in parasuicide. Statistically, Hungarian men kill themselves three times as often as women. However, the canonical validity of this "second law" (as well as generalizations about higher rates in urban areas) has been challenged by recent findings from rural China; see Elisabeth Rosenthal, "Suicide Gains Ground on Women in Rural China," *New York Times,* 24 January 1999, 1, 8.

13. Ede Böszörményi, "A Magyarországi Öngyilkosságok Történetéhez," *Demográfia* 19 (1976): 478–88; Lendvai, *Hungary,* 102. In 1996, the southern towns of Csongrad and Békés led the country in rates of reported suicide with 75 men and 25 women per 100,000 (on average 49 per 100,000) and 85 men and 28 women per 100,000 (on average 56 per 100,000), respectively. In comparison, the highly urbanized capital city, Budapest, had rates half that size, with 36 men and 21 women per 100,000 (on average, 28 suicides per 100,000); see *Központi Statisztikai Hivatal, Demográfiai Évkönyu 1996 Magyarország Nepesedéje* (Budapest, 1998), 256.

14. Zonda, *Öngyilkos Nép-e a Magyar?* 65; Böszörményi, *Az öngyilkosságok,* 43–44.

15. *Hetilap* (1846): 1091–92.

16. Zonda, *Öngyilkos Nép-e a Magyar?* 33, 62, 110–11, 238–40

17. Richard Aczel, *National Character and European Identity in Hungarian Literature 1772–1848* (Budapest, 1996), 7.

18. Ibid., 239–41.

19. This has been demonstrated often enough in regard to (what we view as) functional/dysfunctional relationships with cultural outsiders, i.e., the history of the "other"; one obvious example is the myth of blood libel and ritual murder leveled against the European Jewry from the Middle Ages until the twentieth century.

20. J. C. Nyíri, introduction in Thomas G. Masaryk, *Der Selbstmord als sociale Massenerscheinung der modernen Civilisation* (Munich, 1991), 25.

21. Ibid., 31–32.

22. Ibid.

23. Christian Pfister, Rudolf Brázdil, and Rüdiger Glaser (eds.), *Climatic Variability in Sixteenth-Century Europe and its Social Dimension* (Dordrecht, 1999), 80.

24. A linguistic indication that the original pre-1800 term contained no pejorative implications. Many thanks to Thomas Kabdebo of Maynooth for this information.

25. *Das Ofener Stadtrecht: Eine deutschsprachige Rechtssamlung des 15. Jahrhunderts aus Ungarn,* ed. Karl Mollay (Budapest, 1959), 147.

26. A wide range of procedures are graphically illustrated in Lieven Vandekerckhove, *On Punishment: The Confrontation of Suicide in Old-Europe* (Leuven, 2000), 47–68.

27. Generally, on the Middle Ages, see Alexander Murray, *Suicide in the Middle Ages,* vol. 2, *The Curse on Self-Murder* (Oxford, 2000), 63–85. In Flanders and France, confiscation remained common into the eighteenth century; see Vandekerckhove, *Punishment,* 95–120; an examination of suicide records in the Rijksarchief Gent, Raad van Vlaanderen (21256, 23176, 23266, 23689, 31105–66) confirms cases of confiscation for persons not suspected of other crimes in the late-eighteenth century. In England, attitudes toward forfeiture began to change in the seventeenth century with the rise of the insanity defense; see Michael MacDonald and Terence Murphy, *Sleepless Souls: Suicide in Early Modern England* (Oxford, 1990), 78–89.

28. For example, Murray, *Suicide in Middle Ages,* vol. 2, *Curse on Self-Murder,* 23–26, found customs pertaining to suicides that were unique to Germanic areas.

29. *Der Sachsenspiegel* (Stuttgart, 1999), II, 31, §1; *Die Peinliche Gerichtsordnung Kaiser Karls V. von 1532 (Carolina)* (Stuttgart, 1975), 90, Art. 135.

30. Vera Lind, *Selbstmord in der Frühen Neuzeit: Diskurs, Lebenswelt und kultureller Wandel am Beispiel der Herzogtümer Schleswig und Holstein,* Veröffentlichungen des Max-Planck-Instituts für Geschichte, vol. 146 (Göttingen, 1999), 344–47.

31. Walter Ziegler, *Dokumente zur Geschichte von Staat und Gesellschaft in Bayern: Altbayern von 1550–1651* (Munich, 1992), 1: 165, "Letzte Freiheitserklärung von 10.1.1553." The practical application of a general policy of nonconfiscation in Bavaria from 1610 onwards is verified by the records of the Bavarian Court Council and the Provincial Administrator in Landshut. The quarterly volumes of the Aulic Council protocols (Bayerisches Hauptstaatsarchiv München, Kurbayern Hofrat) were examined systematically for the years 1610–1670, but reported confiscations were few, despite recent claims by Richard Heydenreutter, *Kriminalgeschichte Bayerns* (Munich, 2003), 137–38. From 1621 to 1681, for example, the *Rentmeister* of Landshut also investigated numerous cases of suicide, but regularly refused to order confiscations for self-murderers not accused of any other felony—Staatsarchiv Landshut B 21, Einziehung deren Vermögen. This evidence from such an early period is obviously at odds with Vandekerckhove's generalizations of confiscation as a universal penalty under the ancien régime.

32. *Corpus Statutorum Hungariae Municipalium* (Budapest, 1890), 5: 348–49, #12.

33. *Corpus Statutorum,* 2: Pars 1, 484. In a footnote, the nineteenth-century editors of the edition expressed their surprise that suicide was ever considered a crime.

34. Mátyás Bodo, *De Jurisprudentia criminalis, Pars II: De Jure & Processu Criminali, in Specie* (Pressburg, 1752), 205–6, Article LXIII.

35. As prosecutions for infanticide increased during the eighteenth century, judicial reformers clamored for an end to the death penalty, alarmed by "indirect suicides," i.e., the commission of homicide or infanticide to receive a death sentence; see Arne Jansson's chapter in this volume (chap. 5) and his *From Swords to Sorrow: Homicide and Suicide in Early Modern Stockholm* (Stockholm, 1998); also, more generally, Lind, *Selbstmord,* 163–66.

36. Bodo, *De Jurisprudentia criminalis,* 206, Art. LXIII, XVI, §XVI. Note that unbaptized children were also not generally eligible for burial in the communal cemetery.

37. On "despair" as a religiously grounded category see David Lederer, "The Dishonorable Dead: Elite and Popular Perceptions of Suicide in Early Modern Germany," in *Ehrekonzepte in der Frühen Neuzeit: Identität und Abgrenzungen,* ed. Sibylle Backmann, Hans-Jörg Künast, B. Ann Tlusty, and Sabine Ullmann (Augsburg, 1998), 352–54; on the origins of the term in medieval theology, see Murray, *Suicide in Middle Ages,* vol. 2, *Curse on Self-Murder,* 369–95.

38. *Magyar Jogi Lexikon* (Budapest, 1904), 5: 752.

39. Magyar Országos Levéltár, Helztartótanácsi levéltár, Magyar Királyi Helytartótanács (Departementum politiae in genere et civitatum), C51, 1801–43.

40. This is surely not to say that they do not exist, but they must be rare. Indeed, the criminal records in the civic archive of Budapest are very rich for the period after 1700 and a serial analysis of these German-language documents could form the basis of a well-needed study in historical criminology for eighteenth-century Hungary. However, they have little to say about suicide.

41. E.g., Gyula Ortutay, *Hungarian Folklore* (Budapest, 1972); Linda Dégh, *Folktales and Society: Story-Telling in a Hungarian Peasant Community* (Bloomington, 1969).

42. Kristóf describes the 147 trials in Debrecen from 1575 to 1759 as small scale (1–3 trials a year), with some medium-sized hunts (5–10 trials a year); Ildikó Kristof, "Elements of Demonology in Hungarian Calvinist Literature Printed in Debrecen in the Sixteenth and Seventeenth Centuries," in *Cauda Pavonis: Studies in Hermeticism* 16 (1997): 9–17. Eva Pócs, *Between the Living and the Dead: A Perspective on Witches and Seers in the Early Modern Age* (Budapest, 1999), suggests that approximately 2,000 witch trials occurred in Hungary from the sixteenth to the eighteenth century. Gábor Klaniczay, "The Decline of Witches and the Rise of Vampires under Eighteenth-Century Habsburg Monarchy," in idem, *The Uses of Supernatural Power: The Transformation of Popular Religion in Medieval and Early-Modern Europe* (Oxford, 1990), 168–88, suggests, "It would be a mistake to underestimate the gravity and the destructive effect of witch persecution in Hungary" (169), and reckons about 1,700 trials occurred, half of which left the accused dead or imprisoned. Based on the work of Andor Komáromy and Ferenc Schram, an earlier work placed the total number of trials at 926; Tekla Dömötör, *Hungarian Folk Beliefs* (Budapest, 1981), 63.

43. Henry Marczali, *Hungary in the Eighteenth Century* (Cambridge, 1910), 182, n. 1. The *táltos,* or "cunning-people," "tended overwhelmingly to be male"; Dömötör, *Hungarian Folk Beliefs,* 67.

44. Lederer, "Selbstmord im frühneuzeitlichen Deutschland," 196–202; idem, "Dishonorable Dead," 349–65; idem, "Aufruhr auf dem Friedhof: Pfarrer, Gemeinde und Selbstmord im frühneuzeitlichen Bayern," in *Trauer, Verzweiflung und Anfechtung: Selbstmord und Selbstmordversuche in mittelalterlichen und frühneuzeitlichen Gesellschaften,* ed. Gabriela Signori (Tübingen, 1994), 189–209.

45. Ildikó Kristóf, "The Plague of the Plagues: Epidemic and Riot in Debrecen in 1739–1742," in *The Third Finnish-Hungarian Symposium on Ethnology in Konnevesi 20.-25.8.1989,* vol. 1, *Historical Sources* (Ulvila, 1991), 64–77.

46. Debrecen Civic Archive, SAHBC, IV A. 1018/e.

47. Mircea Eliade, ed., *Encyclopedia of Religion* (New York, 1996), s.v. "Suicide," by Marilyn Harran; s.v. "Martyrdom," by Samuel Klausner.

48. Ibid., s.v. "Martyrdom," by Klausner.

49. Paperno, *Suicide,* 16. Whereas Western European romantics dwelled on suicide as a method of individual self-determination, the Hungarian romantics stressed group-oriented self-sacrifice with nationalist aspirations.

50. E.g., Alexander Murray, *Suicide in the Middle Ages,* vol. 1, *The Violent against Themselves* (Oxford, 1998), 61–70.

51. Johannes De Thurocz, *Chronica Hungarorum* (Budapest, 1985), 150–53. Here, it is possible to suggest parallels to the *Chansons de Geste,* in particular the *Song of Roland,* although clearly Deszö was not guilty of hubris.

52. Heinrich Wilhelm Heller, *Über den Selbstmord in Teutschland* (Frankfurt am Main, 1787), iv.

53. Tibor Klaniczay, ed., *Old Hungarian Literary Reader, 11th–18th Centuries* (Békéscsaba, 1985), 111–31, here 126–27.

54. Tibor Klaniczay, ed., *A History of Hungarian Literature* (Gyomaendrőd, 1983), 89–92. On Pázmány, his ambivalent relationship to the works of Seneca and his relationship to the Zrínyi clan, see István Bitskey, *Konfession und literarische Gattungen der frühen Neuzeit in Ungarn: Beiträge zur mitteleuropäischen vergleichenden Kulturgeschichte* (Frankfurt am Main, 1999), 91–122.

55. Nikolaus Zrínyi, *Der Fall von Sziget* (Budapest, 1944), here 253–54 (author's translation).

56. Bitskey, *Konfession,* 123–36.

57. By the mid-seventeenth century, the younger Zrínyi continued to favor the hit-and-run delaying tactics of his grandfather with the intention of slowing the fall of Eastern Hungary, which he viewed as inevitable: Àgnes R.Várkonyi, "Die Belagerung von Ofen im Rahmen der Pläne zur Zurückdrängung der osmanischen Macht," in *Laurus Austriaco-Hungarica: Literarische Gattungen und Politik in der zweiten Hälfte des 17. Jahrhunderts,* ed. Béla Köpeczi and Andor Tarnai (Vienna, 1988), 7.

58. Klaniczay, *History of Hungarian Literature,* 93; Lóránt Czigány, ed., *The Oxford History of Hungarian Literature: From the Earliest Times to the Present* (Oxford, 1984), 59–60. Excerpts of the original text are translated in Klaniczay, *Hungarian Reader,* 231–33.

59. Péter Hanák, ed., *The Corvina History of Hungary: From the Earliest Times to the Present Day* (Gyomaendrőd, 1991), 63.

60. In the index to the German edition of the Corvina History, Péter Zrínyi is explicitly described as a "Martyr"; Péter Hanák (ed.), *Die Geschichte Ungarns: Von den Anfängen bis zur Gegenwart* (Gyomaendrőd, 1991), 281.

61. Many Hungarians became Ottomanized. Although the case of the Venetian Lodovico Gritti, who transferred from the services of the Hungarians to become a direct subject of the Sultan—see Ferenc Szakály, *Lodovico Gritti in Hungary, 1529–1534* (Budapest, 1995)—is perhaps an extreme example of collaboration, it raises interesting questions about the extent to which other Turkic and Islamic customs, such as the concept of holy war, may have either been taken on or even rekindled common Altaic cultural roots.

62. Bóld'isar Barta, *Rövid Chronica, Avagy Oly Beszélgetés Melly A' Közelebb Elmúlt Száz Esztendők Alatt Debreczenben* (Debrecen, 1666), 42–49. Many thanks to János Barta for this reference.

63. Barta, *Rövid Chronica,* 46.

64. Ibid.

65. Ibid., 48.

66. Ibid., 60–64.

67. For the authoritative bibliography, see Tibor Klaniczay, *A bibliotheca Zriniana története és állománya* (Budapest, 1991).

68. Klaniczay, *History of Hungarian Literature,* 184.

69. Hanák, *Geschichte Ungarns,* 116; Aczel, *National Character,* 241.

70. One example of a successful integration of the numerous ethnic minorities in Hungary into a national ethos.

71. Czigány, *Oxford History,* 191.

72. Ibid., 227.

73. Anton van Hooff, "Glorie aan de verslagenen," *Trouw,* 7 March 2003, 12.

74. Aczel, *National Character,* 251.

Chapter 8. Suicide, Gender, and Religion

Material for this chapter has been taken from *Choosing Death: Suicide and Calvinism in Early Modern Geneva* (Kirksville, 2001). I warmly thank Truman State University Press for permission to reproduce this material here.

1. Arthur J. Droge and James D. Tabor, *A Noble Death: Suicide and Martyrdom among Christians and Jews of Antiquity* (New York, 1992), 167–83; Georges Minois, *History of Suicide: Voluntary Death in Western Culture,* trans. Lydia G. Cochrane (Baltimore, 1999), 7–41; Alexander Murray, *Suicide in the Middle Ages,* vol. 2, *The Curse on Self-Murder* (Oxford, 2000). A classic sociological study is Thomas Masaryk, *Suicide and the Meaning of Civilization,* trans. William B. Weist and Robert G. Batson (Chicago, 1970).

2. Statistics show men outnumbering women among self-inflicted deaths in all Western countries. In 1990, for example, these countries recorded the following suicide rates (per 100,000 people) for men and women, respectively: Austria, 34.8 and 13.4; United Kingdom, 12.6 and 3.8; Switzerland, 31.5 and 12.7; U.S.A., 20.1 and 5.0; Silvia Sara Canetto and David Lester, "The Epidemiology of Women's Suicidal Behavior," in *Women and Suicidal Behavior,* ed. Silvia Sara Canetto and David Lester (New York, 1996), 44–45.

3. Even certain statistical works tell us more about changes in the judicial treatment of suicide than in the frequency of self-inflicted deaths. S. J. Stevenson believes that the recorded increase in suicide verdicts in the late sixteenth century was likely the result of more systematic investigations; "The Rise of Suicide Verdicts in South-East England, 1530–1590: The Legal Process," *Continuity and Change* 2 (1987): 37–75; idem, "Social and Economic Contributions to the Pattern of 'Suicide' in South-East England, 1530–1590," *Continuity and Change* 2 (1987): 225–62.

4. I am convinced that explanations for suicides offered by witnesses and survivors bore some relation to the causes of suicide. The explanations proffered were shaped by contemporary shared values, an understanding of the social changes then at work, and familiarity with the personality and mental and physical health of those who chose death.

5. Emile Durkheim, *Suicide: A Case Study in Sociology,* trans. John A. Spaulding and George Simpson, ed. George Simpson (New York, 1951), 272.

6. For an important critique of official suicide statistics, see Jack D. Douglas, *The Social Meanings of Suicide* (Princeton, 1967), 163–231.

7. Archives d'Etat de Genève (hereafter AEG), Procès Criminel (hereafter PC) Juridiction Pénale Lc No. 59, Landecy.

8. For a detailed analysis of unnatural deaths in early modern Geneva, see Watt, *Choosing Death,* 15–66. Other work on suicide in early modern Geneva includes Laurent Haeberli, "Le suicide à Genève au XVIIIe siècle," in *Pour une Histoire Qualitative* (Geneva, 1975), 115–29, a Durkheimian study which attempts to trace changes in suicide rates in the 1700s. Since he studied only criminal proceedings, relying heavily on the Archives' handwritten *inventaires* to identify self-inflicted deaths, Haeberli missed a large number of suicides. Michel Porret has also authored several articles on suicide, such as "Solitude, mélancolie, souffrance: Le suicide à Genève durant l'Ancien Régime (XVIIe-XVIIIe siècles)," *Cahiers Psychiatriques Genevois* 16 (1994): 9–21. Though of some value from the juridical-medical point of view, Porret's works are based on selected sources and make little attempt to analyze suicide as a social phenomenon.

9. Suicide had also been rare in the previous century, amounting to a rate of only 2.9 per 100,000 for the years 1651–1700. Population estimates from Alfred Perrenoud, *La population de Genève XVIe–XIXe siècles* (Geneva, 1979), 37.

10. Jean-Claude Chesnais, "Géographie du suicide," *Histoire* 189 (1995): 30.

11. AEG, Registres du Consistoire 89: 452; Registres du Petit Conseil (hereafter RC) 259: 57; this latter cited in Haeberli, "Suicide à Genève," 116, n. 6.

12. Voltaire, *Les Oeuvres complètes de Voltaire,* ed. Theodore Bestermann et al. (Banbury, 1968–77), 115: 389, D 13995; see also Haeberli, "Suicide à Genève," 116. Voltaire was repeating the stereotype, now viewed as unwarranted, that the English of the eighteenth century were especially prone to suicide.

13. Voltaire, *Oeuvres,* 123: 431–32, D 18376, n. 1.

14. Henri Brunschwig, *Enlightenment and Romanticism in Eighteenth-Century Prussia,* trans. Frank Jellinek (Chicago, 1974), 220–21; Robert Favre, *La mort dans la littérature et la pensée françaises au siècle des lumières* (Lyon, 1978), 473; Jeffrey Merrick, "Patterns and Prosecution of Suicide in Eighteenth-Century Paris," *Historical Reflections* 16 (1989): 1–53.

15. For a much more thorough discussion of this increase in suicides, see Watt, *Choosing Death,* 67–125. Vera Lind adeptly analyzes the decriminalization of suicide in eighteenth-century Germany; *Selbstmord in der Frühen Neuzeit: Diskurs, Lebenswelt und kultureller Wandel am*

Beispiel der Herzogtümer Schleswig und Holstein, Veröffentlichungen des Max-Planck-Instituts für Geschichte, vol. 146 (Göttingen, 1999). On similar penalties against the corpses of suicides in medieval and early modern Europe, see Alain Joblin, "Le suicide à l'époque moderne: Un exemple dans la France du Nord-Ouest: à Boulogne-sur-Mer," *Revue historique* 589 (1994): 94–95, 117; Michael MacDonald and Terence R. Murphy, *Sleepless Souls: Suicide in Early Modern England* (Oxford, 1990), 44–47; Murray, *Suicide in the Middle Ages,* vol. 2, *Curse on Self-Murder,* 28–53.

16. Françoise Bayard, "Régions et morts subites en Lyonnais et Beaujolais aux XVIIe et XVIIIe siècles," in *Du provincialisme au régionalisme XVIIIe–XXe siècle* (Paris, 1989), 211–22, also found that men and women killed themselves in roughly equal numbers. By contrast, Lind finds that men comprised the large majority of suicides for the period 1600–1820; *Selbstmord,* 190–204.

17. Durkheim, *Suicide,* 272.

18. Philippe Besnard, "Durkheim et les femmes ou le *Suicide* inachevé," *Revue française de sociologie* 14 (1973): 27–61; Louis I. Dublin, *Suicide: A Sociological and Statistical Study* (New York, 1963), 38–41; Maurice Halbwachs, *Les causes du suicide* (Paris, 1930), 43, 75; Howard I. Kushner, "Women and Suicide in Historical Perspective," *Signs* 10 (1985): 537–52; Ronald W. Maris, *Social Forces in Urban Suicide* (Homewood, 1969), 96–98.

19. Perrenoud, *Population de Genève,* 35, 544.

20. Michel Porret, *Le crime et ses circonstances: De l'esprit de l'arbitraire au siècle des Lumières selon les réquisitoires des procureurs généraux de Genève* (Geneva, 1995), 157–60.

21. Jean Baechler, *Suicides,* trans. Barry Cooper (New York, 1979), 290.

22. Another explanation that suicidologists offer for the gender gap is that males are much more prone to toxicomania, especially alcoholism, which greatly increases the risk of self-inflicted death; ibid.; George Howe Colt, *The Enigma of Suicide* (New York, 1991), 266–67. Geneva's criminal records shed little light on the drinking habits of those who took their lives. No evidence suggests that heavy drinking suddenly became a problem for males in the mid-1700s. More broadly, I cannot of course investigate the biochemical aspect of early modern suicide. Though surely important, biochemistry does not alone determine who commits suicide. Depression is by far the mental disorder most often associated with suicide, but only a small percentage of the depressed actually commits suicide—currently in the United States, an estimated 17 million people suffer from depression, and about 40,000 Americans take their lives annually. While some studies have found that suicide is often associated with low levels of the neurotransmitter serotonin, the issue of cause and effect is not clear. Though a low level of serotonin may affect one's behavior, personal experiences, such as job loss or the death of a loved one, may quite plausibly affect one's chemical balance. Quite simply, it seems unlikely that Geneva's explosion in suicides was merely the result of a sudden drop in the serotonin levels of its residents in the mid-eighteenth century. Experts on mental health now generally agree that social factors, such as urbanization and popular values, contribute in an important way to suicide; David Lester, *Why People Kill Themselves: A Summary of Research Findings on Suicidal Behavior* (Springfield, 1972), 33–34, 194; Steve Taylor, *Durkheim and the Study of Suicide* (New York, 1982), 36–37.

23. Durkheim, *Suicide,* 171–89. See also Nick Danigelis and Whitney Pope, "Durkheim's Theory of Suicide as Applied to the Family: An Empirical Test," *Social Forces* 57 (1979): 1081–106; Henry Romilly Fedden, *Suicide: A Social and Historical Study* (New York, 1972), 326; Maris, *Social Forces in Urban Suicide,* 108–10.

24. For a critique, see Kushner, "Women and Suicide," 537–52.

25. For a fuller discussion of the family and suicide, see Watt, *Choosing Death,* 213–51; idem, "The Family, Love, and Suicide in Early Modern Geneva," *Journal of Family History* 21 (1996): 63–86.

26. Dublin, *Suicide,* 17, 65; Halbwachs, *Causes du suicide,* 362–74; Andrew F. Henry and James

Short, "Suicide and External Restraint," in *The Sociology of Suicide: A Selection of Readings,* ed. Anthony Giddens (London, 1971), 63; Steven Stack and Ain Haas, "The Effect of Unemployment Duration on National Suicide Rates: A Time Series Analysis, 1948–1982," *Sociological Focus* 17 (1984): 17–29.

27. AEG, Etat Civil, Livres des Morts (hereafter EC, LM) 60: 409, 23 September 1747; PC 9411.

28. AEG, EC, LM 65: 249, 13 January 1779; PC 13265.

29. Liliane Mottu-Weber, "Les activités manufacturières" and "La conjoncture de l'économie genevoise, XVIe–XVIIIe siècles," in *L'économie genevoise, de la Réforme à la fin de l'Ancien Régime, XVIe–XVIIIe siècles,* ed. Anne-Marie Piuz and Liliane Mottu-Weber (Geneva, 1990), 423–99, 615–48.

30. Perrenoud, *Population de Genève,* 170.

31. AEG, PC 15188.

32. Liliane Mottu-Weber, "Women's Place of Work in Geneva under the Old Regime (16th–18th Centuries)," in *Forgotten Women of Geneva,* ed. Anne-Marie Kappëli, trans. Rebecca Zorac (Geneva, 1993), 100–103.

33. See Natalie Zemon Davis, "Women in the Crafts in Sixteenth-Century Lyon," in *Women and Work in Preindustrial Europe,* ed. Barbara A. Hanawalt (Bloomington, 1986), 167–97; Peter Earle, "The Female Labour Market in London in the Late Seventeenth and Early Eighteenth Centuries," in *Women's Work: The English Experience 1650–1914,* ed. Pamela Sharpe (London, 1988), 134–35; Olwen H. Hufton, "Women and the Family Economy in Eighteenth-Century France," *French Historical Studies* 9 (1975): 1–23; idem, "Women without Men: Widows and Spinsters in Britain and France in the Eighteenth Century," *Journal of Family History* 9 (1984): 355–76; idem, "Women, Work and Marriage in Eighteenth-Century France," in *Marriage and Society: Studies in the Social History of Marriage,* ed. R. B. Outhwaite (New York, 1981), 186–203; Merry E. Wiesner, *Women and Gender in Early Modern Europe* (Cambridge, 1993), 83–86; idem, *Working Women in Renaissance Germany* (New Brunswick, 1986), 4, 33, 185–87, 192–97.

34. Mottu-Weber, "Activités manufacturières," in *Economie genevoise,* ed. Anne-Marie Piuz and Liliane Mottu-Weber, 488; Perrenoud, *Population de Genève,* 170, 176, 178. For women and work in early modern Geneva, see Liliane Mottu-Weber, "L'évolution des activités professionnelles des femmes à Genève du XVIe au XVIIIe siècle," in *La Donna nell'economia, secc. XVIII– XVIII,* ed. Simonetta Cavaciocchi (Florence, 1990), 345–57; idem, "Les femmes dans la vie économique de Genève, XVIe–XVIIe siècles," *Bulletin de la Société d'histoire et d'archéologie de Genève* 16 (1979): 381–401.

35. Dennis A. Ahlburg, and Morton Owen Schapiro, "Socioeconomic Ramifications of Changing Cohort Size: An Analysis of U.S. Postwar Suicide Rates by Age and Sex," *Demography* 21 (1984): 97–105; Warren Breed, "Occupational Mobility and Suicide among White Males," *American Sociological Review* 28 (1963): 188; Dublin, *Suicide,* 66; Maris, *Social Forces in Urban Suicide,* 95; Elwin Powell, "Occupations, Status, and Suicide," *American Sociological Review* 23 (1958): 131–39.

36. Suzanne Desan, *Reclaiming the Sacred: Lay Religion and Popular Politics in Revolutionary France* (Ithaca, 1992), 199–200, 205–7; Olwen H. Hufton, "Women in Revolution, 1789–1796," *Past and Present* 53 (1971): 104–8.

37. See Hermann Blanc, *La Chambre des Blés de Genève 1628–1798* (Geneva, 1941). On the whole, Genevans were remarkably well fed, consuming unusually large quantities of meat: 83– 88 kilograms per capita in 1780. By comparison, residents in the Department of Le Léman consumed on the average only 6.5 kilograms annually in 1813; David Hiler, "Permanences et innovations alimentaires: L'évolution de la consommation des Genevois pendant le XVIIIe siècle," *Bulletin de la Société d'histoire et d'archéologie de Genève* 18 (1984): 31.

38. AEG, EC, LM 68: 78, 13 September 1793; PC 17057; RC 302: 956.

39. Patrice Louis Higonnet, "Du suicide sentimental au suicide politique," in *La Révolution*

et la mort, ed. Elisabeth Liris and Jean Maurice Bizière (Toulouse, 1991), 137–50; John McManners, *Death and the Enlightenment: Changing Attitudes to Death in Eighteenth-Century France* (Oxford, 1981), 417.

40. AEG, PC 17079.

41. AEG, PC 16769.

42. See, for example, Judith M. Bennett, *Ale, Beer, and Brewsters in England: Women's Work in a Changing World, 1300–1600* (Oxford, 1996), 152; Ralph A. Houlbrooke, "Women's Social Life and Common Action in England from the Fifteenth Century to the Eve of the Civil War," *Continuity and Change* 1 (1986): 171–89.

43. On the role of women and attitudes toward women in the French Revolution, see Jane Abray, "Feminism in the French Revolution," *American Historical Review* 80 (1975): 43–62; Darline Levy, Harriet Applewhite, and Mary Johnson, eds. and trans., *Women in Revolutionary Paris* (Urbana, 1979); Linda Kelly, *Women of the French Revolution* (London, 1977); Annette Rosa, *Citoyennes: Les femmes et la Révolution française* (Paris, 1988). In Revolutionary Geneva, only a couple incidents bear even the slightest trace of feminism. In 1794 a Genevan Jacobin complained about the presence of women at the Great Fraternal Club, provoking the wrath of some female members who came close to beating him up; in 1797 a group of women proposed a new liturgy for marriage which "would better respect the rights of *homesses* (sic)"; E. William Monter, "Women in Calvinist Geneva (1550–1800)," *Signs* 6 (1980): 207, n. 76.

44. François Lebrun, *Les hommes et la mort en Anjou aux 17e et 18e siècles* (Paris, 1971), 136, 338–47; Pierre Goubert, *Louis XIV and Twenty Million Frenchmen,* trans. Anne Carter (New York, 1970), 215–19.

45. Anne-Marie Piuz, "Chertés et disettes," in *Economie genevoise,* ed. Piuz and Mottu-Weber, 372–78.

46. AEG, EC, LM 51: 64v, 19 January 1699.

47. Fedden, *Suicide,* 54

48. See Corinne Walker, "Les pratiques de la richesse: Riches Genevois au XVIIIe siècle," in *Etre riche au siècle de Voltaire,* ed. Jacques Berchtold and Michel Porret (Geneva, 1996), 135–60.

49. Charron, *De la Sagesse* (Bordeaux, 1601), book 2, chapter 11; John Donne, *Biathanatos: A Declaration of the Paradox or Thesis That Self-Homicide Is Not So Naturally a Sin That It May Never Be Otherwise* (London, 1647); Montaigne, "Coustume de l'Isle de Céa," in *Essais* (Paris, 1588), book 2, chapter 3. For analyses of medieval literature on suicide, see Albert Bayet, *Le Suicide et la morale* (Paris, 1922; reprint, New York, 1975), 532–36; Murray, *Suicide in the Middle Ages,* vol. 2, *Curse on Self-Murder.*

50. S. E. Sprott, *The English Debate on Suicide from Donne to Hume* (La Salle, 1961), 128–34.

51. Michael MacDonald, "The Medicalization of Suicide in England: Laymen, Physicians, and Cultural Change, 1500–1870," in *Framing Disease: Studies in Cultural History,* ed. Charles E. Rosenberg and Janet Golden (New Brunswick, 1992), 94; Stephen L. Trainor, "Suicide and Seneca in Two Eighteenth Century Tragedies," in *Drama and the Classical Heritage,* ed. Clifford Davidson, Rand Johnson, and John H. Stroupe (New York, 1993), 227–40.

52. Cesare Beccaria, *Dei delitti e delle pene,* ed. Franco Venturi (Milan, 1991), 85–88; Lester G. Crocker, "The Discussion of Suicide in the Eighteenth Century," *Journal of the History of Ideas* 13 (1952): 47–72; Favre, *Mort,* 469–96; McManners, *Death and the Enlightenment,* 409–37.

53. Joseph-Albert Bédé, "Madame de Staël, Rousseau, et le suicide," *Revue d'histoire littéraire de la France* 66 (1966): 55; Denis Diderot and Jean Le Rond d'Alembert, eds., *Encyclopédie, ou Dictionnaire raisonné des sciences, des arts et des métiers,* 28 vols. (Paris, 1751–1772), s.v. "Suicide"; Favre, *Mort,* 473–83; Fedden, *Suicide,* 224–25; Lind, *Selbstmord,* 45–151; McManners, *Death and the Enlightenment,* 424–25; Merrick, "Patterns of Suicide," 2–3; idem, "Suicide, Society, and History: The Case of Bourdeaux and Humain, 25 December 1773," *Studies on Voltaire and the Eighteenth Century* 8 (2000): 75–76; Minois, *History of Suicide,* 179–209; Jean-Jacques Rousseau, *Julie ou La Nouvelle Héloïse,* ed. René Pomeau (Paris, 1960), part 3, letters 21–23; Michael J. Seidler, "Kant and the Stoics on Suicide," *Journal of the History of Ideas* 44 (1983): 429–53.

54. Dublin, *Suicide,* 189; Masaryk, *Suicide;* Bernice A. Pescolido and Sharon Georgianna, "Durkheim, Suicide, and Religion: Toward a Network Theory of Suicide," *American Sociological Review* 54 (1989): 33–48.

55. Durkheim, *Suicide,* 152–64.

56. Steven Stack, "The Effect of Domestic/Religious Individualism on Suicide, 1954–1978," *Journal of Marriage and the Family* 47 (1985): 431–47.

57. Jean Delumeau, *Sin and Fear: The Emergence of a Western Guilt Culture 13th–18th Centuries,* trans. Eric Nicholson (New York, 1990), 168–85, 523–54; H. C. Erik Midelfort, *A History of Madness in Sixteenth-Century Germany* (Stanford, 1999), 51–58, 376–81; idem, "Sin, Melancholy, Obsession: Insanity and Culture in 16th Century Germany," in *Understanding Popular Culture: Europe from the Middle Ages to the Nineteenth Century,* ed. Steven L. Kaplan (Berlin, 1984), 113–45. For a contemporary account, see John Sym, *Lifes Preservative Against Self-Killing,* ed. and Introduction by Michael MacDonald (London, 1989).

58. AEG, PC 552; RC 50: 23v, 25v, 27–28.

59. AEG, PC 2681bis. By placing the origins of her illness in her sin, Dauphin differs somewhat from German physicians who, according to Midelfort, from the mid-sixteenth century increasingly asserted that all diseases were physical in origin and accordingly prescribed humoral treatments, such as bleedings, for patients suffering from melancholy; "Sin, Melancholy, Obsession," 115–25. In another work, Midelfort provides a nuanced view, avowing that physicians attributed German princes' insanity to demon possession only after medical cures had failed—if no natural cause could be found, then the madness must be of supernatural origin; *Mad Princes of Renaissance Germany* (Charlottesville, 1994), 149.

60. AEG, PC 4679; RC 186: 23–24.

61. AEG, PC 4712.

62. See *Registres du Consistoire de Genève au temps de Calvin, 1542–1544,* ed. and Introduction by Thomas A. Lambert and Isabella M. Watt (Geneva, 1996). See also a number of works by Robert M. Kingdon, such as *Adultery and Divorce in Calvin's Geneva* (Cambridge, Mass., 1995); "Social Control and Political Control in Calvin's Geneva," *Archive for Reformation History* (special volume, 1993): 521–32.

63. AEG, EC, LM 43: 98, 14 March 1679; PC 4451; RC 179: 82–83, 91, 95–96.

64. See Jeffrey R. Watt, "Calvin on Suicide," *Church History* 66 (1997): 463–76; idem, "Suicide in Reformation Geneva," *Archive for Reformation History* 89 (1998): 227–46. These findings do not support the claim that Calvinist religiosity nurtured suicidal proclivities, allegedly because people felt a spiritual void after the elimination of Catholic rituals and were so obsessed with their sinfulness that they were driven to suicide; Markus Schär, *Seelennöte der Untertanen: Selbstmord, Melancholie und Religion im Alten Zürich, 1500–1800* (Zurich, 1985); Sprott, *English Debate,* 29–54. See also Midelfort, *History of Madness,* 80–139; idem, "Religious Melancholy and Suicide: On the Reformation Origins of a Sociological Stereotype," in *Madness, Melancholy, and the Limits of the Self,* ed. Andrew D. Weiner and Leonard V. Kaplan, vol. 3 of *Graven Images: Studies in Culture, Law, and the Sacred* (Madison, 1996), 41–42; John Stachniewski, *The Persecutory Imagination: English Puritanism and the Literature of Religious Despair* (Oxford, 1991), esp. 46–52.

65. See C. John Sommerville, *The Secularization of Early Modern England: From Religious Culture to Religious Faith* (Oxford, 1992), 9, 16–17.

66. Graham Gargett, *Jacob Vernet, Geneva and the Philosophes* (Oxford, 1994); Martin I. Klauber, *Between Reformed Scholasticism and Pan-Protestantism: Jean-Alphonse Turretin (1671–1737) and Enlightened Orthodoxy at the Academy of Geneva* (Selinsgrove, 1994); idem, "The Eclipse of Reformed Scholasticism in Eighteenth-Century Geneva: Natural Theology from Jean-Alphonse Turretin to Jacob Vernet," in *The Identity of Geneva: The Christian Commonwealth, 1564–1864,* ed. John B. Roney and Martin I. Klauber (Westport, 1998), 129–42.

67. Favre, *Mort,* 482; Jeffrey Burton Russell, *Mephistopheles: The Devil in the Modern World* (Ithaca, 1986), 128–31, 149.

68. Geneva's *Liturgy* of 1543 warned of the great risk that the devil might seize the souls of

sick people during their last miserable hours. By contrast, official prayers of the eighteenth century besought God to heal the afflicted, if that be his will, or to accept their souls into eternal paradise. No mention at all is made of the devil; Linda Kirk, "'Going Soft': Genevan Decadence in the Eighteenth Century," in *Identity of Geneva,* ed. Roney and Klauber, 148.

69. Gargett, *Jacob Vernet,* 144–51.

70. Watt, *Choosing Death,* 284–98.

71. MacDonald, "Medicalization of Suicide," 98–99; idem, "The Secularization of Suicide in England 1660–1800," *Past and Present* 111 (1986): 50–100; MacDonald and Murphy, *Sleepless Souls,* 109–216. See also Lind, *Selbstmord,* 159–81.

72. See Michael Heyd, *Between Orthodoxy and the Enlightenment: Jean-Robert Chouet and the Introduction of Cartesian Science in the Academy of Geneva* (The Hague, 1982), 9–10; Michel Vovelle, *Piété baroque et déchristianisation en Provence au XVIIIe siècle: Les attitudes devant la mort d'après les clauses de testaments* (Paris, 1973).

73. Pierre Chaunu, *La mort à Paris aux XVIe, XVIIe, et XVIIIe siècles* (Paris, 1978), 434–36; Desan, *Reclaiming the Sacred,* 210–16; Philip T. Hoffman, *Church and Community in the Diocese of Lyon, 1500–1789* (New Haven, 1984), 144–45; Kathryn Norberg, *Rich and Poor in Grenoble, 1600–1814* (Berkeley, 1985), 250–52; Bonnie Smith, *Ladies of Leisure: The Bourgeoises of the Nord* (Princeton, 1982); Vovelle, *Piété baroque,* 322.

74. Fedden, *Suicide,* 326.

75. Durkheim, *Suicide,* 168.

76. Roger Girod, "Le recul de l'analphabétisme dans la région de Genève, de la fin du XVIIe au milieu du XIXe siècle," in *Mélanges d'histoire économique et sociale* (Geneva, 1963), 2: 179–89; François Grounauer, "Livre et société à Genève au XVIIIe siècle: Essai d'étude socio-culturelle à partir des inventaires après décès" (Mémoire de licence, Université de Genève, 1969); Laurent Haeberli, "Le taux d'alphabétisation à Genève au XVIIIe siècle," *Revue de Vieux Genève* 12 (1984): 59–64.

77. Monter, "Women in Calvinist Geneva (1550–1800)," 205–7.

78. AEG, PC 13346, 14170, 17092.

79. AEG, PC 11902. See also Michel Porret, "Mourir l'âme angoissée: Les 'reflexions sur le suicide' de l'horloger genevois J.-J. Mellaret (1769)," *Revue d'histoire moderne et contemporaine* 42 (1995): 71–90.

80. AEG, PC 15188.

81. AEG, PC 17079.

82. Merrick, "Patterns of Suicide," 19–22.

83. Nor were the philosophes instrumental in the disappearance of penalties against the bodies and estates of suicides in Geneva. While the most important writings against these practices date from the second half of the eighteenth century, with a handful of exceptions, as previously noted, the penalties stopped in Geneva a century earlier. The evidence from Geneva suggests that the views on penal reform of Beccaria and other Enlightened thinkers were more the effect of changing mentalities already under way than the agents of change themselves.

84. Daniel Aquillon, "'Celui qui se cache bien vit heureux' ou l'exposition d'enfant à Genève entre 1765 et 1785," *Revue de Vieux Genève* 13 (1983): 22–27; Monter, "Women in Calvinist Geneva (1550–1800)," 198; Watt, *Choosing Death,* 53–61.

85. For a fuller discussion, see Watt, *Choosing Death,* 252–320.

Chapter 9. Suicide in Paris, 1775

1. Louis Sébastien Mercier, *Le Tableau de Paris,* ed. Jean-Claude Bonnet (Paris, 1994), 1: 655–57.

2. Siméon Prosper Hardy, "Mes Loisirs, ou Journal des événements tels qu'ils parviennent

à ma connaissance," Bibliothèque Nationale (hereafter BN), Cabinet des Manuscrits (hereafter Ms), Fonds Français 6681: 16 and 6683: 149. On this source, see Valérie Goutal-Arnal, "Mes Loisirs, ou Journal d'événements tels qu'ils parviennent à ma connaissance, chronique (1753 – 1789) du libraire Siméon-Prosper Hardy," *Revue d'histoire moderne et contemporaine* 46 (1999): 457–77.

3. Albert Bayet, *Le Suicide et la morale* (Paris, 1922), chapter 3. See, most notably, Robert Favre, *La Mort dans la littérature et la pensée française au siècle des lumières* (Lyon, 1978), chapter 11; John McManners, *Death and the Enlightenment: Changing Attitudes to Death among Christians and Unbelievers in Eighteenth-Century France* (Oxford, 1982), chapter 12; and Georges Minois, *History of Suicide: Voluntary Death in Western Culture*, trans. Lydia Cochrane (Baltimore, 1999), chapters 8–11.

4. The book by Patrice and Margaret Higonnet forthcoming from Harvard University Press will supersede all previous work on the intellectual history of the subject. For examples of published research on suicide in the provinces, see Monique Lemière, "Morts violents, morts subites dans le bailliage d'Orbec au XVIIIe siècle," in Paul Dartiguenave et al., *Marginalité, déviance, pauvreté en France, XIVe-XIXe siècles* (Caen, 1981), 82–115; and Alain Joblin, "Le Suicide à l'époque moderne: Un Exemple dans la France du Nord-Ouest, à Boulogne-sur-Mer," *Revue historique* 589 (1994): 85–120.

5. On the Châtelet and the Parlement, see Gérard Aubry, *La Jurisprudence criminelle du Châtelet sous le règne de Louis XVI* (Paris, 1971); Porphyre Petrovich, "Recherches sur la criminalité à Paris dans la seconde moitié du XVIIIe siècle," in André Abbiatéci et al., *Crimes et criminalité en France au XVIIIe siècle* (Paris, 1971), 187–261; Richard Andrews, *Law, Magistracy, and Crime in Old Regime Paris, 1735–1789*, vol. 1, *The System of Criminal Justice* (Cambridge, 1994).

6. See Jeffrey Merrick, "Patterns and Prosecution of Suicide in Eighteenth-Century Paris," *Historical Reflection / Réflexions historiques* 16 (1989): 1–53.

7. The so-called Inventory 450 in the Salle des inventaires at the Archives Nationales (hereafter AN).

8. See Jeffrey Merrick, "Suicide, Society, and History: The Case of Bourdeaux and Humain, 25 December 1773," *Studies on Voltaire and the Eighteenth Century* 8 (2000): 113–57. An additional source: Marie-Jeanne Laboras de Mézières, "Madame Riccoboni to Robert Liston, 7 January 1774, in *Madame Riccoboni's Letters to David Hume, David Garrick, and Sir Robert Liston, 1764–1783*, ed. James Nicholls, *Studies on Voltaire and the Eighteenth Century* 149 (1976): 328.

9. On the insanity defense, see case 92 ("Is Suicide a Proof of Madness?"), decided in 1777, in the popular collection of jurisprudence entitled *Causes célèbres, curieuses, et intéressantes de toutes les cours souveraines du royaume*, ed. Nicolas Toussaint Lemoyne Desessarts, 196 vol. in 98 (Paris, 1775–89), vol. 35.

10. *Mémoires secrets pour servir à l'histoire de la république des lettres en France depuis 1762 jusqu'à nos jours*, 36 vols. (London, 1777–89). For the other cases, see 8: 12 (a talented naval surgeon who was "attacked by the madness of suicide"), 79 (two Englishmen who crossed the Channel "to confirm themselves in the madness that the French have contracted from their country"), and 215–16 (a wealthy and greedy farmer who regretted his decision to sell a load of grain at a modest price in order to please the government). On this source, see *The Mémoires secrets and the Culture of Publicity in Eighteenth-Century France*, ed. Jeremy Popkin and Bernadette Fort (Oxford, 1998).

11. *Mémoires secrets*, 8: 80.

12. Ibid., 158.

13. Hardy, "Mes Loisirs," 6682: 119 and 153. Hardy also reported (f. 72) that a sixty-year-old peasant who might have participated in recent bread riots hanged himself in the Bois de Boulogne. This man's corpse and case must have been handled by the *maréchaussée*, the mounted constabulary with jurisdiction over the suburbs.

14. See Alan Williams, *The Police of Paris, 1718–1789* (Baton Rouge, 1979); and Steven Kap-

lan, "Note sur les commissaires de police de Paris au XVIIIe siècle," *Revue d'histoire moderne et contemporaine* 28 (1981): 669–86.

15. This declaration and others are conveniently collected in the dossier on suicide in BN, Ms, Collection Joly de Fleury (hereafter JF) 2342. In some cases the commissioner drafted a *procès-verbal* (report) on the spot and an *information* (investigation) after the fact. See Appendix I for examples. In other cases one of the two documents is missing or one document includes both the description of the body and the testimony of witnesses.

16. For flagrant examples, see the cases reported in Hardy, "Mes Loisirs," 6680: 282, and discussed in BN, Ms, JF 447, dossier 5540.

17. AN, Y 11091, 17 January 1775. The doctor identified the cause of death as a ruptured abscess.

18. AN, Y 14338, 6 May 1775. In this case, the wife allayed suspicions by declaring that her husband had been absent-minded during his illness. In another case, the wife aroused suspicions by stating that she had shut the window before leaving her sick husband in their room on the fourth floor. Y 14102, 3 June 1775.

19. According to Petrovich, "Recherches," 221, the commissioners attributed fourteen of the forty-two drownings in the first four months of 1785 to suicide.

20. AN, Y 10642. These registers list forty-four men and four women drowned in 1775.

21. AN, Y 10907, 6 May 1775.

22. AN, Y 14560, 11 and 30 June 1775. According to Nicolas Toussaint Lemoyne Desessarts, *Dictionnaire universel de police* (Paris, 1786–89), 7: 313, the police retrieved forty-one people from the Seine in 1775, and all but six of them survived.

23. On bodies, clothing, and possessions, see Richard Cobb, *Death in Paris: The Records of the Basse-Geôle de la Seine, October 1795–September 1801, Vendémiaire Year IV–Fructidor Year IX* (Oxford, 1978).

24. Time: morning, 6; afternoon, 4; night, 4. Day: Monday, 0; Tuesday, 3; Wednesday, 2; Thursday, 5; Friday, 3; Saturday, 1; Sunday, 5. Month: January, 0; February, 0; March, 1; April, 3; May, 0; June, 3; July, 1; August, 2; September, 2; October, 3; November, 0; December, 4.

25. The usual emotional and economic motives, for example, play surprisingly small roles in the documented explanations of suicide in 1775, in part, no doubt, because of the necessary exclusion of (and limited information about) individuals who drowned themselves. For more about these motives in other years and other sources, see Merrick, "Patterns and Prosecution."

26. On networks and attitudes, see Arlette Farge, *Fragile Lives: Violence, Power, and Solidarity in Eighteenth-Century Paris,* trans. Carol Shelton (Cambridge, Mass., 1993); and David Garrioch, *Neighborhood and Community in Paris, 1740–1790* (Cambridge, 1986), both based on extensive research in the papers of the commissioners.

27. AN, Y 13127, 25 June 1775.

28. AN, Y 15977, 19 July 1775.

29. AN, Y 13685, 24 March 1775.

30. AN, Y 13790, 8 June 1775.

31. Ibid., 19 April and 15 May 1775. One witness declared that Louis Olivier Joseph Ledos never beat Dominique, as if to dispel any suspicions that the father might have been responsible for the boy's death.

32. Noël Pelletier, who drank so much that he sometimes slept on the floor, might belong in the same category. AN, Y 11494, 26 September 1775.

33. AN, Y 12791, 22 September 1775.

34. AN, Y 11016, 22 August 1775.

35. AN, Y 14102, 30 December 1775.

36. AN, Y 15076, 30 August and 2 September 1775.

37. AN, Y 12185, 8 April 1775; Y 14102, 6 October 1775; and Y 14824, 15 December 1775.

38. AN, Y 15977, 19 July 1775. Nathan Lifman also beat his wife, who told the commissioner

that he was "out of his mind." AN, Y 12186, 26 October 1775. Like the other witnesses, she signed the report and investigation in Hebrew characters.

39. AN, Y 11400, 26 April 1775.

40. The reports contain only one other reference to religion: Giraudier had a copy of *The Imitation of Christ* and a plaster Virgin in his room.

41. Giraudier's brother knew about his problems, and Fournier's father knew about his delusions, but both testified that they were "surprised."

42. One witnessed testified that he had feared that Lepelletier might drink himself to death. AN, Y 11494, 26 September 1775.

43. AN, Y 11402, 31 December 1775. For the basic biographical information about Journet, see Michel Antoine, *Le Gouvernement et l'administration de Louis XV: Dictionnaire biographique* (Paris, 1978), 133.

44. Hardy, "Mes Loisirs," 6682: 153.

45. According to another account dated 4 January 1776, the lieutenant-general of police (Joseph François Raymond d'Albert) was nowhere to be found, so Parlongue next sent a message to the minister of the royal household (Chrétien Guillaume de Lamoignon de Malesherbes) and eventually secured permission to have the door opened from the royal attorney general in the Parlement (Guillaume François Louis Joly de Fleury). "Journal de nouvelles formé pour le marquis d'Albertas," BN, Ms, Nouvelles Acquisitions Françaises 4390, 2453–55.

46. For the text of the inconsequential letter from Journet to a banker in Bordeaux, dated 18 December 1775 and found in the valet's pocket, see AN, Y 11403, 5 January 1776.

47. Matthieu François Pidansat de Mairobert, *L'Espion anglais, ou Correspondance secrète entre Milord All'Eye et Milord All'Ear* (London, 1784–86), 3: 54–56. The first edition of this work was published in four volumes in 1777–78 with the title *L'Observateur hollandais*.

48. Turgot tempered criticism with reassurance in seven letters to Journet dated from 4 April to 7 December, in *Oeuvres de Turgot et documents le concernant,* ed. Gustave Schelle (Paris, 1913–23), 5: 82–89. For Turgot's comments about Journet after his death, in letters to Clugny, see 329–32.

49. *Journal de l'abbé de Véri,* ed. Jehan de Witte (Paris, 1928–30), 1: 391.

50. Implicated in and disgraced by a financial scandal, Mairobert himself committed suicide at the end of March 1779. See Jeffrey Merrick, "Le Suicide de Pidansat de Mairobert," *XVIIIe siècle* 35 (2003): 331–40.

51. François Marie Arouet de Voltaire to Alexandre Marie François de Paule de Dompierre d'Hornoy, 15 January 1776, in *Les Oeuvres complètes de Voltaire,* ed. Theodore Besterman et al. (Banbury, 1968–77), 126: 343, D 19865.

52. For another example of posthumous appropriation, see Jeffrey Merrick, "Rousseau's Suicide Note," *Rethinking History: The Journal of Theory and Practice* 5 (2001): 447–50.

53. For a colorful compilation of news and gossip about private and public affairs, see Pierre Rétat, *Le Dernier règne: Chronique de la France de Louis XVI, 1774–1789* (Paris, 1995).

54. On public opinion in practice rather than principle, see Arlette Farge, *Subversive Words: Public Opinion in Eighteenth-Century France,* trans. Rosemary Morris (University Park, 1995); Gilles Maladin, "Les Mouches de police ou le vol des mots: Les Gazetins de la police secrète et la surveillance de l'opinion publique, Paris, deuxième quart du dix-huitième siècle," *Revue d'histoire moderne et contemporaine* 42 (1995): 376–404; Robert Darnton, "An Early Information Society: News and the Media in Eighteenth-Century Paris," *American Historical Review* 105 (2000): 1–35; and Lisa Graham, *If Only the King Knew: Seditious Speech in the Reign of Louis XV* (Charlottesville, 2000).

55. The *nouvelles* contain other examples, from other years, of connections between suicide and politics. When Jacques Alexandre César learned that Louis XVI had forbidden him to launch his "aerostatic machine" in the Tuileries garden, he told the minister of the royal house-

hold that the king was "the master of his life but not his honor" and that he would shoot himself unless he was allowed to satisfy the "public" assembled there to watch him ascend into the clouds. When an "obscure author" was imprisoned for having discussed "public affairs" and criticized royal policies in his clandestine newsletters, his wife told the controller-general that she would make a scene by killing herself on the spot unless he was released. Both threats apparently worked. *Mémoires secrets,* 24: 64–66, 31: 93–94.

56. AN, Y 12185, 8 April 1775.

57. The original list and note, both spelled phonetically, have survived in the dossier transmitted to the Châtelet, in AN, Y 9535, 8 April 1775. The list includes: 17 fine shirts, 2 of them of cotton and 2 of them not trimmed; 22 coarse shirts, 10 [of them with?] collars; 2 tablecloths, 12 napkins, 7 cotton caps; 6 pairs of sheets, 6 pillowcases; 11 colored handkerchiefs, 2 old white ones; 4 clean handkerchiefs, 10 kerchiefs; 7 pairs of white cotton and linen stockings [illegible words]; 2 packets of cloths; 1 bundle of blouses; 22 collars.

58. In this case, as in others, the royal prosecutor most likely ordered the investigation to be continued without really expecting it to produce any further results. The medical report, dated 8 April and included in the dossier transmitted to the Châtelet, indicated that Cellier died as a result of the loss of blood caused by the wound in his throat.

Chapter 10. The Suicide of Sir Samuel Romilly

1. William Combe, "The Suicide" in *The English Dance of Death* (London, 1815), 2: 11–12.

2. "Sir Samuel Romilly" in *Dictionary of National Biography,* 17: 188–91. Most biographies of Romilly were written in the nineteenth and early twentieth century. The only reasonable recent account is Patrick Medd, *Romilly* (London, 1968); *Times,* 3 November 1818.

3. *Bell's Weekly Messenger,* 8 November 1818, 358.

4. Ibid., 353.

5. *British Review and Critical Journal,* February 1819, 1. See also similar sentiments in the *Monthly Repository,* November 1818, 725; and the *Morning Post,* 5 November 1818.

6. *Bell's Weekly Messenger,* 8 November 1818, 357; *Sunday Advertiser,* 8 November 1818.

7. *Imperial Weekly Gazette,* 7 November 1818.

8. *Monthly Repository,* November 1818, 721.

9. *Belle Assemblee,* November 1818, 227. See also *British Luminary and Weekly Intelligence,* 7 November 1818, 41; and *Evening Star,* 3 November 1818.

10. For commendations of Romilly's devotion to ameliorating social conditions, see *Country Herald and Weekly Advertiser,* 7 November 1818; *British Luminary and Weekly Intelligence,* 7 November 1818, 41; *Evening Star,* 3 November 1818; *Lady's Magazine,* December 1818, 549; and *Morning Post,* 5 November 1818.

11. *British Press,* 3 November 1818; *Weekly Dispatch,* 8 November 1818, 356.

12. *Lady's Magazine,* December 1818, 549.

13. *British Press,* 3 November 1818; *Monthly Magazine,* December 1818, 421. See also *British Luminary and Weekly Intelligence,* 7 November 1818, 45; *Lady's Magazine,* December 1818, 549; and *European Magazine,* November 1818, 422.

14. *Constitution,* 8 November 1818.

15. *British Luminary and Weekly Intelligence,* 7 November 1818, 45; *British Press,* 5 November 1818.

16. *Constitution,* 15 November 1818.

17. *Monthly Magazine,* December 1818, 421.

18. *Monthly Repository,* November 1818, 725; *Imperial Weekly Gazette,* 7 November 1818. *Bell's Weekly Messenger,* 3 November 1818, 356, commented that "no one in private life, for so he might be considered, ever excited so strong and so universal an interest," while the *Morning*

Post, 5 November 1818, said that "perhaps a deeper gloom never pervaded the public mind on the sudden death of an individual in the same sphere of life."

19. *Monthly Magazine,* December 1818, 426; *Times,* 5 June 1790; *Lady's Magazine,* December 1818, 549. See also John Barrell, *Imagining the King's Death: Figurative Treason, Fantasies of Regicide 1793 – 1796* (Oxford, 2000), esp. chapter 1, and Philip Carter, *Men and the Emergence of Polite Society, Britain 1660 – 1800* (London, 2001), esp. chapter 3.

20. See for example the *British Press,* 3 November 1818; the *British Review and Critical Journal,* February 1819; and the *Monthly Magazine* December 1818, 426.

21. *British Review and Critical Journal,* February 1819, 9.

22. George Crabbe, from *Poems* (1905), vol. 3, "Miscellaneous Verses Previously Printed: On the Death of Sir Samuel Romilly" (*Chadwyck-Healey English Poetry Full-Text Database*); see also Bernard Barton, "Stanzas on the Death of Sir Samuel Romilly" in *Poems* (London, 1825); *British Press,* 5 November 1818; *Monthly Magazine,* December 1818, 426.

23. *Morning Chronicle,* 7 November 1818.

24. Although this chapter spends little time on this aspect of his death, there were a number of comments on it. See, for example, the *Champion and Sunday Review,* 8 November 1818, 705; *British Press,* 3 November 1818 and 7 November 1818.

25. *Constitution,* 8 November 1818.

26. *British Neptune,* 9 November 1818, 249.

27. *Constitution,* 15 November 1818.

28. *Courier,* 4 November 1818; *British Press,* 7 November 1818, was only one of the papers in which these sentences were found.

29. *Country Herald and Weekly Advertiser,* 7 November 1818; *Gentleman's Magazine,* November 1818, 466; *Monthly Repository,* November 1818, 721; *Examiner,* 9 November 1818, 705, 706.

30. *Lady's Magazine,* December 1818, 549; *Bell's Weekly Messenger,* 8 November 1818, 358; *British Luminary and Weekly Intelligence,* 7 November 1818, 42, and see also *Lady's Magazine,* December 1818, 550.

31. *British Press,* 5 November 1818.

32. *Globe,* 4 November 1818; *New Times,* 3 November 1818. A classic contemporary statement of the view that deep feelings are the source both of public virtue and private misery was published as part of the explanation of Romilly's act: "The affections of the heart borrow their sensibility from the refinements of the soul, which, like treacherous servants, often point the sharpest weapons against those breasts which have most cherished and indulged them. The innumerable accidents and infirmities . . . deeply wound those hearts . . . while they hardly ruffle vulgar minds. . . . Yet these fine feelings, however painful to the *possessor,* are the parents of all that virtue, compassion and benevolence, which humanize the heart and are the best bonds of society; *Morning Post,* 5 November 1818. For other press comments of a similar sort, see the *Constitution,* 8 November 1818; and the *Examiner,* 9 November 1818, 705. Even the *Courier,* which had started all of this, admitted the danger of hyperactive sensibility, see 3 November 1818.

33. *Monthly Repository,* November 1818, 721; *Examiner,* 9 November 1818, 705; *News,* 8 November 1818, 348. Though John Barrell's recent *Imagining the King's Death* is a tour de force, and enormously useful in connecting the notion of "imagination" with political and social discourse, its consolatory role is not discussed.

34. *British Review and Critical Journal,* February 1819, 15; *Morning Advertiser,* 3 November 1818; *Philanthropic Gazette,* 4 November 1818, 368.

35. *Constitution,* 15 November 1818 for the "disappearance" and "eagle" references; *Imperial Weekly Gazette,* 7 November 1818; *Monthly Repository,* 18 November 1818, 725; *Morning Chronicle,* 3 November 1818. For more "providential" explanations, see *Gentleman's Magazine,* November 1818, 465; *Imperial Weekly Gazette,* 7 November 1818; *New Times,* 4 November 1818.

36. *News,* 8 November 1818.

37. *Independent Whig,* 8 November 1818, 712; *Monthly Repository,* November 181, 701; *Black Dwarf,* 11 November 1818, 716.

38. *Morning Chronicle,* 7 November 1818.

39. Although several of the papers reported the public's sorrow about Romilly's death or lauded his accomplishments and also criticized and censured his self-inflicted end, only one that I have found, the *British Neptune,* printed both sympathetic and critical paragraphs about the act. Most papers took one side of the controversy or the other.

40. *Bell's Weekly Messenger,* 8 November 1818, 354; *British Review and Critical Journal,* February 1819, 10; *St. James's Chronicle,* 3−5 November 1818. See also *Independent Whig,* 15 November 1818.

41. *Philanthropic Gazette,* 4 November 1818, 368. For Whitbread's life, and death, see Roger Fulford, *Samuel Whitbread 1764−1815: A Study in Opposition* (London, 1967), esp. chapter 26.

42. *Morning Post,* 5 November 1818; *British Review and Critical Journal* (review of Belsham's sermon), February 1819, 6; *Anti-Jacobin Review* (review of Belsham's sermon), December 1818, 353. Oddly enough, J. M. Rigg, the author of the biography of Samuel Romilly in the *Dictionary of National Biography,* blamed "the morbid bias . . . given to his mind" and "the gloom . . . [which] haunted him at intervals throughout life" to the supernatural stories told him by a "methodist maid-servant" (188).

43. In fact, it was said that a Mr. Elliot, while breakfasting, was brought the newspaper on the day after Romilly's death. "When, after reading the melancholy fate of Sir Samuel Romilly, he suddenly put a period to his own existence by cutting his throat with a razor"; *Traveller,* 4 November 1818.

44. *Morning Post,* 5 November 1818; *Independent Whig,* 15 November 1818; *Bell's Weekly Messenger,* 8 November 1818, 354.

45. The *Courier,* discussing the death of Romilly, noted that "The character of a public man, when its lineaments have been fixed by the hand of death, become as it were a part of public history"; 6 November 1818; ibid., 3 November 1818; the *British Monitor,* 8 November 1818, 656, "Varieties"; *Times,* 31 December 1818, letter to the editor signed, "Ordovex."

46. For more on the origins of this view, see S. E. Sprott, *The English Debate on Suicide from Donne to Hume* (LaSalle, 1961); and Michael MacDonald and Terence R. Murphy, *Sleepless Souls: Suicide in Early Modern England* (Oxford, 1990).

47. X.Y. in the *Sunday Advertiser,* 15 November 1818; the *British Monitor,* 8 November 1818. See also Donna T. Andrew, "Debate: The Secularization of Suicide in England 1660−1800," *Past and Present* 119 (1988): 158−65.

48. *Bell's Weekly Messenger,* 8 November 1818, 358.

49. *European Magazine,* November 1818, 423.

50. Roy Porter comments that England's medical men had already diagnosed such a malady: "The Enlightenment thus formulated not just progress but its verso: the idea of diseases of civilization, afflicting meritocrats of feeling"; *The Creation of the Modern World* (New York, 2000), 282. See also John Mullan, *Sentiment and Sociability: The Language of Feeling in the Eighteenth Century* (Oxford, 1988).

DONNA T. ANDREW is Professor of Modern British History at the University of Guelph in Canada. She is the author of *Philanthropy and Police: London Charity in the Eighteenth Century* (Princeton, 1989), the compiler and editor of *London Debating Societies 1776–1799* (London Record Society, 1994), and, with Randall McGowen, joint author of *The Perreaus and Mrs. Rudd: Forgery and Betrayal in Eighteenth Century London* (Berkeley, 2001).

MACHIEL BOSMAN studied history at the University of Amsterdam. Currently working as a freelance scholar, he does research in the field of social history. He has authored a book about an orphanage in Amsterdam and is presently fulfilling a commission to write the history of a Dutch orphanage in Culemborg (1560–1950).

JAMES M. BOYDEN is Associate Professor of History at Tulane University, and the author of *The Courtier and the King: Ruy Gómez de Silva, Philip II, and the Court of Spain* (Berkeley, 1995), and of a number of essays on the social and political history of early modern Spain.

ELIZABETH G. DICKENSON is pursuing a Ph.D. in medieval history at the University of Texas at Austin. Specializing in premodern Spain, she is currently working as a historian in the Speaker's Office of the Texas House of Representatives and as an aide to the House Select Committee on School Finance.

ARNE JANSSON received his Ph.D. in history from Stockholm University in 1991. In addition to numerous articles, he is the author of *Bördor och bärkraft. Borgare och kronotjänare i Stockholm 1644–1672* [*Public Burdens and the Ability to Bear Them: Burghers and Crown Servants in Stockholm 1644–1672*] (Stockholm, 1991) and *From Swords to Sorrow: Homicide and Suicide in Early Modern Stockholm* (Stockholm, 1998), and the editor of *Johan Rosenhanes dagbok 1652–1661* [*Diary of Johan Rosenhane, 1652–1661*] (Stockholm, 1995).

CRAIG M. KOSLOFSKY is Associate Professor of History at the University of Illinois, Urbana-Champaign. His publications include *The Reformation of the Dead: Death and Ritual in Early Modern Germany* (Macmillan Press/St. Martin's Press, 2000) and a book co-edited with Bernhard Jussen, *Kulturelle Reformation: Sinnformationen im Umbruch 1400–1600* (Vandenhoeck & Ruprecht, 1999).

DAVID LEDERER is Lecturer of Modern History at the National University of Ireland, Maynooth. He is completing a book on the history of madness, has published numerous articles on the history of suicide, and, as an Alexander von Humboldt fellow, is currently engaged in writing a book on suicide in the Holy Roman Empire, 1500–1800.

VERA LIND received her Ph.D. from the University of Kiel in 1997. She is the author of *Selbstmord in der Frühen Neuzeit. Diskurs, Lebenswelt und kultureller Wandel* (Vandenhoeck & Ruprecht, 1999), which will be published in English as *Suicide in the Early Modern Period* by Berghahn Press. Currently a research fellow at the German Historical Institute in Washington, D.C., Lind is working on a book-length study on Africans in early modern Germany.

JEFFREY MERRICK, Professor of History at the University of Wisconsin–Milwaukee, is the author of *The Desacralization of the French Monarchy in the Eighteenth Century* and co-editor of five books: two on André Morellet and three on homosexuality in French history.

PAUL S. SEAVER gained his doctorate at Harvard and has taught since 1964 in the history department at Stanford University, where he now has emeritus status. He is the author of *The Puritan Lectureships* (1970), *Wallington's World* (1985), and a number of articles.

JEFFREY R. WATT, Professor of History at the University of Mississippi, is the author of *The Making of Modern Marriage: Matrimonial Control and the Rise of Sentiment in Neuchâtel, 1550–1800* (Cornell, 1992) and *Choosing Death: Suicide and Calvinism in Early Modern Geneva* (Truman State, 2001).